RELIGION WITHIN THE LIMITS OF REASON ALONE

By IMMANUEL KANT

Translated by J. W. SEMPLE

Religion within the Limits of Reason Alone
By Immanuel Kant
Translated by J. W. Semple

Print ISBN 13: 978-1-4209-8196-4
eBook ISBN 13: 978-1-4209-8222-0

This edition copyright © 2024. Digireads.com Publishing.

All rights reserved. No part of this publication may be reproduced, distributed, or transmitted in any form or by any means, including photocopying, recording, or other electronic or mechanical methods, without the prior written permission of the publisher, except in the case of brief quotations embodied in critical reviews and certain other noncommercial uses permitted by copyright law.

Cover Image: a detail of a colored engraving of Immanuel Kant, by an unknown artist, c. 19th century / Stefano Bianchetti / Bridgeman Images.

Please visit *www.digireads.com*

CONTENTS

The Translator to the Reader. 5

Author's Preface. 7

Preface to the Second Edition. 13

Book I. 15

Book II. 43

Book III. 71

Book IV 118

C. CORNELIUS TACITUS

DE MORIBUS GERMANORUM.

HAUD DEFUIT AUDENTIA *GERMANICO:* SED OBSTITIT OCEANUS IN SE, SIMUL ATQUE IN HERCULEM INQUIRI. MOX NEMO TENTAVIT. SANCTIUSQUE AC REVERENTIUS VISUM, DE ACTIS DEORUM CREDERE QUAM SCIRE.

The Translator to the Reader.

DURING the six-and-forty years that FREDERICK THE GREAT reigned over Prussia, his subjects enjoyed unrestricted liberty of the press. But upon the death of that illustrious monarch in 1786, and the accession of F. William II., a different order of affairs began. An edict was published shortly after (in 1788), greatly hampering, or even suppressing, freedom of debate, especially in matters theological; and this edict had very nearly the effect of stifling Kant's work on religion. Kant had sent the first book to the Editor of the *Berlin Monthly Magazine*, and this part was allowed by the PHILOSOPHICAL censor, Mr. G. R. Hillmer, to pass to the public, when it appeared in April 1792. Book II. was forwarded to Berlin, with the view of being published in some subsequent number. Upon reading it, however, Mr. Hillmer considered the treatise theological, not philosophical, and therefore sent it for inspection to Air O. C. R. Hermes, the THEOLOGIC censor, who most unhesitatingly refused his *imprimatur*, and took Book II. into custody, as illicitly poaching on the preserves of theology. In Germany, the ancient universities possess several immunities and many important privileges and jurisdictions of their own. Some of them have even rights of appellate jurisdiction. To this latter class belongs the university at Königsberg; and before the university of Königsberg Kant resolved to bring his case. He completed his Philosophical Theory of Religion, and sent it to the theological faculty, contending that the investigation did not fall under their jurisdiction, as it was merely a philosophical speculation upon theology. After mature deliberation, the theological faculty of Königsberg found that the volume was not one that could fall under their cognizance, and remitted it to the philosophical faculty, who at once sanctioned its publication. Thus a work suppressed by the royal censorship at Berlin, was printed notwithstanding in the same year at Königsberg, with the express consent both of the theological and philosophical faculties.

This account of the present volume I have thought it necessary to prefix, to enable readers to understand the allusions in the Preface, and also some expressions in the text. The preposterous behaviour of Mr.

Hermes furnishes ns with a very satisfactory scale by which to estimate the justness of the lashing inflicted by Kant in Book IV. on churchmen bigoted, superstitious, and despotic. It must be admitted, Hermes had afforded ample room for even a severer reprimand. The pointed passage at p. 242, where the Author complains of churchmen attempting to give the go-by at once to biblical learning and to reason,—thinking that they need only to *command*, but not *convince*,—I understand as a direct allusion to Mr. Hermes.

Touching the Treatise itself, the Germans hold that this volume is the most important disquisition that ever appeared upon RELIGION *generally*, and upon the CHRISTIAN RELIGION in particular; ail opinion in which I think every person must concur, whether he accept or decline the singularities and originalities of Rationalism. That it concerns us islanders TO KNOW the religious or quasi-religious opinions entertained by our next-door neighbours on the Continent, no sane man, I apprehend, can doubt. Journeys are made to China and Hindostan to learn the metaphysical and ethical speculations there prevalent. Even the books of CON-FU-TSZEE are translated, and deemed not unworthy of sifting comment. How much more nearly are we called upon to study opinions which, to use the words of Sir James Macintosh, "have now exclusive possession of Europe to the north of the Rhine—have been welcomed by the French youth with open arms—have roused in some measure the languishing genius of Italy; but are still little known, and unjustly estimated, by the mere English reader;"[1]—more especially when we reflect that those opinions are the cherished and valued sentiments of a race who, both by speech and blood, are our nearest kinsfolk.

To contribute in some measure, however slender, toward removing the ignorance so justly lamented by the polished writer whose words I have quoted above, is the humble aim of the few following sheets, as well as of the volume which I previously ventured to lay before the public. I have only yet farther, before concluding, to thank my readers, both on this and the other side of the Atlantic, for the very courteous reception with which they have deigned to countenance my labours.

Edinburgh, 1st *November* 1838.

---

[1] Prelim. Dissertat. to 7th ed. of Encyc. Brit. p. 412.

Author's Preface.

ETHIC, in so far as founded on the Idea of Humanity as a free Agent, binding himself, by virtue of that very Freedom, to an unconditionate Law of Reason, is by itself complete and entire; so that mankind neither requires the idea of any Superior Person to enable him to investigate his duty, nor does he need any incentive or spring to its execution other than the law itself. At least it must be his own fault if there exist any such want or need; a defect, however, quite without remedy from any foreign sources; since, whatsoever is not originated by himself from his own freedom, cannot supply or make up the want of his own morality.

A System of Ethics, therefore, needs no Religion, neither *objectively* to aid man's WILL, nor *subjectively*, as respects his ability, to aid his POWER; but stands, by force of pure practical reason, self-sufficient and independent: for, since its decrees have ethical virtue to oblige by the bare form of that universal legality wherewith all maxims must coincide, such formal fitness for law universal, being the supreme and unconditionate condition of the intent of all actions whatsoever, it results that Ethic needs no material determinator of choice, *i. e.* requires no ulterior end, either to recognise what is duty, or to excite toward its execution, but, on the contrary, can and ought, in a question regarding duty, to abstract from all ends whatsoever. To take an instance, suppose I wish to know, if I SHOULD (or can) speak truth in the witness-box, or re-deliver a deposite intrusted to my care, then I require to make no inquiry concerning any end or purpose which my evidence or re-delivery may accomplish; for he who in such a case should cast about for some ulterior motive, would show by doing so that he is a villain.

But although Ethics require no representation of an end, as a condition antecedent to the determination of the will, yet it is possible that it may have a necessary reference to an end; not, indeed, as the groundwork, but as the sequent of maxims adopted in harmony with the law: for no determination of will can exist in man entirely devoid of all reference to ends, since no volition can remain without effect; the representation of which effect will no doubt not be the determinator of the choice, nor yet an end extant in the formal intent how to act; but which effect must be adopted by the will, as an end emerging in consequence of its determination by the law, apart from which a will could not satisfy itself; for, being left destitute of every, whether objectively or subjectively, assigned end, in an intended action, the will would be commanded *how*, but not *whitherwards*, it had to act. Thus, for morality no end is required, only the law, which is the formal condition of the use of freedom; but Ethic gives birth to an end: nor can reason remain indifferent to the question, WHAT IS TO BE THE RESULT

OF ALL HER RIGHT ACTING? toward which final result as a goal (even supposing that goal beyond our reach) she might direct all her actions, as toward a common centre.

This end is no more than the idea of an object which comprises in itself, 1. The formal condition of the ends we ought to have (duty); and, 2. Also the thereby conditioned aggregate of the ends we actually have (the happiness proportioned to our observance of the former); that is, in other words, the idea of the SUMMUM BONUM, to realize which best possible world (*Summum Bonum*), we must postulate a Supreme, Moral, Most Holy, and All-mighty Being, as he who is alone able to unite these two elements. But this idea is practically not void, for it aids the need we feel to figure to ourselves some last end as the final scope and aim of our exertions;—the absence of which end would be an impediment to ethical determinations. But the main point observable is, that the idea takes its rise from Ethic, and is not its groundwork; for to adopt this end, pre-requires ethic principles in the person who does so. It is therefore nowise indifferent to the moralist whether he frame to himself the notion of a final scope and chief end of all things or not (to harmonize with which does not increase the number of his duties, but supplies a common point where all his exertions are ultimately to terminate and coincide); for it is only by force of this idea, that objective practical reality can be given to our notion of the conjungibility of the *formal symmetry* of actions originated by freedom, with the *material symmetry* of objects in the physical system; a conjunction which is an indispensable postulate of reason. Let us figure to ourselves an Intelligent, a reverer of the moral law, revolving in thought what kind of world he would create if guided singly by practical reason (a cogitation man can hardly avoid), of which world he himself should be a part; then he would not only choose (supposing a wish only were left to him) just such a world as that ethical idea of the summum bonum brings along with it, but he would likewise WILL (had he the power) such a world into existence, because the moral law ordains that he effectuate the highest good possible by his exertions, even although he would see himself in great danger of losing his own personal happiness, by the hazard he might run, of not being found adequate to that idea to which, as a condition, reason restrains the distribution of happiness. This judgment would be impartial as if passed by another, and yet his reason would force him to recognise it as his own too; by all which the Intelligent would evince his ethical need, to figure to himself a final or last end, as the sequent of his duties.

ETHIC issues, then, inevitably in RELIGION, by extending itself to the idea of an Omnipotent Moral Lawgiver, in whose will, *that* is the end of the creation, which at the same time can and ought to be likewise mankind's chief end.[2]

---

[2] The position THERE IS A GOD, consequently there is a *Summum Bonum*, in the universe, if it as a belief is to rest on pure morals, is a synthetic *a priori* proposition, which, although adopted singly for a practical behoof, extends beyond the notion duty (which notion supposes no matter of choice, only its formal (negative) laws), and consequently cannot be evolved analytically from it: coincidence with the *mere Idea* of a Moral Lawgiver of Mankind, is no doubt identic with the ethical conception DUTY; and to this extent a proposition ordaining such coincidence were *analytic:* but to assume HIS existence, says more than is expressed by the bare idea of the possibility of such an object. The key to the unfolding of this matter, I can only here sketch in skeleton, without applying it to the intricacies of the wards.

AN END, or AIM WILLED, is always the object of AFFECTION, *i. e.* of immediate desire to possess something by means of an action, in the same way as the LAW is always ail object of REVERENCE: an objective end (*i. e.* one which we ought to have), is one objected to the mind (as such by reason). That end, which is the indispensable and sufficient condition of all other ends, is the last end or SCOPE: proper happiness is the subjective end of finite intelligents (which end all HAVE by force of their sensitive economy, and of which end it were contradictory to say that they OUGHT to have it), and all propositions which rest on this ground are synthetic, and *a posteriori*. But that every person should make the HIGHEST GOOD possible in the world, his LAST END and aim, is a synthetic practical proposition *a priori;* and further, is an objectively practical one, proposed by reason; for it is a position which goes beyond the conception of the duty to be performed in this world, and superadds to it a sequent, *i. e.* an effect not involved or contained in the moral law, and which, consequently, cannot be evolved analytically from it. The law commands categorically, be the effect what it may; nay, it necessitates man to abstract altogether from such effect, when it calls for any given act; and does, by this very circumstance, make duty an object of the highest veneration, that it assigns neither end nor scope which might recommend it, or become an incentive towards the performance of duty. All men would find mobilé enough, in the law, if they adhered (*as they should*) to the decrees of pure Reason. What need have they to know what issue of their exertions the course of things may bring about? for them it is enough that they have done their duty, whether all things expire with this earthly existence, and although happiness and desert never coincide. It happens, however, to be one of the limits put to man's reason, that he always casts about for some effect resulting from his actions, in order to find in this effect an end and aim such as may prove the purity of his will, which end, although last in execution, was, notwithstanding, first in his intention. In this end, even when assigned by reason, mankind seeks something that he can LOVE. Consequently the law, which begets REVERENCE only, and cannot recognise the need or want of the latter, does nevertheless extend itself for the behoof of this want, so as to adopt the ethical scope of reason among its determinators, *i. e.* the position, "MAKE THE HIGHEST GOOD POSSIBLE IN THE WORLD BY THY EXERTIONS, THY LAST END AND SCOPE," is a synthetic a priori proposition, introduced by the moral law itself, although, by doing so, reason extends itself beyond its law; and the synthetical extension is possible, by the law's being applied to that physical predisposition of man's nature, whereby he is forced to think an end out of, and beyond, the law (which physical property makes man an object of experience), and is, in fact (like the speculative synthetic propositions *a priori*), only *thus* possible, viz. by containing the *a priori* principle, whereby we know the material conditions of freedom as exhibited in practice, so far forth as experience and observation, exhibiting in their results the effects of morality, procure objective though only practical reality to the idea morality, as a causality acting in upon the world. But if the rigid observance of the law is to be considered as the cause of the production of that end, the *Summum Bonum*, then must we (man's power being inadequate to that effect) assume an Omnipotent Moral Being as Governor of the World, under w hose Providence this conjunction of felicity with desert is effected, *i. e.* Ethic issues necessarily in Religion.

If Ethic recognise in the Holiness of its Law an object of the greatest veneration, it doth farther, when on the grade of religion, it exhibits as an object of Adoration—a Supreme Cause, executive and upholder of the Law—enrobe itself with majesty, and appear in state. But every thing, even the most exalted, dwindles to insignificance in the hands of man, when its idea is applied to use. Even that which can only be truly venerated, in so far as the reverence bestowed on it is free, is necessitated to accommodate itself to such shapes and forms as co-active laws ordain; and that which offers itself to the free unreserved critique of every man, is constrained to yield to a critique *par force*, i. e. to a censorship.

Nevertheless, since the commandment, "OBEY THE GOVERNMENT!" is also of moral obligation; and since its observance may, as indeed may that of every other duty, be reckoned under the head of religion; it is but seemly that a treatise devoted to the investigation of this latter idea, should itself exemplify this ordained obedience—a thing not to be accomplished by observing merely one single statutable decree of the state, but only by devoting a united reverence to them all. Now, a Theologian who sits in judgment on a book may be invested with a post where lie is merely intrusted with the cure of souls, or else with one, where he is also concerned with the advancement of the sciences: the former judge is only a clergyman, the second is at the same time one of the learned. As a member of a learned institution (*called a University*), where the sciences are nurtured, and guarded against hurt, it is incumbent upon the latter to curb the excessive Censorship of the former, so far, at least, as to prevent the sciences from receiving any damage. Suppose, now, that both censors are BIBLICAL THEOLOGIANS; then will to the latter, as member of that Academic Faculty which has pre-eminently to deal with University Theology, belong the right of appellate jurisdiction: for, so far forth as the cure of souls is at stake, both being clergymen, are equally concerned; but as for the interest of the sciences, the Theological Teacher at the University has a yet farther and peculiar province to administer. If this rule be set aside, then we shall ultimately come to that pass (which in the days of GALILEO really happened), that the BIBLICAL THEOLOGIAN, in order to humble the pride of the sciences, and to save himself the trouble of learning them, will, by a crusading inroad against physical astronomy, ancient geology, or whatever else the science may be (just like those savage hordes who, to defend themselves against the dreaded attacks of an enemy, lay waste beforehand whole territories around them), endeavour to blockade every outlet against the forthcoming operations of the human understanding.

Moreover, in the field of the sciences there stands over against biblical theology, a philosophical theology, as a good intrusted to a particular faculty. Now, so long as this branch of philosophic speculation remains "WITHIN THE BOUNDS OF NAKED REASON," and uses toward the confirmation and establishment of its positions, history, languages, the old writings of various nations—the Bible not excepted,—without, however, attempting to intrude its opinions into biblical theology, or to alter those public doctrines which stand under the privileged guardianship of the clergy; then must it have full freedom to extend itself as far as its scientific grasp can reach: and should it perchance even happen that the philosopher had wandered beyond his boundary, and invaded unawares the domain of the biblical theologian, then would this last, in his capacity of clergyman, be entitled to subject the intruder to his cognizance. But were it at all doubtful whether or not the due boundary really had been overstepped, and question arose if such trespass actually had been committed, whether by writing or by any spoken lecture, then would the supreme or appellate censorship devolve on that biblical theologian alone, who might be likewise MEMBER OF AN ACADEMICAL FACULTY; for then only would he have the ulterior interests of the commonwealth to study,— holding his appointment from the state, in order that he might attend to the sciences, and their growth.

Unquestionably, in such a case as is here supposed, the Censorship would devolve, in the last resort, on the Theological, not on the Philosophical Faculty; for the former alone can claim a monopoly of certain doctrines, whereas the latter always leaves its tenets open to general debate, and can consequently never complain that any new speculation diminishes the traffic of the guild. Any doubt, however, as to a territorial invasion, is, notwithstanding the approximation of the two doctrines, and apprehended trespass on the part of Philosophical Theology, very easily removed, when we consider that the mischief arises, not from the Philosopher's borrowing any thing from Biblical Theology, but from his thrusting speculations upon Divinity, whereby this last is bent to ends foreign to her established constitution. Thus no one would ever think of saying, that Teachers of International Law, when citing classical passages or formulae out of the Code or Digest, for the behoof of a philosophical theory of their subject, are guilty of invading or violating the majesty of the CORPUS JURIS, although those passages be accommodated and understood in a sense slightly varying from that in which Justinian and Ulpian may have employed them; nor could they, with any colour of reason, be accused of tampering with, or trespassing on, the Civil Law, provided they did not insist that the Bench and Bar should receive their gloss as the strict and proper meaning of the words. For, were not each faculty entitled to borrow occasionally from the other, then, conversely, we might accuse the Biblical Theologian, or the Statutable Jurist, of making innumerable inroads into the territory of philosophy (seeing that neither can dispense with reason, nor, where a scientific pre-exercitation is required, with philosophy), and bearing hence treasures for their own use. And yet were the first-named faculty to aim at having nothing to do with reason or philosophy in religious matters, soon would it appear which party suffered the greater damage; for a religion which should declare and wage an uncompromising war against reason, must, in the long run, be worsted. I would even venture to ask, if it were not advisable that the student should, after completing his studies in the Hall, hear a course on the Philosophy of Biblical Theology, or, indeed, of any other Theology, in order to give the last finish to his preparation for his work? In truth, the sciences advance only when elaborated separately, so far forth as each constitutes a whole by itself, and when subsequently an architectonic survey is made in order to arrange and display them in systematic harmony. It is immaterial whether the Biblical Theologian agree or differ with the Philosopher, and so deem it needful to confute his tenets, provided that he only hear and know them; for thus alone can he become thoroughly fore-armed against all difficulties, open or latent, strown by the philosopher in his path; whereas, to conceal objections, or which, if possible, is worse, to decry them as impious, is a wretched stratagem, that can only fail: while, on the other hand, to weld both parts together, and only occasionally exhibit an amalgam of philosophy, betrays want of intellectual depth, and brings the public at length to such a pass that they cannot well divine where Theology is going, or what it is about.

Of the following four books,—where, in order to make perceptible the relation obtaining betwixt religion and humanity, affected as it is, in part with good, in part with evil, predispositions, I have represented the Good and the Evil Principles as two self-subsisting causes, operating outside of, and bearing in upon man,—the first has already appeared in the Berlin Monthly Magazine for April 1792. I was, however, under the necessity of republishing it now, on account of its intimate connection with the remaining three, which, indeed, contain the development and application of the notions therein set abroach.

Preface to the Second Edition.

IN this edition no alterations have been made; only the misprints, and some few faulty expressions, have been amended. One or two additional notes have been subjoined to the text. They are indicated by a star, thus[3]. Those in the old edition bore a cross[4]f.

Touching the title of the book (RELIGION WITHIN THE BOUNDS OF NAKED REASON, for it seems I have been accused of some; latent design), I beg leave to say in explanation, that since a REVELATION may comprehend *inter alia* as its object-matter the doctrines of NATURAL RELIGION, while, conversely, this last cannot possibly contain the historical details of the former, it may be permitted us to regard the one as a larger sphere of belief, containing within it the other as a less (*i. e.* as orbs concentric, consequently not without and outside of one another). Within the bounds of this last—the smaller sphere—may the philosopher, as an inquirer into pure reason, proceeding singly upon principles *a priori*, confine himself; where, consequently, he must abstract from all experience and observation. Leaving this position, he may make the farther experiment of beginning at any supposed revelation (abstracting in the meanwhile from pure natural Religion, as an independent and self-subsisting system), and of holding it, as a historical system, bit by bit, up to the moral notions, for the purpose of comparison; in order to see if it do not lead back eventually to the self-same system of Natural Theology, which, though incomplete in itself in a theoretical point of view (for it would require to embrace and contain a technico-practical part, for the purpose of instruction), is, nevertheless, for every ethico-practical purpose, complete, and quite sufficient for religion properly so called; which, as a notion *a priori* (remaining after abstraction has been made from every *a posteriori* part), has significancy only when understood in this reference. Should this turn out really to be the case, then may it be said that reason and revelation are not only in harmony, but identic; so that whoever should, under guidance of ethical notions, follow the one, would find himself eventually at the same goal with the other. And were it not so, then would there exist either two religions in the same person, which is absurd, or there would be one religion and one ceremonial worship; and since the latter is not, like religion, an end-in-itself, but has value only as a mean, then they might, no doubt, like heterogeneous elements, be for a while confounded, but would, as oil from water, soon become separate—pure ethic, the religion of nature, floating above, while the ceremonials are precipitated.

---

[3]
[4]

That this union, or attempt to bring it about, is a task quite allowed to one who makes a philosophical scrutiny into Religion, and no inroad into the province of Biblical Theology, was shown in the preface to the first edition. Since then, I have seen my assertion quoted by the celebrated MICHAELIS in his *Morals* (Part. I. p. 5-11),—a man equally conversant with either faculty. In fact, this principle pervades his whole work; and yet the Theological Faculty have not complained, so far as I know, of finding in his book any thing prejudicial to their rights.

Writings by the learned, whether named or innominate, arrive so tardily at this farther corner of the globe, that I have not been enabled to notice in this second edition, the reviews which I understand have been passed upon this my Philosophical Theory of Revelation. It was my anxious wish to have replied to the celebrated Dr Storr of Tubingen, who, in his "*Annotationes quædam Theologicæ,*" has subjected my opinions to a very sifting scrutiny, conducted at the same time with such extreme attention and candour as to have earned my warmest thanks. Some intention of answering him I even yet entertain, but venture not to promise a rejoinder, on account of the impediments which great age now throws in my way, especially when engaged in elaborating abstract ideas. One *Critique*, namely, that published in "*No. 29 of the Greifswald New Critical Reporter*," I may discuss with that curt brevity wherewith my Reviewer has handled me. According to his judgment, the present treatise is merely an attempt to solve, for my own satisfaction, a self-proposed problem, viz. "HOW, UPON GROUNDS OF PURE THEORETICAL AND PRACTICAL REASON, ARE THE NOTIONS AND POSITIONS CONTAINED IN THE ARTICLES OF THE CHURCH CREED POSSIBLE?" "This, consequently," says he, "is an investigation wherewith they cannot be concerned who know his (KANT'S) system as little as they care about it. The question, in fine, is for them inexistent."—Upon this I remark—there are needed for comprehending the substance of the present book, only the most ordinary notices of Ethic, without the slightest acquaintance with the "INQUIRY INTO THE WILL," and still less without any reference to the *Critique of Speculative Reason*. True, I sometimes speak of *virtue*, when understood as a readiness in performing actions outwardly in harmony with the law, as *virtus phænomenon*, and contradistinguish it from virtue as a steadfast moral mindedness or intent, of executing those acts OUT OF DUTY, called *virtus noumenon;* but then these expressions arc used merely for the sake of scholastic uniformity. The thing indicated by those terms is stated daily in every child's catechism or sermon, and, be the vocables what they may, is easily understood. Would to heaven as much could be said in praise of the mysteries touching the Godhead, reckoned by the church integrant parts of our religion, which, as were they on a level with every one's common sense, are thrust into catechisms for the young; although eventually they must, by a metempsychosis, pass into the form of moral notions, if they are ever to become generally intelligible.

Königsberg, 26th January 1794.

Book I.

ON THE RADICAL EVIL OF HUMAN NATURE.

EXORDIUM.

THAT THE WORLD LIETH IN WICKEDNESS, is a complaint as ancient as any HISTORIC record, or even as that still older VOLUME, the fictions of the POETS—nay, it is equally old with that oldest of all figments, the fabulous mythical religions of priestcraft. All three concur in giving the world at its outset a good beginning: be it a golden age—a life in Paradise—or one still more happy—communion with Celestials. But this welfare speedily disappears. A lapse into evil immediately hurries mankind from bad to worse with accelerated speed.[5] So that we NOW (*which now*, however, is as old as either history or fable) live in the latter times. The last day and destruction of the world lie even at the door, so much so that SIVA, the Destroyer and future Judge of the earth, is already in some parts of Hindustan, worshipped as the God to whom all power in heaven and earth has been delegated; VISHNU having in fatigue thrown up, some centuries ago, the post of governor of the world, which in the beginning he received from the Creator BRAHMA.

A contrary opinion has obtained in modern times. It is, however, far less prevalent, being confined mainly to philosophers and pedagogues, viz. that the world is moving in the opposite direction, being constantly, though imperceptibly, on the advance from bad to better. At least it is contended that the predispositions of human nature are originally so constituted as to tend that way. But this assumption was certainly never taken from experience and observation; for, so long as question is made of MORAL GOOD AND EVIL, and not merely of the refinements of civilization, authentic history in every age declares against it. Probably, therefore, it is only a good-natured HYPOTHESIS, first started by SENECA, and handed down from him through intervening Moralists to ROUSSEAU, in order by its means, to goad mankind on, to the unwearied culture and development of every latent germ, that may perchance one day bring forth good fruit. And, indeed, since man comes into the world usually hale and sound in body at his

---

[5] Ætas parentum, pejor avis, tulit
  Nos nequiores, mox daturos
  Progeniem vitiosiorem.—HORAT.

birth, it is not easy to imagine why the inner man—his soul—should not be deemed by parity of reason just as healthy. Upon this view, nature herself is waiting and ever ready to assist the efforts made for forwarding our moral growth. "*Sanabilibus ægrotamus malis, nosque IN RECTUM GENITOS, natura si sanari velimus, adjurat.*" So SENECA of this matter, and so others.

Since, however, nothing is more likely than that both poets and philosophers are in the wrong, it would at once occur to any bystander to inquire, if no medium could be found betwixt the two extremes, and if there were not room to say, that mankind as a race are neither good nor bad; or otherwise, that man is as much the one as the other, being in part good and in part evil. But a person is called *evil*, not merely because he performs actions that are *bad, i. e.* illegal; but only then, when his actions are of such a stamp, as to enable and entitle us to conclude upon the *evil* maxims of his will. Now, though experience and observation may make us acquainted with actions repugnant to the law, and may even (*at least in our own case*) teach knowledge of illegal acts, perpetrated with the full consciousness that they are so; still the regulating maxims of the will are no object of possible experience (not *always* even the maxims of one's own will); whence, by consequence, the judgment, that AN AGENT IS AN EVIL PERSON, never can, with certainty, be rested on experience and observation. We must, therefore, from *sundry*, or even *one* evil act, done with the consciousness of its being so, be able to conclude *a priori* upon an evil maxim giving it birth; and from thence yet farther, upon a *general* ground of every *particular* morally-evil maxim extant in the thinking Subject; which universal ground is again itself a maxim, before we can deem ourselves entitled to predicate of a person that he is by nature EVIL.

That no occasion of stumbling may be furnished by the word NATURE, which, when used to signify the *Physical System*, is the veriest anti-part of a ground of acting out of freedom, and wherewith the predicates GOOD and EVIL would stand in open contradiction: it is to be observed, that by the *nature* of man we here mean only *that subjective ground of the use of his freedom* precedent to any act falling under sense—let this ground be what it may. Farther, *this subjective ground* must be figured to be AN ACT OF FREEDOM; for if otherwise, neither the use nor abuse made by man of his free choice could be imputed to him as his deed; and his indwelling good or evil would not be moral. Consequently the ground of moral evil can lie in no OBJECT determinative of the will through the intervention of an appetite; neither can it lie in any physical instinct, but only in a *rule, i. e.* in a *maxim* self-appointed by choice to its own freedom. But what now may be the subjective ground of adopting such a maxim, and discarding its contrary, is an ulterior question, that cannot be resolved. For were this last ground, concerning which question is made, no longer a general maxim, but a mere physical determination, then would the use of our freedom be explicable upon mere *natural causes*, which, however, is repugnant to the very idea of a *supersensible causality*. When, therefore, it is said, "Mankind is by Nature Good," or "He is by Nature Evil," those positions merely mean "he contains within him an *unsearchable* last ground[6] of adopting good or of adopting bad maxims;" which ground, unfathomable even by his own reason, pervades and tinges so universally the species, as to serve for an exponent whereby to indicate the character of the whole race.

We shall also farther say, of one or other of those ethic characters, and that, too, with the view of distinguishing *mankind* from other possibly-existing *intelligents*, that with him it is CONGENITE. Notwithstanding, nature is not chargeable with his guilt (should man be evil), nor with his good-desert (should he turn out good): for the man himself is at all times the sole author of his character; but, because the last ground whereby we appoint to ourselves our maxims, seeing that they must always emanate from our free choice, never can be an event given in experience and observation, upon that account it is that man's good or evil (as a good or evil last ground of adopting this or that maxim in harmony with, or militating against the law) is said to be *born with him*, so far forth as at his birth it is already a ground extant, and precedent of all experimental exercise of his freedom. And since this is the case, even from the earliest acts of youth backward to his birth, this ground must be cogitated as co-existing with and in man, even at his birth,—which, however, does not mean that his birth is the cause of it.

EXPLANATORY SCHOLION.

At the bottom of the two just stated hypotheses there lies a disjunctive proposition, "MAN IS BY NATURE EITHER MORALLY GOOD OR MORALLY EVIL;" and it will immediately occur to every one to ask if this disjunction be correct? Some one might say, that there is room for maintaining that "MAN IS BY NATURE NEITHER ONE NOR OTHER;" and a third party might contend that "HE IS BOTH AT ONCE," namely, good in some points, and in others evil. Experience and observation would even seem to declare for this intermediary betwixt the extremes.

Ethic, however, admits only unwillingly of moral *media*, either in

---

[6] That the last subjective ground of adopting moral maxims must be inscrutable (*by man*), is already self-evident from this consideration, viz. that since their appointment is FREE, the ground of such a choice cannot be sought in any physical spring. It can lie only in a maxim. Now, since this maxim must have its ground, and since out of and beyond maxims no DETERMINATIVES of free choice can be assigned, it is manifest that we may recede backwards *in infinitum* along ibis subjective chain, without ever arriving at the last link, *i.e.* without ever fathoming a maxim's absolutely last ground.

actions or in characters: since, were such ambiguity to prevail, all maxims would be in danger of losing both fixity and precision. Those who profess severer sentiments are usually called RIGORISTS, a name which, though intended to convey censure, does in fact praise: their adversaries are styled LATITUDINARIANS, who again are divided into latitudinarians of *neutrality* and of *coalition*. We may call the one INDIFFERENTISTS; the other SYNCRETISTS.[7]

The answer to that disjunctive interrogatory, if it is to fall out agreeably to a rigorous[8] method of deciding, bottoms itself on this

---

[7] If GOOD = a, then is its contradictory the NOT-GOOD; and this again results either from a mere absence of a ground impelling towards good = 0, or from the positive presence of a ground the *antipodes* of good = — a. In this latter case the not-good may be spoken of as positive evil. (With respect to pleasure and pain, there can be assigned an intermediate state, so that pleasure = a pain = — a, and that state wherein neither is felt, viz. a state of indifference, = 0.) This would also be the case in ethics, were not the law itself the spring of will; for then the moral good (*i. e.* the harmony of the will with the law) would be = a, the not-good = 0; which last, however, would only be the consequence of the want of any moral spring = $a \times 0$. But because the law is a moral spring = a, it follows that 0 = the want of the will's harmony with the law is the effect of a contrary and opposite determination of choice, *i. e.* of a counteracting of the law = — a; that is, can only happen through a positively evil will. Wherefore, betwixt a good and an evil *moral-mindedness* (*inward principle of maxims*), according to which an act's morality must be judged, no intermediate cast or bent of volition can be found. A morally-indifferent action (*Adiaphoron Morale*) would be an act brought about simply by physic causes, and would stand, upon that account, unrelated to the Moral Law as the Law of Freedom. An ACT of this sort would not be a DEED; and regarding it there could neither be COMMAND nor PROHIBITION, nor yet PERMISSION.

[8] SCHILLER, in that exquisite masterpiece "ON GRACE AND DIGNITY," disapproves highly of my rigorous representation of obligation, and maintains (vol. xvii. p. 221-4, 1820) that such tenets, if acted on, can only beget manners fitted for the cloister. But since I find that we are at one on every other point, even in the most weighty principles, I am unwilling to allow that there can be here any discrepancy, provided only we can mutually understand each other. I at once admit that I cannot associate *grace* with the *dignity* of the IDEA DUTY; for this idea imports co-action, *i. e.* unconditionate necessitation, wherewith the ease of grace is quite inconjungible. The Majesty of the Law (like that on SINAI) inspires AWE (not dread that daunts, nor yet charms that invite), *i. e.* REVERENCE felt by a subject towards his Governor; which, however, in the present case, since the Commander lies *within* ourselves, is A FEELING OF THE SUBLIMITY OF OUR OWN DESTINY, transfixing and transporting the mind far more intensely than any beauty. And yet VIRTUE, *i. e.* the well-grounded intent of invariably discharging all one's duties, is productive of most beneficial effects, more so than all that nature or art in the world can accomplish; and so fair, or even glorious, a portraiture of humanity admits very well of being accompanied by the GRACES, who, so long as *mere* duty is concerned, stand reverently aside. When regard is had to the physical grace wherewithal virtue would enrobe the world, were it universally pursued; then does moral legislative reason call on fancy and the powers of sense for aid. But it is only after having overcome the Hydra that Hercules can attend the Muses—a toil from which the graceful sisters shrink. So that, were the question put, what AESTHETIC CHARACTER, or, as it were, what TEMPERAMENT BELONGS TO VIRTUE?—valiant, and by consequence JOYOUS, or anxious and dejected? scarce any answer would be needed. The latter slavish tone of soul never can be where there is not a latent HATRED of the Law; and the joyous heart, in DISCHARGING duty (not complacency in RECOGNISING it), betokens that the virtuous sentiments are genuine, nay, is the test that PIETY is real—piety consisting not in the *self-reproachings of a whining*

remark, which is of the most vital moment in ethics, viz. that the freedom of the will is endowed with this peculiar property, that it never can be determined by any spring to any act, EXCEPT IN SO FAR AS MANKIND HAVE HIMSELF ADOPTED, AND TAKEN UP THAT SPRING INTO HIS MAXIM, *i. e.* have transformed it into a universal rule, according to which he wills to conduct himself. In no other manner can a spring, be it what it may, consist with the absolute spontaneity of a free choice. Again, the moral law is,—our own reason being judge,—itself the originary spring, and whoso makes it his maxim, is MORALLY good. But if, notwithstanding, the law does not determine a person's choice, then some contrary spring must influence the will; and since, by hypothesis, this can only happen by a man's adopting this spring, and along with it its necessary effect, viz. the swerving from the Law, into his maxim (in which latter case the man is evil), it follows that Ins inward mindedness to observe or depart from the law is never in a state of equilibrious indifference, and that mankind never can be neither good nor evil.

Neither can man be in some points good, and at the same time in others morally evil. For is he in any one point morally good, then has he made the Moral Law his maxim; but should he at the same time be in some other points bad, then would,—since the Moral Law is but one and yet universal,—the maxim referring to it, be at once a general and a particular maxim, which is a contradiction.[9]

To have one or other of those sentiments, as a connate property by NATURE, does not mean to say that the man who entertains them is not their author, *i. e.* has not himself acquired them, but signifies that they have not been acquired *in time*, so that he must be regarded as one or other of them, FROM YOUTH UP CONTINUALLY. The turn of mind (called its *sentiment or mindedness*), *i. e.* the last subjective ground of adopting

---

sinner (a state of mind I look upon as exceedingly equivocal, and which is for the most part the man's inward upbraidings at having erred against a dictate of prudential expediency), but in the steadfast unfaltering determination to make the matter better in all time to come; and this purpose gaining in life and force by the constancy wherewith the ethical ascetic knows he has adhered to his predeterminate resolves, must needs beget a joyful disposition, apart from which no one can be certain that he LOVES the moral good, *i. e.* has adopted it into his maxims.

[9] The Moral Philosophers of Antiquity, who nearly exhausted every question that can be raised in ethic, did not forget to discuss the branches of the above dilemma. The first query was worded thus: "MUST VIRTUE BE LEARNED?" *i. e. Is man by nature indifferent alike to vice or its opposite?* the second, "CAN THERE BE MORE THAN ONE VIRTUE?" *i. e. Can virtue subsist fragmentarily in the mind, and man be virtuous and vicious by halves?* Both were denied with peremptory and rigoristical precision, and rightly; for they considered virtue as it is in the idea of reason. And yet, on the other hand, when we contemplate this moral being AS A PHENOMENON, *i. e.* according to what experience and observation teach, then may either question be answered in the affirmative; for then he is not weighed in the balance of pure reason (*before a Divine Tribunal*), but measured by an *a posteriori* standard (*before a Human Court*), of which more anon in the sequel.

maxims, can be but one, and goes universally to the whole use of freedom. Farther, this ground must itself have been adopted by one's own free choice, otherwise it could not be imputed. Again, the ulterior subjective ground or inward cause of such adoption cannot be known, although it is impossible not to inquire after it; since, to account for it, all that could be done, would be to assign another maxim, into which that sentiment had been adopted, and which maxim, again, must have had a farther ground; wherefore, seeing that this sentiment, or rather its last ground, cannot be deduced nor explained from any act of choice, as a *first act in time*, we call it a property of Will, belonging *by Nature* to the appetitive faculty, although, in point of fact, it arises from the Will's own Freedom. Moreover, when we say of mankind that he is by Nature good or evil, those moral properties are not predicated of him individually, as if some particulars were by nature good, and only others evil; although, to become entitled to understand those terms as applicable generally to the whole race, can take place only then, when anthropological investigations show, that the grounds entitling us to ascribe to one single man, either of those characters, are such as to leave no room for excepting *any* from their influence.

SECTION I.

OF MANKIND'S ORIGINARY PREDISPOSITION TOWARD GOOD.

This aboriginal substratum may be fitly brought all under review, when classed according to the three following heads:

I. The substratum of man's ANIMALITY as a living being.

II. The substratum of his HUMANITY as a living, and at the same time intelligent being.

III. The substratum of his PERSONALITY as an intelligent and accountable being.[10]

---

[10] The third predisposition cannot be regarded as already exhausted by either or both of the two former; for although an animal may have reason, it follows not, from that circumstance alone, that his intellect should possess the ability of determining unconditionally his will, and that too by the mere representing of the fitness of a maxim for universal legislation; *i. e.* it does not follow, because man has reason, *that reason* should be self-practical, at least not so far as we can see. How intelligent soever a creature might be, it might very possibly still stand in need of certain springs taken from desired objects, in order to determine its volitions; nay, it might bestow the most prudent and deliberate judgment both on the springs and means of action, so as thereby most commodiously to reach the end willed, without ever awaking to the reality, or even dreaming the possibility, of such a thing as a moral unconditionally-commanding law, which should announce itself at once as the determinator and supreme spring. Were not this law really given within us, never could we have quibbled into existence such a legislation by any stretch of reason, much less have wheedled our will into the belief of its authority. This law alone it is, that convinces us of the independency of our will on every outward and foreign determinative, and, along with this, of the imputability of all

1. The predisposition for mankind's ANIMALITY may be stated under the general denomination of MECHANICAL or instinctive self-love, *i. e.* such self-love as needs no exercise of reason, and is threefold; *first*, the appetite for self-preservation; *second*, toward the propagation of one's species by means of the connubial affections, and toward rearing whatever progeny may be procreated by inter-sexual commixtion; *third*, the taste for society, and general intercourse with one's fellow-men. Upon these, various sorts of vices may be ingrafted, though they spring not spontaneously from those predispositions as a root. They are the vices of an unpruned and uncultivated sensory, and may, when swerving farthest from the ends proposed by nature in giving man those appetites, be called BEASTLY VICES, viz. those of gluttony, drunkenness, voluptuousness, and that savage contempt of law exhibited in the life of systematic freebooters, pirates, and the like.

2. Man's HUMANITY may be all classed under the general title of COMPARATIVE self-love, for which theoretic reason is required, whereby we deem ourselves happy or the reverse, when compared with others as a standard. Hence springs the appetite for being thought to be some one in the eyes of others; this appetite, at first no more than a wish to be deemed their equal, so as not to allow to any one a superiority over us, attended, however, with the continual apprehension that others may seek to subject us to their sway, passes at last into a state of mind where we cherish an unjust desire of lording it over others. Upon this spirit of rivalry and emulation may be grafted the most enormous vices, bursting out into animosities, open or concealed, against all whom we look upon as *strangers*. And yet those vices do not sprout naturally from the soil of our humanity, but are re-agent vices, occasioned by our anxiety lest others should obtain a hateful authority over us, and impelling us, as a measure of precaution, to anticipate them, by usurping to ourselves the power we dread may be employed against us. Whereas nature, in implanting within us an emulous spirit— (a thing by no means inconsistent with mutual love)—aimed only at supplying a spur towards self-culture. Vices engraffed on this appetite may therefore be called CIVILIZED VICES, and are, when luxuriant in wickedness, known by the name of the DEVILISH VICES,—ENVY; INGRATITUDE; and MALICE.

3. Man's predisposition for PERSONALITY consists in his susceptibility for such reverence toward the moral law as is of itself sufficient to make the law the immediate spring of will. Merc susceptibility for reverence toward the law is the moral sense; but this in itself would not justify us in taking it for any particular predisposition pointing to any particular end; it can be held so only so far forth as it is an original spring of will. Again, since reverence can

---

our actions.

only be constituted such a spring by the will's freely adopting it into its maxim, which, when done, imparts to the person whose choice is so regulated, a good character, and this, like every character belonging to a free choice, is something that must always be acquired; it follows that for the possibility of such acquisition a predisposition of some sort or other, in our ethical economy, is demanded, whereupon nothing that is evil can be grafted. The naked idea of the moral law, even with the reverence inseparably attaching to it, cannot with propriety be looked upon as the substratum of man's personality—on the contrary, it is itself his personality—is the very idea of a man's humanity considered quite intellectually. That we are able to adopt this reverence into our maxims, thereby making it a spring, must rest upon some subjective ground; and this would seem to be somewhat additional, superinduced on our personality, and this *surplus* is what may be fitly termed a predisposition toward, and for behoof of, our moral personality.

Recapitulating the three aforesaid aboriginal substrata according to the conditions of their possibility, it is apparent that the FIRST needs no rational power of any sort; that the second does indeed require a practical exercise of reason, but only in subservience to physical springs; while the third alone is self-practical, *i. e.* has unconditionally-legislative reason working at the root. All these predispositions of humanity are not only *negatively* GOOD, *i. e.* so far forth as they are in no wise repugnant to the moral law; but they even tend positively toward good, so far forth as they actually advance and assist in its execution. They are all ORIGINARY; for human nature would be impossible without them, and though the two former may be abused and perverted, none of them can be extirpated. The term *predisposition*, applied to any being, must be understood to mean not only the elements essential to its constitution, but also that FORM of their arrangement whereby the agent is made what he is. Such elements are ORIGINARY when they are of necessity pre-required toward the possibility of a creature's being precisely what he is: CONTINGENT could the Being still be essentially the same without them. Finally, let it be remarked, that in this section no predispositions have been spoken of, except such as immediately refer to the faculty of appetition, and the determinableness of its choice.

SECTION II.

OF THE BIAS TO EVIL IN HUMAN NATURE.

By the term BIAS (*propensity or proneness*), I understand the subjective ground of the possibility of acquiring all at once inveterate habits, so far forth as such habitual desire is in itself only adventitious, and casually superinduced upon human nature. A Bias[11] must not be confounded with a predisposition; for though both may be brought by mankind into the world with him at his birth, still the bias must not be regarded as merely congenite or innate; but must—be the bias to good or to evil—be farther looked upon as matter of acquisition, and entailed by the man upon himself. At present we speak only of a Bias to Moral Evil; and since evil can arise only from a perverse determination of one's free choice, which choice again can only be deemed good or evil when regard is had to the maxims it has adopted, it follows that the bias to evil can only consist in the subjective ground of the possibility of an Agent-Intelligent's maxims swerving from the Moral Law; and if this bias can be predicated of mankind universally, *i. e.* as marking and making part of the character of the race, then may it be fitly called a NATURAL BIAS of mankind to evil. To all which is to be added, that the hence arising ability or disability of the choice to make the Moral Law its maxim, is what is called the having of A GOOD OR EVIL HEART.

We may figure to ourselves three different degrees of this badness of heart: *FIRST*, it is the general weakness of man's heart in not adhering to good maxims originally determined on, or, in other words, THE FRAILTY OF OUR NATURE. *SECOND*, the tendency to mix up immoral with the moral springs, which, even although this admixture should take place with a good intention, and from (*supposed?* TR.) maxims of good, must nevertheless be called IMPURITY. *LASTLY*, the bias to adopt merely evil maxims, which is the DEPRAVITY of man's nature, or of his heart.

---

[11] BIAS (*Hang*) is, strictly speaking, the *susceptibility* of so liking an object of desire, as that when once the Subject has tasted the enjoyment, a permanent appetite toward it is thereby forthwith established. Thus all savages carry about with them a Bias toward intoxicating liquors; for though there be many among them who know not the excitement of inebriation, and so by consequence entertain no desire for those things which produce it, still it is only necessary to allow them this gratification *for a single time*, in order to found an almost ineradicable appetite for spirits. Midway betwixt appetite and bias (both which presuppose acquaintance with the object desired) lies INSTINCT, a want felt to do or enjoy something yet unknown (*e. g.* the plastic instincts of animals or our own for sex). Lastly, there is a stage of desire above appetite, viz. PASSION (not *emotion*, for emotions, whether affectionate or disaffected, belong to the feelings of pain and pleasure), which is an appetite that excludes and takes away all self-command.—[Compare Kant's *Introduction to the Elementology of Ethics*, § xvi. and Anthropologic, § 77. Tr.]

FIRST, the frailty of human nature afforded matter of complaint even to an Apostle: "What I would, that I do not." Willing I am, but the execution follows not, *i. e.* I adopt the good (tire law) into the maxim of my choice; but this, which is objectively in idea (*in thesi*) an irresistible spring, is notwithstanding subjectively (*in hypothesi*), when the maxim is to be acted on, the weaker, when compared with the appetitive springs.

SECOND, The IMPURITY of the human heart consists in this: The maxim is very likely, in regard of its nature and end aimed at (viz. the intended observance of the law) good, and even a sufficiently powerful mobile to action; but then it is not purely moral, *i. e.* the law is not, as it should be, stated in the maxim as of itself ALONE the SUFFICIENT spring, but there are required at times (*perhaps at all times*) other springs different from the law to assist in bending the choice toward that which duty would demand. In other words, conduct, although dutiful, has not been performed purely out of duty.

THIRD, the DEPRAVITY, or, if the term be preferred, the CORRUPTION, of the Human Heart, is the bias whereby the choice leans to maxims that postpone the spring afforded by the Moral Law in favour of other and immoral springs. It may be likewise called the PERVERSITY of the Human Heart, inasmuch as it inverts or perverts the ethical order of a FREE will's springs; and although legally good actions may still be exhibited notwithstanding that inward disorder, the cast of thinking is (*so far as the moral-mindedness of the Agent is concerned*) corrupted at its root, and the man must upon that account be characterized as evil.

The reader will have observed that the bias to evil is here charged upon all men, even the best in outward actions, which moreover must be done, if the universality of a bias to evil is to be proved as extant among all men, or, which says the same thing, if we are to show that the bias is interwoven with the nature of man.

There is, however, betwixt a man of good morals (*bene moratus*) and a morally good man (*moraliter bonus*) no difference, so far at least as the harmony of their actions with the law is concerned, except this, that with the one the law is not always, perhaps never, whereas with the other it is AT ALL TIMES, the alone and supreme spring. Of the first we may say, HE OBSERVES THE LETTER OF THE LAW (*i. e.* so far forth as regards the act commanded by the law), of the other, however, HE HAS OBSERVED ITS SPIRIT; (the spirit of the law consists herein, that it be alone and by itself a sufficient spring) AND THAT WHATEVER IS NOT OF THIS FAITH, IS SIN (*in respect of the Formal of the intent*). For whenever ulterior springs are required to determine the choice to make its election of legi-conform acts, such, for instance, as ambition, self-love, a good-natured instinct, or sympathy, all which obviously differ from the law, then is it merely accidental that these coincide in any given conjuncture with the same; and they might possibly just as easily invite to transgression. The maxim according to whose worth all moral value of the person must be estimated, is notwithstanding itself *illegal;* and the man remains, in the midst of merely good deeds all the while evil.

Farther explanation may be needful to clear up the notion of a BIAS. Every bias is either physical, *i. e.* belongs to man's choice as an organized product of the physical system, or it is ethical, *i. e.* affects his choice as a Moral Agent. In the former sense, there can be no bias to moral evil, for a bias of this sort must arise from freedom; and a physical bias (resting upon sensitive excitement) toward any use of freedom—be it good or bad—is a contradiction. An indwelling bias toward evil can therefore cleave only to the moral faculty of choice. Again, nothing can be morally (*i. e.* imputably) evil that is not our own DEED. Contrariwise, however, is understood by a *bias*, a subjective determinator of choice antecedent to every deed, which bias, therefore, is not yet itself a deed. The bare representation of a bias to evil, would, by consequence, contain a contradiction, were not the expression taken in a twofold sense, either adapting itself to the idea freedom. Now, the term "*deed*" or "*act*" may signify that primordial use of freedom whereby the supreme and ruling maxim—contrary to, or in harmony with, the law—was determined on, or it may equally well denote that derived exercise of will whereby outward actions themselves (*i. e.* acts materially considered, so far forth as they are objects of choice), are actually brought forth, conformably to such maxim. The indwelling bias toward evil is a deed in the former sense (*peccatum originarium*), and at the same time the formal ground of every illegal deed in the second sense (*peccatum derivativum*), when it is called VICE. The guilty demerit of the first subsists even while that of the second is most carefully and successfully eschewed by dint of springs differing from the law. The one act is a *deed cogitable*, patent to reason *a priori*, independently of all conditions of time; the other is a *deed sensible*, *a posteriori*, exhibited in time (*Factum Phenomenon*). It is the former, as more particularly contradistinguished from the latter, that is a bias, and held connate, chiefly because it never can be extirpated (which uprooting would demand a supreme maxim morally good, a thing impossible, since, owing to the presence of the bias, the uppermost and ruling bent is already figured as morally evil); and also because the question, why evil should have corrupted our dominant and last maxim of choice? is as unanswerable (although the corruption be our own deed) as is the inquiry after the causes of any other fundamental property, now once for all belonging to our being. What has just been here advanced assigns the ground, why in this section we at once sought the three sources of moral evil only there, where, agreeably to laws of freedom, was to be sought the ultimate ground of choosing or of observing our practical maxims,—overlooking the sensory as mere receptivity.

SECTION III.

MAN IS BY NATURE EVIL.

Vitiis nemo sine nascitur. HORAT.

THE position, MAN IS EVIL, can consequently signify nothing more than this: He is inwardly aware of the authority of the moral law, and has, notwithstanding, adopted the intent of occasionally swerving from it into his maxim. To say that BY NATURE he is evil, imports that evil can be predicated of him, considered as a race; not however as if such wicked quality could be concluded upon from the general notion of humanity, for in this latter event his indwelling evil would be necessary, *i. e.* mankind, as known by us from observation and experience, cannot be otherwise judged of; *or thus*—we may presuppose this evil as subjectively-necessary, in every, even the best man. Again, since the bias must itself be regarded as morally evil, consequently as no gift of nature, but as something that may be imputed, it must consist in illegal maxims of choice. Farther, since this illegality must,—the will being free,—be regarded as fortuitous; which contingency, however, would seem to be at variance and incompatible with this evil's universality, unless the first subjective ground of appointing maxims be interwoven, somehow or other, and, as it were, rooted, in the substratum of humanity: we shall therefore call this bent a natural bias to evil; and since it is self-demerited, we shall moreover call it a RADICAL EVIL, inborn in the nature of man, and yet nevertheless entailed by him upon himself.

That such a corrupt bias must really be rooted in mankind, scarce needs a regular proof, when we reflect on the multitude of crying instances, thrown by the observed ACTIONS of man into our hands. Do we prefer examples from that state of society philosophers have eulogized as setting forth the primeval good-natured dispositions of the race? then we need only to contrast with this hypothesis the scenes of wanton and unprovoked cruelty in the murderous dramas enacted on the stage of TOFOA, NEW ZEALAND, and the NAVIGATORS' ISLANDS, or the ceaseless feuds[12] that devastate (*according to Captain Hearne*)

---

[12] Like the perpetual war betwixt the Arathavesqwa, and the dog-ribbed Indians,—a war having no other end in view than mutual murder. In their opinion, martial valour is the chief virtue of savage life. Even in civilized states, warlike intrepidity is an object of admiration, and the ground of an especial regard expected by that profession who deem courage their only boast; and not without reason: for, that mankind can propose to himself something as his end, prized by him even higher than life (HONOUR), and where he divests himself of every interested aim, demonstrates a certain sublimity in his internal

whole tracts of North-West America,—from which deadly havock not one individual derives the smallest gain,—and we have vices of the savage more than enough to make us abandon that assumption. Think we, on the other hand, to find a more favourable portrait of human nature among civilized nations (where their faculties are better and more fully developed), and we shall straightway hear a long melancholy litany, whose stanzas contain nothing but indictments against humanity: we shall hear of a secret guile betwixt even the most cordial friends, so that a certain moderation and reserve of confidence is recommended even in friendship, as an indispensable rule of prudence; of a propensity to hate those who have obliged us, and for which return every benefactor must be prepared; of a hearty good-will, which still leaves room for the remark, that there is something in the misfortunes of a very dear friend not altogether displeasing to us, of many other vices cloaked with a specious and dissembled mantle of virtue; to say nothing of those open faults which disdain all secrecy; and we shall have enough of the civilized vices (the most mortifying of all) to cause us to avert our view from the faulty conduct of our fellows, lest we superinduce upon us a still farther, and perhaps more hateful vice, that of misanthropy. Should this catalogue, however, not yet suffice, then let any one attend to the vices curiously compounded out of both at once, obtaining betwixt states in their outward international relations, where countries, although civilized, place themselves to one another in the relation of savage hordes, *i. e.* into a state of continual readiness for war, and that, too, with such forethought obstinacy, that they seem to have taken up the rooted opinion, that standing armies never are to be abandoned; and be will immediately perceive, that those great societies called NATIONS[13] proceed upon principles diametrically

---

predispositions. And yet the complacency wherewith conquerors extol their mighty feats of destruction and implacable death, shows but too clearly, that mere violent superiority, and the havock they can effect, even apart from every other view is precisely that whereon they most plume themselves.

[13] Looking at the historical progress of states as the phenomenal exhibition of those internal predispositions of our humanity that are for the most part hidden from our own view, we become aware of a certain mechanical precession, whereby nature advances her own ends, even while defeating and disappointing nations of theirs. Every state endeavours to enlarge its territories by overrunning all adjacent whom it hopes to conquer, and so, if possible, to erect a universal monarchy; a state of matters where all freedom, and along with it its fruits, viz. virtue, taste, and science, must expire. But the monster, after having devoured all its neighbours, explodes by and by of itself,—its laws losing by degrees all co-active power,—and becoming broken up by insurrection and revolt into several lesser states., These, instead of combining in a *civitas maxima* (*i. e.* a commonwealth of free confederate peoples), begin in turn the same game of new, lest war (that scourge of our species) should cease; a thing, which, although by no means so Incurably evil as the deadly sepulture of a universal empire (or even as A HOLY ALLIANCE, to guarantee to DESPOTS their respective DESPOTISMS for ever), docs, nevertheless, as was remarked by one of the ancients, *make* far more wicked men than it removes.

contrary to their professed objects—principles whereof they know not how to divest themselves,—which no philosopher has yet been able to bring into harmony with morality, nor (which is worst) in exchange for which has he been able to propose any better, that would be in unison with human nature; from whence it has happened, that the philosophical MILLENNIUM, which expects a period of perpetual peace, grounded on a universal league of nations, constituting themselves into a grand cosmical republic, is—just like the THEOLOGICAL, which tarries for the complete moral amendment of the whole human race,—universally derided as a fanatical delusion.

The ground of this evil cannot be placed (*first*), as is commonly done, in the HUMAN SENSORY, and the thence arising natural appetites and wants; for not only have the appetites no immediate reference to evil (on the contrary, by allowing the moral sentiment to appear in its force, they afford opportunity to good); but farther, we are not accountable for their existence (neither can we impute them to ourselves; for, as *con-created*, we are not their author); but what we are by all means accountable for, is the bias to evil, which, as it affects the morality of our own subject, *i. e.* that wherein and whereby we are free agents, must, as self-demerited, by all means be imputed to us, notwithstanding the deep inrooting of that bias into our choice; upon account of which bias, we must say that evil is by nature indwelling in man. Neither can (*secondly*) the ground of this evil be placed in a corruption of moral-legislative reason, as if reason had abrogated and defaced within itself the authority of the law, and rebelled against the obligation founded on it; for this last is absolutely impossible. An agent, free, and at the same time absolved from his corresponding Moral Law of Liberty, is a manifest contradiction, and tantamount to fancying a cause in operation without efficient laws. So then, to explain the ground of moral evil in man, the sensory contains too little; for the sensory, by itself alone, and abstractedly from those springs originated by freedom, lowers man merely to an ANIMAL; whereas the hypothesis of an absolutely wicked will, and a reason renouncing the government of its own laws, contains too much; since, in this latter case, a principle of antagonism against the law would be constituted the ruling spring, and the person would be transformed to a DEVIL. Neither of these characters, however, can properly be applied to mankind.

Although the existence of a bias to evil can be sufficiently set forth by the proved collision of man's choice with the law, still such phenomena, experienced and observed in time, do not acquaint us with the inward nature nor the true ground of this enmity; for, since this antagonism obtains betwixt free choice (*i. e.* such a choice as can only be cogitated by an *a priori* notion), and the moral law, so far forth as it is a spring (where, again, we have still to deal with a pure intellectual conception), it follows, that it must be cognisable *a priori*, and be

Immanuel Kant 29

deduced from the idea EVIL, so far as such evil is possible according to freedom's laws of obligation and imputability. What follows is the evolution of this idea.

No man (not even the worst) does in any maxim state a rebellion against the moral law by a studied renunciation, and, as it were, disclamation of his due obedience. On the contrary, the law does, by force of his moral nature, thrust itself irresistibly upon him; and were no oilier spring astir in the mind, he would adopt it as a sufficient determinator into his uppermost maxim, *i. e.* he would be morally good. But, by means of his physical nature, although equally harmless with the other, he leans toward the springs of sense, and, agreeably to the subjective principles of self love, adopts these also into his maxims of life. But were he to do so irrespectively of the law, and make them by themselves alone, the singly-sufficient determinators of his acts, then he would be morally evil. Since now he naturally adopts both into his maxims, and since either, when alone, would be found quite enough to afford a ground of voluntary determination; he would,—if the moral difference of maxims depended only on the difference of their contained springs (*i. e. on the matter of those maxims*), viz. whether the law, or an impulse of sense, were such matter,—be at once both morally good and evil, which, however agreeably to what was laid down in the exordium, is a contradiction. Consequently, that whereby a man is morally good or evil, cannot depend on the *difference* of the springs adopted by him into his maxims (*not on their matter*), but on their *subordination* (on their FORM), namely, WHICH ONE HE CHOOSES TO MAKE THE CONDITION OF THE OTHERS.

Hence it appears that mankind is only evil so far forth as he inverts the ethical order of those springs which he adopts into his maxims. In choosing his principles of life, he begins by attempting to place self-love and the moral law alongside of one another; and on becoming aware that they cannot subsist as co-ordinates, but that one must necessarily be subordinated to the other as its condition, he makes the selfish spring condition his observance of the law; whereas the latter it is that ought to be the condition precedent of his gratifying the former, and stated as the alone and exclusively prior spring in his supreme and most universal maxim.

Notwithstanding this invertedness of the will's springs, contrary to their legitimate ethical order, actions may outwardly be as much in harmony with the law as if they had sprung from genuine motives; so long as reason lends to the appetitive springs, when integrated as greatest-happiness principles, that unity which would otherwise belong to the moral law—a case where a man's outward and observed character is good, although his intelligible remain all the while evil.

If, now, there be in human nature a *proneness* to this inverting of the proper order of the will's springs, then is there in man a natural bias toward evil; and such bias is itself morally evil, for it must be regarded as seated in the will's free causality, and consequently as imputable. This evil is RADICAL, for it corrupts man's maxims in their last ground. Moreover, as a natural bias, it never can be extirpated by any exertions of the human subject, for this could only take place by force of good maxims, which, when the supreme subjective ground of all maxims is already corrupt, never can occur; nevertheless it can be OUTWEIGHED, being met with in mankind who are free agents.

The vitiosity of human nature is, therefore, not so much WICKEDNESS—this word being understood in its severest sense, namely, as an inward wickedness, or intent of choosing evil as evil (for that were diabolical),—as rather PERVERSITY of heart, which, on account of the consequences flowing from it, is called AN EVIL HEART. This, however, is not inconsistent with a state of Will that may generally and on the whole be good, and arises from the infirmity of human nature, which is not sufficiently strong to adhere to the good principles it may once for all have adopted; coupled, however, with the impurity (insincerity) of not duly sifting and arranging the springs according to their ethic content, and of having an eye mainly to this, that actions quadrate with the Law, although they have not been originated by it. Now, although from such a state of matters VICE may not immediately arise, still the cast of thinking, whereby the absence of vice is looked upon as virtue, is already a radical perversity of the human heart.

This guilt, called connate, because it shows itself as early as the first utterances of Mankind's Freedom, though sprung from it and imputable, may, in its two first stages of frailty and impurity, be regarded as unintentional (*culpa*), and only in the third as forethought crime (*dolus*); for it bears the character of a certain GUILE (*dolus malus*) of heart, whereby we deceive ourselves as to the state of our own good or evil sentiments, and, instead of troubling ourselves about our moral or immoral mindedness, deem ourselves rather justified before the Law, so long as our actions draw after them no bad effects—a case which, for any thing that the maxims are worth, might very well happen. Hence comes the peace of conscience of many who think themselves religious: in the midst of actions where no consideration was had of the Law, or, however, where the Law had not preponderating sway, they luckily escape from all unpleasant sequents, and hence have not only a tranquil mind, but perhaps even a self-opinion of their own merit, by feeling themselves guiltless of those transgressions wherewith they observe others to be stained. Nor do they think it needful to inquire whether this exemption be owing merely to the bounty of fortune, or whether the very same vices might not have been committed by them, had not imbecility, constitutional temperament, education, or circumstances of time and place (all things quite unimputable), led them to refrain. This insincerity, shrouding our real inward character from our view, prevents the founding of genuine moral principles within, and spreads, after having deceived ourselves, so as next to beguile and impose upon others, which, if not wickedness, is at least worthlessness, and proceeds from the radical evil of human nature, which, by distorting and untuning our moral understanding in regard of what a man is to be taken for, renders slippery and uncertain all ethical imputation, and constitutes that rotten spot in humanity, which, until entirely severed, keeps back the germ of good from unfolding itself, as it otherwise infallibly would do.

A member of the British Parliament once, in the heat of debate, threw out the remark, *"Every one has a price, for which he is certainly to be had."* Should this indeed be true (and let each determine for himself), and if there is absolutely no virtue for which a grade of temptation cannot be assigned sufficient for its overthrow; and if our enlisting under the banners of the good or the evil principle depend on the highest bidder and quickest payment; then may that be universally true of all men, once taught by an Apostle, *"There is here no difference, for all are gone astray. There is none that doeth good* (according to the spirit of the Law); no, not one."[14]

SECTION IV.

OF THE ORIGIN OF EVIL IN HUMAN NATURE.

A FIRST BEGINNING is that origination of an effect by a cause, where the cause is not itself the effect of any other cause of the like kind. A COMMENCEMENT may be considered as being either a cogitable or a sensible original. In the former respect, we consider only the EXISTENCE of the effect; but in the latter, the HAPPENING of the effect, where consequently the effect is as an event referred to its CAUSE IN

---

[14] Of this condemnatory sentence of morally judging reason, the proof is contained, not in this, but in the former section; the above confirms only by experience the accuracy of the previous deduction. But experience and observation cannot unveil the original of this evil, lying, as it does, in the uppermost maxim regulating our free choice, the appointment or adopting of which governing principle is AN INTELLIGIBLE ACT, anterior to all experience. Hence, likewise, viz. from the incomplex unity of the uppermost maxim and the similarly' uncompounded unity' of the standard law, we comprehend why the pure intellectual judgment of mankind's morality proceeds on the principle of excluding any intermediary betwixt good and evil; although, when judging of actions *merely as deeds exhibited to sense,* the position is quite admissible that there may be a mean betwixt the moral extremes. Thus, we may hold *negatively,* that, prior to any education, man is indifferent to both good and evil; or *positively,* that his moral actions are mixed, being partly good and partly bad. But these experimental judgments speak of the character of man so far forth only as it is A SENSIBLE PHENOMENON, and must give place to the pure *a priori* intellectual decision when a final and conclusive adjudication of the whole case is required.

TIME. When an effect is referred to a cause wherewith it stands connected agreeably to the laws of freedom, as is the case with moral evil, then is the determination of choice toward its production, viewed in connection, not with its determining grounds in time, but with those in pure *a priori* reason only, and can consequently not be deduced from any ANTECEDENT state; although this last must always be done when an evil action is as an EVENT in the external world referred to its efficient cause in the physical system. To search for an origin in time, of free actions as such, is a contradiction; and it is equally a contradiction to inquire after any such origin of the moral peculiarities of man so far forth as these last are regarded as contingent; the last ground of the use of freedom must, like every determinative of free choice whatsoever, be sought for exclusively in intellectual representations.

Whatever the origin of the moral evil of humanity may be, assuredly, of all representations, the most improper and inept is that whereby its propagation over the race is figured as if it descended to us BY INHERITANCE from our first parents; for of moral evil we may well say what the poet affirms of mankind's good-desert, "*Genus, et proavos, et quæ non fecimus ipsi, vix ea nostra voco.*"[15] Farther, it is to be noted, that in investigating the origin of evil, we do not at first take into consideration the bias toward it (as *peccatum in potentia*); but sift only the internal possibility of the true and actual evil of given actions, and those conditions of choice that must concur and co-operate with that possibility, before such evil can be perpetrated.

Every wicked action whatsoever must, when we consider its cogitable original, be so depictured to the mind as if the person had fallen directly into it, out of a state of innocence: for, let a man's previous deportment have been what it may, and whatsoever may have been the physical force bearing in upon him; nay, whether those physic forces be entirely without, or, moreover, also within the man; nevertheless Iris act is free and undetermined by any one of those

---

[15] The three academical faculties would make intelligible, each after its own fashion, this hereditary transmission, viz. as HEREDITARY DISEASE, as A HERITABLE DEBT, or as INHERITED DEPRAVITY. (1.) The medical faculty would figure to themselves this heir-loom of evil as something like a tape-worm, concerning which many natural historians are of opinion, that since nothing like it is found elsewhere, not even in any other animal, this insect must have been pre-existent in our first parents. (2.) Lawyers would regard it as the legal consequence of our succeeding to a patrimony burdened severely with sundry casualties of superiority, or other monstrous *debita fundi*. (To be born is nothing else than to acquire possession of the goods of the earth, in so far as those are indispensably requisite to our support.) We must now discharge (suffer for) those obligations, and are notwithstanding eventually torn by death from our possessions. (3.) Theologians regard this evil as the personal participation of our first parents in the apostacy of an outcast rebel, and that we either then (although now no longer aware of it) joined his party, or that, born at present under his dominion, we take more pleasure in the Prince of this World's goods than in the sovereign behest of our Heavenly Lawgiver; by which breach of allegiance, however, we can only expect hereafter to share his destiny.

invading causes; and hence such deed not only *can*, but in truth *must*, be held AN ORIGINARY USE OF CHOICE. He ought to have eschewed it, in what conjunctures and circumstances soever he may have been placed; for by no cause in the world can he ever cease to be a free, *i, e.* a spontaneously acting being. Farther, we rightly say, that we impute to every man the CONSEQUENCES arising from his former free immoral acts, and by this we obviate an evasion that might otherwise be attempted, by inquiring whether those sequents themselves be not beyond our control; because in the primary free act giving them birth, there is already extant sufficient ground of imputing them *likewise*. What although an intelligent may have been never so inveterately wicked, even up to his present and immediately instant act? what though his evil habits, long a second nature, should have grown into a first? still, notwithstanding, it has not only been all along incumbent on him to act otherwise, but it is likewise even NOW his immediate duty to amend; consequently such indebted change must be fully within his power, and he is, in the very moment of not altering his inner man, as open to an imputation of transgressing, as if endowed with a natural predisposition toward good—(a thing inseparable from freedom)—he were now, by an original lapse, falling from his pristine state of innocence into evil. We cannot therefore raise any question as to such deed's origin in time (*i. e. its chronic origin*), but can investigate only its origin in reason (*i. e. its cogitable origin*), when we wish to look into, and, if possible, explain the bias, *i. e.* the general subjective ground whereby we adopt into our maxim an intent of transgressing.

Quite analogous to what is here advanced is the representation of this matter given by the Scripture, when it describes the origin of evil as *chronologically* BEGINNING in the human race, and narrates what in the nature of things must have gone FIRST (apart from all conditions of time) as a commencement in time only. Agreeably to this ancient Chronicle, evil commences not from any indwelling bias toward it, for then its rise and spring would not be from the causality of freedom, but takes its origin from SIN, *i. e.* from the transgression of the Moral Law *qua* Divine Commandment. Again, the state of mankind antecedent to all bias toward evil is called the STATE OF INNOCENCE. In this state the Moral Law first announced itself to mankind by its VETO (Genesis, ii. 16, 17), as indeed it must do in the case of every agent not altogether pure, but exposed to the solicitations of appetite. But instead of exclusively giving ear to this law as the only unconditionately good spring, mankind began to beat about for sundry other springs (Ibid. iii. 6), which are no more than hypothetically good (viz. so far forth as they encroach not on the law), and made it his maxim (if we cogitate the act as emanating with full consciousness from freedom) to obey the Law of Duty, not singly out of *Duty*, but perchance with a view to some ulterior ends. Hence he began to quibble[16] away the severity of that commandment which secludes the influence of every other spring. By and by he degraded OBEDIENCE to the rank of a mere mean or condition subservient to principles of self-love; thus finally an undue weight of sensitive impulses became introduced into the maxims of life, the springs arising from the law were overbalanced, AND SO MANKIND SINNED. *Mutato nomine de te fabida narratur.* That we daily and hourly do just so; and that consequently "*in Adam all have sinned,*" and "*still sin,*" is self-evident from our previous remarks; with this difference, however, that WE come into the world with a connate bias to transgression, whereas in the first created pair no such bias—only innocence—is conceivable; wherefore a transit into evil is in their case spoken of as A FALL—in us as proceeding from the already extant and ingenite DEPRAVITY of our nature. This bias, however, signifies nothing farther, than that when we endeavour to unravel and retrace THE CHRONIC ORIGIN of evil, we must, for the cause of every predeterminate transgression, recede toward the sources of evil, along the links of time, backwards to that period when our rational faculties were as yet undeveloped; for the groundwork of which development we must assume a bias somewhere as a natural bent toward evil, called upon that account *connate*—a mode of figuring to ourselves the matter, that, since our first parents are held to have been created with, and instated in, the complete possession of all their faculties, is in their case quite impracticable. For had our progenitors brought with them into the world any such indwelling bias, then it would have been, not indeed connate, but, what is far worse, CONCREATED, and part of their aboriginal subsistency; whereas, as it is, their SIN is proposed to us as a FALL out of innocence.—Of a moral property imputable to our account, no origin in time is therefore to be sought, although it is quite inevitable not to attempt such an investigation when we wish to EXPLAIN to ourselves its contingent presence with our race. Whence perhaps also the Scripture, in condescension to our frailty, may have thought fit thus to represent the matter.

The cogitable origin of this disjointing of our choice, whereby subordinate springs have come to be uppermost, is inscrutable; for this bias to evil must itself be imputed to us, and consequently the ground of choosing evil maxims would itself need to be accounted for by presupposing some ulterior maxim to adopt such evil ground. Evil can

---

[16] All homage demonstrated toward the law, so long as we give it not, as by and for itself the sufficient spring, preponderating weight over every other determinative of choice, is HYPOCRITICAL, and the BIAS to pay such abortive homage INWARD GUILE, *i. e.* a bias to *self-deceit*, when quadrating ourselves with the moral law; upon which account it is that the Bible calls the Author of Evil (who, however, resides in ourselves) THE LIAR FROM THE BEGINNING; and thus characterizes mankind by what seems the main ground of his evil conduct.

only take its rise from what is morally bad, and cannot have the bounds of our finite nature for its source; and yet, since the originary predispositions of humanity (which, if this corruption is to be imputed to him, no one save mankind himself could destroy) are all substrata toward good, there remains no assignable ground whence moral evil can at first have flowed. This incomprehensibility, together with the more exact specifying of the grade of mankind's wickedness, is what is suggested by Holy Writ,[17] when it sets forth EVIL as coeval with the beginning of the world, though not yet to be met with in man, but pre-existent in a SPIRIT once of a most excellent and lofty nature; whereby is foreshadowed to us just this FIRST beginning of all evil as utterly unfathomable: for whence can have come the evil of this spirit?—as also farther, that since 'twas only BY HIS SEDUCTION that mankind lapsed into evil, we are not out-and-out corrupted, but still capable of amendment, and thereby contradistinguished from a seducing SPIRIT, in whose favour no fleshly appetites can be counted as an alleviation of his guilt; whereas with us, amid the ruin of our hearts there are remains of a good will, and consequently room for the not ungrounded hope of our return to that good from which we have swerved.

GENERAL SCHOLION.

OF RE-INSTATING THE PREDISPOSITION TOWARD GOOD, INTO ITS ORIGINARY POWER.

Whatever, in a moral sense, man is, or ought to be, whether good or evil, *that* must he either have made, or have still to make, OUT OF HIMSELF; either product must be the effect of his own free choice, since, if otherwise, it could not be imputed, and the man himself would consequently be MORALLY neither good nor evil: When it is said "mankind was created good," that can mean no more than that he was destined FOR GOOD by his Creator, and that his originary

---

[17] What is here said is not to be understood as if it were intended for Scriptural exegesis,—a thing quite beyond the legitimate boundary of pure reason. People may come to a general understanding as to the best mode of making available, for purposes of moral instruction, any historic document, without undertaking to say whether the interpretation is really the writer's meaning, or only one we put upon him; provided only that such interpretation contain what is in itself true, even independently of all historic evidence, and be moreover the only sense by dint of which we can extract from a passage somewhat conducive to moral edification;—since otherwise the narrative could be no more than a fruitless augmentation of our historical knowledge. People ought not needlessly to dispute about a document, and its historical authority, when that document's contents, how multiform soever they may be, tend in nowise to make us better men, or when, if they have that tendency, they can be known *aliunde* without documentary proof, and indeed *must* be so cognizable. Historical knowledge, which cannot have any inward reference to morality, nor validity for *every one*, falls under the class of *ethical adiaphora*, whereof each may take just as much as he finds edifying.

predispositions are good. Man is not, by force of these, already good, but only so far forth as he rejects or adopts the thence arising good springs into his maxims of conduct (which must be left entirely to his option) does he bring it about that he becomes either good or evil. Even admitting that toward his becoming good or better, supernatural co-operation were indispensable, then, whether this aid consist in withdrawing hinderances, or in lending him some positive help, mankind must nevertheless first of all make himself worthy to receive it, and must, by adopting this principle of intensifying strength into his maxim, LAY HOLD ON and appropriate it—which assuredly is no small matter: *thus alone* can such superadded good be adjudged to his account, and the man himself be reckoned morally well-deserving and of ethical desert.

How it is possible that one naturally and radically bad should come to make out of himself a man good—transcends all our information; for how can an evil tree bring forth good fruit? But since a tree confessedly good has, agreeably to our foregoing investigation, brought forth bad fruit;[18] and since the lapse from good into evil (when we bethink ourselves that it must arise from freedom) is not more comprehensible than a return from that evil toward good, the possibility of this latter transformation cannot be denied. Notwithstanding our fall, the commandment, "*it behoves us to become better men,*" resounds unintermittently throughout our soul; consequently we can amend, even were our own endeavour insufficient, and only rendering us susceptible of an unsearchable higher aid. In this assertion, we no doubt assume that a germ of good still subsists in its entire purity, alike uncorrupted and indestructible, which most certainly cannot be self-love;[19] for this

---

[18] A tree predisposed by its constitution toward good is no more than *possibly* good, not yet *really* so; for, were it actually good, then it could not bring forth bad fruit. It is only when mankind avails himself of the latent springs whereby he can act upon the law, that he becomes truly good (the tree an absolutely good tree.)

[19] Words that admit of a double sense not unfrequently prevent even the clearest grounds of reason from begetting a full and permanent conviction. As LOVE, so may SELF-LOVE be divided into that of BENEVOLENCE and COMPLACENCY. Both are quite consistent with reason. To make the former a principle of conduct is quite natural, for who would not wish for perpetual welfare? And yet this selfish good-will is only reasonable in so far as it proposes to itself those ends singly which may consist with the highest and most lasting happiness, and then chooses the fittest and most appropriate means for reaching those elements of well-being. In such circumstances, reason acts merely as a handmaid in the service of our ordinary appetites, and the systematic maxims that may be adopted for appeasing them stand quite unrelated to morality, or do rather, when made the unconditioned principles of volition, utterly subvert it. A reasonable love of SELF-COMPLACENCY may also be understood in a twofold manner: *first*, that we are well-pleased with ourselves in consequence of our gaining the aforementioned ends, and then such complacential self-love is identic with the love of a selfish good-will toward one's self. We take pleasure in ourselves, just as a tradesman, whose mercantile speculations turn out well, congratulates himself on his foresight and skill. Or, *second*, we may mean the self-love of an UNCONDITIONED COMPLACENCY, and this latter self-

last, when made a ruling principle of choice, is precisely the rise and source of every evil.

The redintegration of our aboriginal predisposition toward good, is consequently not the re-acquisition of a lost ethic spring; for this consisting in *reverence toward the moral law*, we never could by any possibility have forfeited; and could such forfeiture at all occur, then never could we again have resuscitated such a feeling within. The renovation of mankind's moral character, is therefore the reviving of reverence in ITS PRIMITIVE PURITY, as a condition precedent, that must qualify every maxim; agreeably to which reverence, the law,—not merely conjunctly with other springs, or perhaps postponed to them—but in its naked integrity, is re-established as of itself the sufficient spring determining our choice. The original good consists in that SANCTITY OF INTENT, which proposes to itself the execution of all duty, whereby whoso entertains such pure maxims, though not yet himself *holy* (for betwixt intent and act there lies a mighty gap), is notwithstanding on the road thitherward, and approximating his goal by endless progression. Readiness in performing dutiful actions is however called VIRTUE, when regard is had merely to the legality of a person's character, so far forth as it can be known from experience and observation (*Virtus Phænomenon*). Such virtuous character is in permanent possession of maxims, whence actions outwardly in harmony with the law arise—only the springs employed for this purpose are borrowed indifferently from any quarter. In this sense, virtue is acquired BIT-BY-BIT, and is defined by many to be a long habit of observing the law, whereby mankind passes, as he gradually reforms his conduct, from a proneness to vice, into a contrary bias toward virtue; for all which, no CHANGE OF HEART is needed, only a CHANGE OF MANNERS. Mankind deems himself virtuous when he feels his habits

---

complacency would not depend on whatever gain or losses might flow from our actions, but on the inward principle of such *self-approbation* as can alone spring from the subordination of all our maxims to the moral law. No one to whom morality is not indifferent, can be well-pleased with himself while conscious of sentiments militating against the law; on the contrary, such inward warfare can only leave room for a feeling of the most bitter self-dislike. Hence we may speak of a PRACTICAL SELF-LOVE, which disdains all admixture of foreign elements of happiness, and seeks satisfaction only in the pure *a priori* spring of choice. Since, however, this last is neither more nor less than immediate reverence toward the law, it is difficult to understand why people embarrass themselves by talking of a REASONABLE ami of a MORAL SELF-LOVE, seeing that ethically mankind can only like himself so far forth as he is aware of having made reverence for the law his ruling motive. Happiness is, agreeably to our sensitive nature, the first object that we unconditionally desire; although, when viewed in connection with our whole rational and free economy, it is neither the first nor yet unconditioned object of choice. This last is OUR WORTHINESS OF BEING RENDERED HAPPY; *i. e.* the harmony o all our maxims with the moral law. That this be made the objective condition, under which alone our wish for happiness can be brought into unison with legislative reason, is the drift and upshot of every ethic rescript; and a moral cast of thought just consists in harbouring only such conditioned wishes.

confirmed of performing what outwardly is duty, although his actions flow not from the supreme principle of morality. On the contrary, the intemperate grows sober for the sake of health: the liar betakes himself to truth, on account of his reputation; the fraudulent returns to municipal honesty from a view to repose or gain; all in conformity with the lauded greatest-happiness-principles. But for any one to become not merely a LEGALLY, but, moreover, a MORALLY-GOOD man (*i. e.* acceptable to God), that is, virtuous according to his intelligible character (*Virtus Noumenon*), and to make himself one who, when he recognises any thing to be his duty, needs no other or farther motive than just this very representation duty, *that* cannot be effected by any gradual reforms, so long as the basis of his maxims remains impure; but can only be accomplished by a TRANSVOLUTION of the sentiments of the inner man (an instant transit to maxims of holiness), and he becomes a new man only through a sort of regeneration, as it were by a new creation (*John*, iii. 5; *Genesis*, i. 2), and change of heart.

But if man is depraved at the bottom of his heart, how is it possible that he, by his own strength, can bring about this revolution within, and become, of his own accord, a good man? Nevertheless, duty thus enjoins; but the law ordains nothing impracticable, wherefore we must hold that the revolving takes place in the cast of thinking; and that the gradual reform affects the bent of the sensory so far forth as this last throws obstacles before the first: that is to say,—when by one single inflexible determination, mankind retroverts his will's perverted bias for choosing evil maxims, he then puts on a new man, and becomes, in regard of his principles and *inward-mindedness*, placed in a capacity for good: while, perceptibly, it is only through a long track of conduct that he can be seen even by himself to have grown into a good man. In a single word, it is to be hoped, that this purity of principle, now chosen as his dominant rule of life, will suffice to keep him unswervingly steady, along the good though narrow railway of a perpetual progression from bad to better. This progression is for him to whom the unknown depths of the heart are patent, and in whose All-Seeing eye the moments of the series are envisaged in their sum, an integral unity, *i. e.* is before God tantamount to being already a really good man, and acceptable in his sight: wherefore, thus far forth the change may be regarded as a finished and entire conversion of the heart. But for mankind, who can only estimate themselves, and the strength of their adopted maxims, by the upperhand they gradually gain *through time* over the sensory, the transition can never be regarded otherwise, than as an ever-enduring striving after what is better, consequently, as no more than a gradual reformation of the bias to evil.

Hence it follows, that the moral education of man cannot begin with correcting his manners, but must take its rise from a transvolving of his cast of thinking, and must set to work by endeavouring to beget and found a character. Commonly, however, people set about this matter otherwise, fighting against singular vices, and leaving the common root, whence they sprout, untouched. And yet mankind, even when gifted with the most scanty intellectuals, is just so much the more readily awakened to deeper feelings of reverence for duty, the more he is taught to withdraw therefrom all foreign motives that self-love might otherwise thrust into the maxims of conduct; even children are quite in a condition to detect any, aye I the smallest vestige, of an admixture of spurious with the genuine springs; whereupon actions, how seemly soever, lose straightway in their eyes all moral worth. This susceptibility for receiving impressions of the unadulterated moral good, admits of being so wonderfully cultivated, as to become stamped indelibly on the heart, when we propose to their youthful notice EXAMPLES of the illustrious dead, and make them sit in judgment on the ethical purity or impurity of their maxims, so far as that can be clearly gathered from the record of their actions;—an occupation of the understanding that soon gives to the naked idea DUTY preponderating weight. Contrariwise, to allow one's ethic pupils to WONDER at deeds of virtue, even though accomplished with the greatest sacrifices, is far from being the right key to which the mind should be attuned, in order to bring it to a moral pitch. It is a mistake to suppose that any good, mankind may do, can surpass his duty. Discharging duty, however, is only that regularity which is of the essence of a moral order of things, and is consequently nothing that deserves to be wondered at. Such wonder is rather mischievous in its effect, and unstrings the reverential chords of duty, by representing its performance, as something meritorious and extraordinary.

One thing, however, there is, which, when rightly apprehended, never ceases to transfix the soul with the highest possible admiration, and where such admiration is not only just, but does likewise clarify and exalt the soul—and that is the originary substratum for morality itself. What is that (mankind may well ask himself) whereby he, dependent by so many wants on the physical system, is, notwithstanding, at the same time raised so far above it, by force of the idea of an original susceptibility within, that all those wants shrink to nothing, and he himself is judged unworthy even to live, if, overcome by pain, or defiled by pleasure, he incline to an enjoyment of them (*which yet alone can render life desirable*), doing despite to a law whereby REASON mightly commands, though annexing to that behest neither bribe nor threat? The weight of this question even the most unlettered must right inly feel, if at all aware of the sanctity attaching to the idea Duty; though as yet unacquainted with that amazing property of our nature—FREEDOM[20]—unfolded singly from the representing of

---

[20] The idea of our freedom is not antecedent to our consciousness of the moral law,

the law. And it is just the incomprehensible of this godlike susceptibility, announcing to man his celestial descent, that does, by breaking on the mind with a force that cannot be resisted, swell and transfix the soul with reverential emotions of the deepest and most enraptured admiration, thereby strengthening him for whatever sacrifices the awe of duty may demand. Again and again to arouse this feeling of the excellent and sublime of our moral destination is especially to be recommended, as the chief mean of begetting moral sentiments, inasmuch as this feeling directly counteracts our inborn bias to pervert the order of our springs of choice; so that, by restoring the unconditioned reverence for the Law as the supreme condition of all maxims we adopt, the originary moral order may be reintroduced among the heart's ravelled springs, and therewith, that the predisposition toward good, at first implanted in the heart of man, may be resuscitated in its pristine purity and vigour.

But is not this redintegration of character by one's own exertions, diametrically opposed by the inborn depravity of man, whereby he is unfitted for good? Doubtless! so far as the COMPREHENSIBILITY of such a change is concerned; and as for any INSIGHT into its possibility, the present case is quite on a par with every other event in time (*change*), which is itself necessary when regard is had to the Physical System, and whose antipart is nevertheless figured, agreeably to the Moral Law,

---

but is inferentially deduced from its unconditioned sway over the determinableness of our choice. This any one may speedily become convinced of, by merely asking himself if he is immediately certain of possessing a power of vanquishing the greatest seductions to transgression by dint of a forethought steadfastness of resolve,

> Phalaris licet imperet ut sis
> Falsus, et admoto dictet perjuria tauro;

and the answer must at once be, that he cannot tell whether, in such event, he might not be shaken from his purpose. But duty demands that he adhere inviolably faithful to its decrees; hence he rightly infers that he CAN do so, *i. e.* that his will is free. They who maintain that this unsearchable property of our nature is quite comprehensible, delude themselves with the word DETERMINISM (*the Principle of the it fill's Determination by sufficient inward grounds*); as if the difficulty consisted in combining this principle with freedom; whereas the difficulty is, how PREDETERMINISM—whereby our voluntary actions, as events, have their sufficient ground in antecedent times that are no longer within our power—can consort with freedom, which last requires that both act and its contrary be at the instant of my acting fully within my own control. That is what people fain would, but never will, comprehend.

There is, however, no difficulty in combining the idea FREEDOM with that of God as a NECESSARY Being. For freedom does not consist in the contingency of an act (*i. e.* in its being undetermined by any grounds), (*i. e.* such a principle of INDETERMINISM as might represent good and evil as equally possible divine acts, if those last are to be free), but in absolute spontaneity, and thus is endangered by predeterminism alone, in as much as there the determinative ground is contained *in time bygone*, is consequently not in MY power, but in the hand of nature, and so drives me irresistibly on to act. But since in the case of the Deity no sequences of time are cogitable, this difficulty entirely falls away.

to be possible and realizable by freedom. The position of mankind's indwelling radical evil does therefore preclude only our seeing into the ground of the possibility of this self-reform. It is not inconsistent with the possibility of a return to good itself; for, so long as the Moral Law commands, "*Thou* SHALT *become a better man*," the conclusion is inevitable "*that thou* CANST." The heart's connate evil is a statement of no practical import in the theory, *i. e.* neither in the ELEMENTOLOGY, nor in the DIDACTIC of MORALS; for the duties imposed by the Law remain the same, and retain the same obligatory force, whether a bias to evade them be co-extant with the Will or not. But in the ASCETIC of MORALS the position does say something, and yet no more than this, viz. that in cultivating our concreated ethical predispositions toward good, we cannot so begin, as were we by nature innocent, but are constrained to set to work by counteracting a vitiosity of choice, subverting our primeval ethical condition, and, because this bias is ineradicable, by unremittingly wrestling, and so making stand against it. Since now this issues in an endless progress from bad to better, it results that the converting of the *sentiments* of the wicked, into those of the good, takes place by so changing the innermost and last ground whereupon maxims of life are determined on, that those last become henceforward conformable to the Law, so far forth at least as this new ground (the new heart) is itself immutable. A conviction of this immutability cannot be attained by man, neither from the immediate witness of his conscience, nor yet from proofs gathered from his experienced and observed life, inasmuch as the depths of his heart (*the last subjective ground of choosing maxims*) are impenetrable. But upon the road leading thither, *i. e. to such immutability*, he must HOPE to get by his OWN exertions, whitherward indeed he is directed by his bettered sentiment, now grounded and rooted in good. It behoves him to become a good man; and he can only be deemed *morally* good, in regard of whatever, as done by himself, can be imputed to his account.

Against this proposal of self-amelioration, Reason, now naturally disinclined to the irksomeness of any moral task, seeks refuge by screening itself under the allegation of mankind's natural imbecility, and there shielding itself by all sorts of impure religious ideas (amongst which is to be reckoned the ascribing to God greatest-happiness-principles as the condition of his Law). Again, all religions may be divided into those of MERE WORSHIP and THE RELIGION OF A MORAL LIFE. Agreeably to the former, mankind either flatters himself that God will provide for his everlasting welfare, quite apart from his becoming a morally better man (by remitting his sins); or, should this last appear to him incredible, that God may perhaps straightway make him better, and that too independently of his own exertions, provided he only earnestly beseech it by instant prayers and supplications; whereby since, in the eye of an all-seeing person, PRAYING can be nothing else than tantamount to WISHING, nothing need at all be done; for indeed if a wish could accomplish such a transformation, then would every one be good. But upon the principles of MORAL RELIGION (which, amid all public ones that have hitherto appeared, THE CHRISTIAN RELIGION alone is), this is the unalterable decree, "*that every one must do as much as in him lies in order to render himself a better man, and only then, when he has not buried his connate talent, nor tied it up in a napkin* (Luke, xix. 12-20) *i. e. when he has unfolded the germs latent in his aboriginal susceptibilities for good, may he hope, that what lies beyond his power may be supplied by a higher co-operation.*" Neither is it absolutely necessary that an individual should know wherein this aid consists, nor how it is afforded; perhaps it is inevitable, that even were all this revealed at some former period, other people should not at some other and future period, come to frame to themselves different opinions, and that too with the greatest possible sincerity, about the matter. But if this be so, then would this farther principle validly apply. "*It is not essential, and consequently not necessary, for* EVERY ONE *to know what God does, or may already have done for his salvation; but it is undoubtedly requisite that all should know* WHAT THEY THEMSELVES HAVE TO DO *in order to render themselves worthy of his aid.*"

This general scholion is the first of those four remarks that are appended, one to each book, of the present treatise, and that might be superscribed respectively, (1.) Works of Grace; (2.) Miracles; (3.) Mysteries; (4.) Means of Grace. They are the outworks (*parerga*) of a RELIGION WITHIN THE BOUNDS OF NAKED REASON; they do not inwardly belong to it, but they are immediately adjoining. Reason, conscious of its inability to satisfy all the mind's moral *needs*, extends itself to transcendent ideas, hoping that they may make up for this defect, without however vindicating any claim of possession to such more extensive territory. Reason impugns neither the POSSIBILITY nor yet the EXISTENCE of objects corresponding to those ideas, but is unable to adopt any motives from them either into its maxims of thinking or acting. Nay, reason rather holds, that if there be in the unsearchable fields of the supersensible, anything more than it can comprehend, but which were nevertheless needful to eke out and fulfil our moral shortcoming, then this would stand us in stead, and be made available to a good will, though all the while unacquainted with the matter; and this it trusts with a FAITH (touching such unknown and inaccessible supersensible supply) which we may call REFLECTIVE; for the DOGMATICAL belief, which gives out these *parerga* as points of KNOWLEDGE, appears in its eye chargeable with either *insincerity* or *temerity*. The removal of difficulties withstanding what has its practical establishment in itself, is, when those difficulties give rise to transcendent questions, no more than a very secondary affair. Again, as to the detriment accruing from those *morally-transcendent* ideas, when incorporated with religion, the baneful results following the above-named four classes, are, (1.) the FANATICISM of supposed inward experiences (*Works of Grace*); (2.) the SUPERSTITION of alleged outward experience (*Miracles*); (3.) the ILLUMINATISM of a supposed enlightening of the eyes of the understanding in regard of the preternatural (*Mysteries*)—the whimseys of *Adepti* in search of the great secret; (4.) the THAUMATURGY of endeavouring to act upon the supersensible (*Means of Grace*)—all wanderings of an understanding that has strayed beyond its legitimate boundary, and that too with the fancied moral view of becoming acceptable to God. Touching the above general scholion to our first book, every one perceives that to bring about within himself a work of grace, is just such an attempt to bestride the supernatural,—a project that never enters into the maxims of reason so long as it remains within its own limits; since the moment we have to deal with the preternatural, all use of understanding comes at once to an end. To assign *theoretically* a test whereby to ascertain that any inward mental experience is a work, not of nature, but of grace, is impossible, because our notions of cause and effect cannot be extended beyond what we have experienced and observed, consequently not beyond the operations of nature, without or within ourselves. Again, the hypothesis of a PRACTICAL application of this idea is no less self-contradictory; for, to make any use of this conception, would render pre-requisite *a rule* fixing what we ourselves had to do in order to acquire some ulterior good. A work of grace, however, signifies the very contrary, viz. that the moral good is not our deed, but that of some other person, and is therefore, by the very idea of it, something only to be got by DOING NOTHING, which is absurd. We can therefore admit such works of grace as somewhat incomprehensible; but never can they afford the groundwork of any maxims, whether regulating the theoretical or practical conduct of the mind.

Book II.

OF THE COMBAT BETWIXT THE GOOD AND THE EVIL PRINCIPLE.

EXORDIUM.

THAT, in order to become morally good men, it is not enough to allow the germs of good implanted in our race to develop themselves with unimpeded force, but that it is further requisite for us to encounter an opposing cause of evil,—is a matter that the Stoics did pre-eminently beyond all Moralists of Antiquity declare loudly by their watchword VIRTUE, which alike in Greek and Latin signifies

FORTITUDE or VALOUR, and does consequently remind us that there is an enemy to be overcome. Regarded in this point of view, VIRTUE is a most praiseworthy name, notwithstanding its having been often boastfully abused, and, more lately still, sneeringly derided. For, to summon up to VALOUR, is almost tantamount to infusing it; as, on the other hand, a lazy self-distrusting reason, pusillanimously waiting for exterior aids in points of ethic and religion, not only unnerves every energy of the mind, but even renders man unworthy of such help.

But those sturdy Sages mistook their enemy, who is not to be sought in the natural, and, though undisciplined, still openly displayed and undisguised, appetites of the sensory; for the inward FOE is an invisible occult enemy, lurking behind the ambushes of reason, and upon that account just so much the more dangerous and deadly. They[21] called on WISDOM to make a stand against FOLLY, which allows itself unawares to be inveigled and worsted by the sensory, instead of calling upon her to wage war upon the WICKEDNESS of the human heart, which, by soul-destroying principles, secretly saps and undermines the moral fortresses of the soul.

Our natural appetites are considered in themselves good, *i. e.* irreproachable, and it is not only fruitless, but even hurtful and blameworthy, to attempt to extirpate them; they need only to be tamed, lest they encroach upon or overthrow each other, and so be prevented from harmonising toward their whole and common last end—HAPPINESS.

---

[21] These philosophers derived their supreme moral principle from the Dignity of Human Nature, viz. FREEDOM, or the mind's independency on the force of appetite; and one better or more noble they could not have proceeded on. The laws of morality they then immediately deduced from reason, thus alone legislatory, and by them unconditionally commanding. Here everything was properly adjusted, not only *objectively*, as regards the RULE, but likewise *subjectively*, with respect to the SPRING, of action: provided only we ascribe to man the incorrupted will to adopt without delay those laws into his maxims. But in this latter supposition lay their cardinal error; for, however early we may throw our inquiring eye over man's moral state, we immediately perceive that with his affairs it is no longer *res integra;* but that a beginning must be made by dislodging EVIL from possessions it has usurped (a usurpation that never could have taken place, had we not ourselves willingly received it into our maxims), *i. e.* that the first real GOOD we can do, is to come forth out of an evil estate, extant not in our appetites and wants, but in a perverse maxim chosen by freedom. Appetites do no more than throw difficulties in the way of EXECUTING maxims that may happen to thwart them: whereas evil consists properly herein, viz. that mankind WILLS not to withstand those appetites when these last invite to transgression; which evil-mindedness it is strictly that is the true inward enemy. Appetites are merely opposed to fixt principles generally, indifferently whether those principles be good or evil, and hence that generous system of antiquity is as a pre-exercitory discipline of appetite whatsoever, useful toward the moderating and self-government of the individual by stable maxims. But, in so far as there ought to be SPECIFIC PRINCIPLES of the moral good within, which as yet are not, then must a very different enemy be pre-supposed, whom virtue has to encounter,—apart from which sustained warfare, all virtues are not indeed, as the Church-Father had it, *shining sins,* but *dazzling frailties;* since thereby the uproar itself is only sometimes hushed, while the Heads of the sedition remain unquelled and at large.

Reason, when administering this physical interest of wellbeing, is called PRUDENCE. Only the morally illegal is in itself bad, absolutely objectionable, and to be eradicated. Reason, when teaching how this is to be done, and, still more fitly, when exerting this information into act, deserves and obtains the name of WISDOM, in comparison wherewith VICE may certainly be termed FOLLY; but only then, when reason finds herself strong enough not merely to HATE and arm herself against it as an object of terror, but thoroughly to DESPISE its charms and artful entanglements.

When, consequently, THE STOICS painted to themselves man's ethical Olympiad as a mere wrestle or gymnastic with his (otherwise harmless) desires and aversions, so far forth as these latter hinderances of his inward freedom were to be overthrown; then, since they assumed no particular positively evil principle, the cause of transgression could only be placed in reason's NEGLECTING to meet them on the battlefield. But since, farther, *this omission* is itself contrary to duty (*i. e.* transgression), its ground cannot (without explaining in a circle) be again placed in the appetites and wants, but only therein, where will's free choice is determinable (*i. e.* in the inmost last ground of appointing rules of life, which rules are observed to have conspired with the inclinations). This being the case, we easily understand how an inevitable though unwelcome explanation, whose last ground must remain perpetually shrouded within the veil of the impenetrable,[22] should induce philosophers to mistake the actual enemy of good, against whom they thought a contest was to be maintained.

None need, therefore, be surprised that an Apostle should have represented this UNSEEN soul-devastating enemy, known only by his effects upon us, as external to our frame, and more particularly as an evil SPIRIT. "*For we wrestle not against flesh and blood* (OUR NATURAL INCLINATIONS), *but against the principalities and powers of spiritual wickedness;—that we may be able to stand against the wiles of the devil*" (Ephes. vi. 12 and 11); an expression that does not appear designed to extend our knowledge beyond the barriers of the world of sense, but to assist us to envisage, for a practical behoof, a notion of the

---

[22] Moral philosophers commonly imagine that the existence of evil in our race admits of easy explication, from the violence of the sensitive springs on the one hand, and the impotency of the rational springs (*reverence*) on the other; *i. e.* is to be accounted for from the FRAILTY or WEAKNESS of our nature. But then the Moral Good (as to its last ground in the ethical predisposition of our personality) ought to be still more easily explicable; for the comprehensibility of the one, apart from that of the other, is absolutely incogitable, whereas Reason's power of mastering all opposing springs by the naked idea of a law is utterly inexplicable; and it is equally incomprehensible how the springs of the sensory ever could gain the ascendency over a preceptive faculty invested with such authority. And, indeed, if every one acted agreeably to the requirements of the law, then it would be said that all followed a common order, neither would it occur to any one to inquire into the cause of this uniformity.

unfathomable supersensible. For, to all practical ends it is quite the same whether we place our Seducer within or also at the same time without us. Our guilt is the same in either event, in as much as we could not fall by his extraneous seduction were we not already secretly banded and in league with him;[23] an affair we shall consider under the two following heads.

APOTOME I.

OF THE TITLE OF THE GOOD PRINCIPLE TO RULE OVER MANKIND.

A. *Impersonated Idea of the Good Principle.*

MANKIND (*i. e.* Agent-Intelligents generally), IN HIS ENTIRE MORAL PERFECTION, is that alone which can render a universe the object of a divine decree, and be the end of its creation; to which morality as a supreme condition, happiness is immediately attached by the Will of the Most High. This Intelligent is the only-beloved of God—*"the same was in the beginning with God."* The idea of such Person emanates from God's very essence, and is therefore no created thing, but his only-begotten Son. *"The* WORD (THE FIAT!) *whereby all things were made, and without which was not any thing made that is made."* For his sake, *i. e.* for the sake of Intelligents, cogitated agreeably to the fulfilment of their moral destiny, every thing has been created. *"He is the brightness of his Father's glory"*—*"In him God loved the world;"* and only through him, and by adopting his sentiments, can we hope to become *"children of God."*

SELF-ELEVATION to this ideal of moral perfection, *i. e.* to the archetype of moral sentiments in their entire purity, is obviously a duty incumbent upon all men, to which ascent, the idea itself, as objected to us by reason for our imitation, gives power. But since we are not the authors of this ideal (and since, on the contrary, it has taken up its abode in human nature without our being able to explain our susceptibility for the indwelling of such an occupant), it may perhaps

---

[23] It is a distinguishing characteristic of the ethic of Christianity, that it represents Moral Good as distant from Moral Evil, not as HEAVEN from EARTH, but as HEAVEN from HELL; a mode of speech figurative, no doubt, and as such revolting, but which is nevertheless, in its spirit and intendment, philosophically correct. It serves to prevent us from regarding good and evil—the kingdoms of light and darkness—as conterminous, and as merging gradually into one another, through imperceptible shades of perpetually decreasing or increasing luminosity, and suggests to us, that those realms are disjoined by an immeasurable gulf. The total dissimilarity and repugnancy of the maxims whereby man is rendered a subject in one or other of these kingdoms, viewed in connection with the danger run of imagining any cognationship betwixt the properties that fit mankind for one or other of those abodes, entitle us to employ these symbolical representations, which are at once dreadful, and at the same time exceedingly sublime.

be more appropriately said, that that archetype has COME DOWN from heaven to us, and assumed our humanity (for it is not so easy to figure to ourselves how MAN, who is BY NATURE BAD, should strip off his evil, and raise himself to a conformity with the Ideal of Holiness, as it is to hold that the latter has invested itself with HUMANITY (*a thing not in itself evil*), and CONDESCENDED unto it). This union with us may therefore be regarded as A STATE OF HUMILIATION OF THE SON OF GOD, when we figure to ourselves such a godlike-minded person as may be our archetype, taking upon him a multitude of sorrows, although himself holy, and therefore exempt from their sufferance, merely with the view of advancing our Sovereign Good; whereas mankind, who never is free from guilt, must, even after he has adopted the sentiments of that ideal, regard whatever sorrows may afflict him, in whatever way, as his merited desert (*i. e. as no undue humiliation? Tr.*), and must consequently deem himself unworthy of entering into an alliance with such an idea, although this last serves for his archetype.

The ideal of humanity as acceptable to God (*i. e.* the idea of an ethical perfection, so far forth as this last may be possible for finite Agent-Intelligents shackled by wants and appetites) can only be cogitated by the representation of a person ready and willing to discharge all the offices of humanity, who not only by doctrine and example spreads abroad the utmost amount of good, but does further, although assaulted by the highest temptations, undergo for the sake of the whole world, his enemies not excepted, the greatest miseries, even an ignominious death. Thus would the matter seem to be figured; for we can frame to ourselves no notion of the degree and *momentum* of a force, such as is the *vis insita* of a moral sentiment, except by observing it warring against antagonists, and standing, amid the greatest possible invasions and extremities, unvanquished and victorious.

Through A PRACTICAL FAITH IN THIS SON OF GOD (FIgured as having taken upon him our nature), mankind may hope to become acceptable to God (and so to enter into everlasting bliss), *i. e.* lie who is conscious of such moral sentiments within, as enable him to believe and to place in himself a well-grounded trust, that he could, under any similar temptations and griefs (considered as the test and touchstone of the genuineness of that idea), adhere unchangeably to the archetype of humanity, and remain true to the exemplar by a steady following of his footsteps—such a person, I say, and he alone, is entitled to look upon himself as one who may be an object not unworthy of the Divine complacency.

B. *Objective Reality of this Idea.*

This idea's reality is, in a practical point of view, contained completely in itself, for it has its rise and spring from our morally legislative Reason. We OUGHT to conform ourselves to it; consequently we CAN. Needed we first of all to prove the possibility of our becoming conformable to this archetype, as is absolutely indispensable in the case of our notions of the physical system, lest we be misled by empty phantasms, to which nothing given can ever correspond; then must we, by parity of reason, pause before we admitted the claim of the Moral Law to be the unconditionally sufficient determinative of our choice; for how it comes to pass that the bare idea of *law whatsoever* should be a far more weighty mover of the will than any utilitarian considerations, cannot be made comprehensible by reason, nor corroborated by observation and experience: for, touching the first, the Law's behest is unconditional; and as for the second, even supposing that there never yet had been a man who rendered unqualified obedience to the Law, the objective necessity of becoming thus unconditionally obedient, shines the same with self-evidence undiminished. We need, therefore, no examples from experience and observation, in order to constitute, that ideal of humanity whereby alone man is acceptable to God, our pre-appointed archetype. It is already extant in the ideal archetypes of reason. Farther, whosoever should, previously to his acknowledging ANY ONE to be in harmony with that idea, and a fit exemplar for imitation, demand more than an unrebukable and well-deserving life, open to every one's inspection; whoso should besides crave signs and wonders performed *by him* or *upon him* for his credentials, would thereby proclaim his own moral UNBELIEF, viz. his want of belief in virtue,—a defect not to be supplied by ANY FAITH grounded on miraculous supports: for this *Faith* could only be *Historical*, whereas the belief in the practical validity of that idea, as seated in reason, alone possesses moral worth; and this idea it is, that must first accredit miracles as signs from on high, not the idea, that from them, is to receive its confirmation.

Upon this same account, the records of experience ought to be able to set forth, as a historical fact, the given and displayed example of some one who had realized this ideal (so far, at least, as we can extract evidence of one's inward moral sentiments from his exterior deportment), although, properly speaking, the law would entitle us to expect from every one an ectypal transcript of this idea, whereof the *Prototype* resides at all times, veiled and latent, in the deeply hidden sanctuary of our own reason, in as much as neither experience nor example can adequately or exhaustively depicture it, those last not unfolding to view the inmost sentiment of the person, and allowing us

Immanuel Kant 49

only to *conclude* upon it, and that uncertainly. (Even mankind's own inward observation of himself does not so enable him to envisage the depths of his heart, that he can attain a confident, settled, and unchanging conviction of the purity and fixity of the maxims he professes.)

And if a person really endowed with such godlike sentiments had at any given epoch appeared, descending AS IT WERE, from heaven to earth, who in doctrine, life, and death, had fully set forth the exemplary PATTERN of a course of life acceptable to God, to the utmost possible extent that outward experience will admit,—the archetype of such conduct being, as we have said, extant, and to be sought for, in naked reason only,—and had he in consequence of this his character and doctrine, achieved a most gigantic revolution in the destinies of our race, scattering abroad the undecaying seeds of a yet uncomputed and indeed incomputable moral good; still that ought not to give us cause to look upon him as any thing else than a naturally-begotten man, seeing that each individual must recognise and feel himself bound to let the light of a similarly bright example so shine before him, although by this I do not mean to assert *simpliciter* that he may not perchance have been a preternaturally begotten Being. In a practical point of view, the supernaturalist hypothesis can benefit us nothing, since the archetype subjected by us in thought, to this phenomenon is to be found *in ourselves* (though ordinary men); and the existence of this ideal in the human soul is in itself sufficiently incomprehensible, without our multiplying difficulties by holding it, in addition to its supersensible original, hypostatised in a particular individual; on the contrary, the advancement of THIS HOLY ONE above the weaknesses of human nature, would,—so far as we can see,—rather impede than assist this idea in exciting our generous emulation to attain it. For how perfectly human soever we cogitate the physical constitution of this morally perfect man, what though he be invested with the same wants, and exposed to the same miseries, and temptations to transgression with ourselves; still, if he is represented as thus far superhuman as, by a purity of will not earned, but immutable and ingenite, to be absolutely exalted beyond the possibility of a lapse, then must this enormous elongation from the common class of men remove him to so infinite a distance, that this godlike man would cease to be fitly proposed to us as an exemplar. Mankind might, in such event, say, let there be given to me a thoroughly holy will, and every seduction to evil must of itself come to nought; give me a perfect inward conviction, that after a brief career on earth, I by force of this connate holiness shall straightway enter into possession of the everlasting glories of the heavenly kingdom, then will I not only willingly but joyously undertake and stand out all grief and pain, how bitter soever, even up to the most contumelious death, seeing, as I do, in near prospect the exhilarating and glorified result. And though unquestionably the cogitation—that this godlike person was from everlasting, in the actual possession of those excelsities and beatitudes, and needed not to earn them by these his sorrows,—that he voluntarily divested himself of such celestial splendours for the sake of the unworthy, even for his enemies, in order to rescue them from everlasting ruin,—must determine our minds to admiration, love, and gratitude toward him,—and although the idea of a deportment regulated upon so perfect a standard of morality would by all means be valid for us as a behest to be observed, still he himself could not be represented as a pattern for our imitation, nor consequently as any evidence to us of the practicability and attainableness of so pure and exalted a moral good.[24]

Such a godlike-minded, though still perfectly human teacher, might nevertheless with the greatest propriety speak of himself as if the ideal of morality dwelt in him bodily, and were fully set forth in his doctrine and life. In using such an expression, he would allude only to the turn of thinking adopted by him as the regulator of his actions; but

---

[24] The limits of the human understanding prevent us from figuring to ourselves any considerable personal worth in the actions of another, unless we have them represented to us after a human fashion; but then such figurative representation ought never to be understood as implying that so the matter (χατ' ἀληζειαν) is, in real fact and event. In order to cogitate supersensible properties, we need always to think them according to an analogy with physical entities. It is thus that our philosophical poet ascribes a higher rank to man, in consequence of his bias to evil, at least in so far as he fights against and overcomes it; than to those celestial spirits who, by force of the sanctity of their nature, are exalted beyond the possibility of seduction.—(*This world, with all its faults, is better than a realm of will-less angels.*—HALLER.) Even the Scripture accommodates itself to this mode of speech, when, explaining to us the intensity of the love borne by God toward the human race, it speaks of his having submitted to the utmost sacrifice that a loving Being can undergo in order to render even the unworthy happy ("*So God loved the world,*" &c.): for reason cannot comprehend in any way how a self-sufficient Being can give up part of what constitutes its own bliss, and deprive itself of its own possessions. This is an ANALOGICAL SCHEMATISM indispensable for illustrating the matter; but when turned into a *Schematism* or *Eiffigiation* for determining an object, it becomes ANTHROPOMORPHISM, which is of the most hurtful consequences in religion—I may here remark, that in passing from the sensible to the supersensible it is quite allowable to SCHEMATISE (*i. e.* explain a conception by help of the analogy it may bear to somewhat sensible); but it is quite disallowed analogically to conclude that what belongs to the one can be predicated of the other. To take an instance: I cannot infer that, because I cannot depicture to myself in thought the cause of a plant except by comparing it with the relation obtaining betwixt an Artist and his Work (*e. g.* a watch), *i. e.* by ascribing intelligence to such cause,—it cannot, I say, be inferred, that therefore the cause of the plant (or of the material universe generally), does itself possess understanding; *i. e.* I am not entitled to say that intelligence, which is a hypothesis necessary for my private explaining to myself the growth and structure of a plant, is likewise a condition precedent of the possibility of the existence and action of such cause itself. The relation obtaining betwixt a SYMBOL and a notion, bears no analogy whatever to the relation obtaining betwixt that symbol and the thing indicated by the notion; and to pass from one to the other is *ingens saltus* (μεταβασις εις αλλα γενος), plunging us at once into the abysses of anthropomorphism—the arguments proving which assertion, I have expounded elsewhere at length.

since these rules of life cannot be forthwith held up to others as exemplars, being in themselves invisible, and capable of outward protraiture only by action and instruction, he might very well say of himself *which of you accuseth me of sin;* for it is but equitable to ascribe that blameless example of a teacher, which illustrates his tenets, to nothing but the purest motives, so long as those tenets treat only of what, at any rate, is every person's duty, and all grounds are awanting for suspecting him of by-views. A cast of thinking such as now described, ready to forego and undergo every thing, in order to forward the general interests of the race, figured as extant in an Ideal of Humanity, is valid for all men, at all times, and throughout all worlds, in the eye of Supreme Justice, whenever mankind makes, as he ought, his own real sentiments conformable to the archetype thus cogitated in idea. Doubtless this will ever remain a righteousness not our own, so far forth as our own righteousness ought to consist in sentiments fully commensurate to the prototype, and in a thence arising course of life tallying with faultless exactness to the standard. There must, however, be an appropriation of this righteousness possible for a person who leads a good life, when viewed in connection with its prototype sentiment; although to make this appropriation comprehensible, is attended with very great difficulties, which we now set ourselves to expound and remove.

C. *Difficulties contrary to the reality of this Idea, together with their Solution.*

The first difficulty, suggesting doubts as to the attainableness of this idea, viz. that of a Humanity morally acceptable to God, springs from the HOLINESS of the lawgiver, taken in connection with the defective state of our own righteousness. The law says, *Be holy* (in your life and conversation) *as your Father which is in Heaven is Holy;* for that is the Ideal of the Son of God proposed to us as our archetype. But the distance of the good we have to attain, from the evil we quit, is infinite, and can consequently not be passed over in any given time; nevertheless, the moral economy of man is destined to coincide with the sacrosanct requirements of the law. This harmony must consequently be looked upon as taking place in the sentiments, *i. e.* in that universal and pure maxim of obedience, whence, as a germ, all good is to be unfolded—a change of character which, being duty, is certainly possible. Here, then, lies the difficulty. How can the sentiment, or formality of the intent, come in the room of deeds that are *at all times* (not throughout the whole of absolute time, but at each point of time) faulty? and the solution is, that good conduct, regarded as a constant progression from bad to better *in infinitum*, must always be estimated by us as defective, in as much as the law of cause and effect fetters us to the conditions of time; whence also it happens that our good deeds, made exhibitive as phenomena, must at all times be held as disconform to the Holy Law. The Searcher of the Heart, however, tests the supersensible sentiment whence such actions flow, and may therefore be cogitated as regarding, in his pure intellectual intuition, such endless progression as a completed whole,[25] and so as somewhat perfect. Thus may mankind trust, notwithstanding his perpetual shortcoming, that he may, *on the whole*, be well pleasing to God, in what point of time soever his existence may be terminated.

The SECOND difficulty emerging, when we contrast the aspirations of mankind after good, with the DIVINE RIGHTEOUSNESS, touches the reaching this moral good itself—a state of MORAL WELFARE, consisting in the reality and CONSTANCY of an ever onward persevering (and kept from falling) sentiment in good, widely different from PHYSICAL WELL-BEING, understood as contentedness with one's outward state, liberation from evils, and enjoyment of perpetually increasing pleasures. For an uninterrupted *striving after the kingdom of God,* could one become confidently assured of the UNCHANGEABLENESS of such a turn of mind, would be tantamount to already knowing one's self to have entered into it; after which mankind might assuredly trust that "*all other things* (requisite for external comfort) *would undoubtedly be added unto him.*"

A soul solicitous on this point, might no doubt be comforted, when told, "*The Spirit beareth witness with our spirit,*" &c.; that is to say, whoever cherishes sufficiently pure sentiments, must of himself be inwardly aware that he never again can fall so low as to be in love with evil; and yet to trust to such supposed feelings of supersensible origin is rather a perilous undertaking. Never are people more apt to deceive themselves than when open to be misled by their own favourable self-opinion. Neither does it seem advisable to summon mankind up to any such confidence; but rather more conducive to morality "to *work out our salvation with fear and trembling*" (a hard saying, which, misunderstood, may goad man on to the blackest fanaticism). And yet if bereft of all confidence in our once adopted maxims, scarcely could we persist in our intended course. But this assurance enters of itself, without having recourse either to a sweet or an anxious fanaticism, from observing the harmony obtaining betwixt our life and previously adopted purpose; for an individual who throughout a considerable tract

---

[25] To prevent mistakes, it may be necessary to add, that the above does not by any means intend to say, that a virtuous sentiment can COMPENSATE for our failing in duty, or serve as an indemnity for the actual evil extant in this endless series; what is said is, that the sentiment which comes in the room of the totality of this indefinite approximation, can supply those defects only, inseparable from the finite existence of Intelligents in time, viz. those defects arising from their never *being* fully, what they are only always on the point of *becoming*. The question of compensating positive transgressions falls under the THIRD difficulty.

of time has seen his forethought principles exerted into act, and is thence enabled to conclude, with tolerable certainty, upon a radical reformation of his character, may reasonably hope that this advancement, provided only its inward principle be good, will so confirm and augment the elastic force wherewith he still presses forward to what is better—as not only to prevent him from quitting while on earth the narrow path of virtue, and urge him with more courageous and unimpeded footstep thitherward—but also, should another life yet await him, still to carry him onward in the same direction toward the unapproachable goal of moral excellence; since, from his own inward experience and observation, he may look upon his character as radically altered. On the contrary, he who, notwithstanding many an attempt at moral amendment, never yet steadfastly persevered in good, but fell perpetually back into evil; or who perhaps is even inwardly aware of having slidden farther, as life advanced, downwards along the devious slope from bad to worse; cannot reasonably entertain the smallest hope, that he would, either in this, or another life, conduct himself better, inasmuch as those malignant symptoms would show that moral corruption had struck deep root in his inmost sentiments. In such circumstances, every one perceives that the former would obtain a vista into an unboundedly opening and happy futurity; the latter, again, a vista into just as inimitably increasing and dimensionless a misery; which two prospects are for us mankind, so far as we can judge, views into a blessed or cursed eternity. Suggestions, enough startling and mighty, to tranquillize and fortify the one in good, as well as to arouse in the other, the condemning voice of conscience, calling on him to halt in his wicked career; nay, such cogency as springs, do those subjective representations possess, as to supersede the necessity of laying down objectively the dogmatical position, that at death, man's future destiny becomes *then* everlastingly foredoomed[26] for either good or evil,—a

---

[26] The question, whether the pains of Hell are finite or eternal, is a CHILDISH question, *i. e.* one which, though answered, could benefit the querist nothing. Were the former alternative taught, then would there be too much ground to fear, that MOST (as indeed is the case with ALL who believe in purgatory) would, like the sailor in Moore's Travels, say, "*Well, I'll do my best to stand it out.*" Again, were the other alternative supported, and incorporated with the Church-Creed, then *might*, even contrary to the intent aimed at by such doctrine, result to the vicious a hope of complete impunity, even after the most abandoned life. The clergyman called to the death-bed of one whose late though avenging conscience urges him to seek advice and consolation, feels it cruel and inhuman to announce eternal reprobation as his lot; and since betwixt this last and plenary absolution no intermediary is admitted by his creed—his church teaching that the culprit is to be punished *either eternally* or *not at all*,—he endeavours to inspire him with hope that his guilt may be forgiven, and promises to transform him in all haste into a new man acceptable to God; and as time is now no more for entering on a walk and conversation well-pleasing to his Judge, rueful confessions, formulas of faith, and vows of amendment if life be spared, are brought in as means to prop up his fainting heart. This is the certain and inevitable consequence whenever the ETERNITY of the future DOOM

adjudged to us as the due recompense of our earthly life is set forth as a DOGMA; and mankind are not rather told to frame to themselves a notion of their hereafter ethical estate, from a careful estimate of their present and previous deportment, and to regard such future lot as the spontaneously arising and naturally to be anticipated consequence of the other. The sight-outrunning extent of the series of sequents to be apprehended, while under the Dominion of the Principle of Evil, will take as effective ethical a purchase on the mind as were that series authentically proclaimed to be interminable; without, however, drawing after it the disadvantages attendant on this portentous dogma (to which, by the way, neither grounds of reason nor warrants of Holy Writ furnish a title). As a specimen of these disadvantages we may note, that since the wicked, even while ALIVE, counts beforehand on this ultimately and easily to be accepted pardon; or, when life is drawing to an end, thinks he has only to do with the claim of God's justice against him, that is to be appeased by words and formularies; it results that the rights of mankind are violated with disregard, and no one ever re-acquires possession of his own: a result this, from those forms of expiation, so extremely common, that an instance to the contrary is almost unheard of; whereas the other vista into the unknown and unfathomable recesses of his awaiting destiny naturally prompt him to repair and counteract what he has done, as much as possible, in order that the *effects* flowing from his evil deeds may, while he is yet alive, be to the very uttermost obliterated. Is there any one who may perchance think that Reason will not, before life has ebbed, prefer against a sinner a sufficiently stern indictment at the bar of his own conscience; if such there be, he would, I apprehend, err exceedingly; for, just because reason is free, its sentence over man cannot be corrupted or bribed. When conscience resumes her rights, and her avenging ministers bring forth in array man's register of crime, and suggest to him, while engaged with this dark review, that he may speedily stand before HIS JUDGE, then needs he only to be left to the forebodings of his own thoughts, which, in my opinion, will judge him with the uttermost severity.——I have only one or two remarks to add. The popular adage, "ALL'S WELL THAT ENDS WELL," cannot be applied to Morals, unless indeed we understand by a good termination, such a close as consists in the person himself becoming a truly good man. But how is any one to know he has become GOOD, seeing that this wished for transformation can only be inferred from the good course of life it subsequently brings forth; for which, at the end of life, no farther space remains. Of HAPPINESS, the remark may hold very well: and yet even then, only when regard is bad to the station whence we review our life, viz. not from its commencement, but from its close. Past griefs leave no painful reminiscences behind when once we know ourselves secured against their return: their departure rather makes way for a gladness that enhances the zest of present good, in as much as pleasure and pain, being seated in the sensory, and floating on the stream of time, vanish with this last's lapse. Neither can they be held to constitute one whole with that happiness of which we are at present in the fruition, but are, on the contrary, expelled and displaced by the now existing occupant of time. If, however, this brocard be understood to refer to a moral estimate of life, then may mankind go very far wrong indeed, if he think *all well* because good actions have wound up its close. The subjective moral principle—(the cast of thinking, or SENTIMENT)— which alone gives or deprives his character of worth, is as *somewhat supersensible*, not capable of being frittered down into fragments of time, but must be cogitated as an *unum quid*, or absolute unity; and since we can only conclude upon our sentiments from actions which are the phenomena of those sentiments, we must, in any such general estimate, take our whole life into consideration; and then the reproaches of conscience, arising from the earlier part of life (previous to repentance), may perhaps drown the self-applause bestowed on the later, and go far to stifle the triumphant exclamation, *all's well that ends well.*——There is connected with the doctrine of eternal punishment another tenet, closely allied, but not identic with it, viz. the dogma that "all sins must be forgiven *here.*" One reckoning is finally summed up when we quit this world—as the tree falls, it must lie; and no one may hope *yonder* to overtake what he has neglected *here*. There is, however, just as little room for confidently asserting this last position as the former; it is fancied knowledge, that only induces the human understanding to overstep the bounds of all allowed insight. A good and pure sentiment (which may be called a good spirit governing us), whereof we are conscious, guides consequently to a conviction of its permanency and steadfastness, although it does so *mediately* only—and is the Comforter (*Paraclete*) re-assuring us, when backslidings make us apprehensive of its constancy. Certain knowledge is, on such a point, unattainable by man; neither is it, as far as we can see, morally desirable. For (be it well noted) this assurance cannot be founded on any immediate consciousness of the unchangeableness of our sentiments, these being no object of intuition; it can only be inferred from their effects experienced and observed in our daily life—a conclusion drawn from the phenomena of that good and evil sentiment, and therefore incapable of acquainting us certainly with the *viz insita* of its causal strength. This deficiency must be still more sensibly felt, when the change of character has taken place only toward the close of life; for then those *a posteriori* proofs of its sincerity altogether fall away, no sufficient trajectory of moral walk and conversation being given, that might serve as a groundwork whereon to rear a satisfactory judgment touching one's moral worth; and INCONSOLABLENESS (which, however, the nature of man, and the obscurity of all trans-sepulchral matters, prevent from passing into WILD DESPAIR) must inevitably spring from any rational estimate that such a person can make of his moral state.

The THIRD, and, as it would seem, the greatest difficulty, that must stand in the way of all men, even after they have struck into the paths of good, and that must represent, as wanting, when weighed in the balance of divine justice, the sum-total of our actions, is as follows. Notwithstanding the adoption of a good sentiment, and with what constancy soever mankind may have persisted in acting on it, STILL HE BEGAN FROM EVIL; and this prior guilt he never can abolish. That, after a change of heart, no new debts are contracted, can never pass for any adequate discharging of his old ones. Neither can there be performed any thing supererogatory, or beyond what is at all times incumbent on

---

nothing more than a principle employed by Practical Reason for *regulating* the use it makes of its notions of the supersensible, reason remaining all the while perfectly aware that we are totally in the dark as to the objective properties of such supersensible; all that reason intends by such a suggestion, is to remind us that since we can infer from our past walk and conversation singly, whether or not we are acceptable to God, and since our allotted space of earthly probation ends when we go hence, we have cause to regard our account as closed, and are led to draw out a balance-sheet to see whether we can then hold ourselves justified or not Generally speaking, were we, instead of aiming at principles CONSTITUENT of knowledge of supersensible objects, contentedly to confine our judgment to REGULATIVE principles that acquiesce in their own possible practical use, then would human wisdom be a great gainer, and mankind would cease to hatch broods of supposed knowledge where nothing can be known; that after all do, in the end, turn out highly pernicious to morality.

him to do; for it is our unremitting duty always to execute all the good possibly in our power. Lastly, neither can this primordial guilt, antecedent to any good ever done by man (styled in the former book the RADICAL evil of Human Nature), be taken away by any other person, so far as all our notices of the law of nature and reason reach; for the obligation thence arising is not transferable like a money debt (where it is indifferent to the creditor whether his debtor or some one else discharge the bond), so as to admit of being devolved upon a cautioner; but is, on the contrary, the most exclusively personal that can be conceived, viz. a debt of sins, and tye to punishment, prestable by the guilty alone, not the guiltless, even though this Innocent were magnanimously willing to offer himself as a substitute. Again, since moral evil (called SIN, when regarded as a transgression of the Moral Law *qua* Divine Commandment) brings along with it an INFINITUDE of violations of THE LAW, consequently an infinity of guilt, not so much on account of the infinity of the Supreme Lawgiver—(of which transcendent relation obtaining betwixt MAN and THE MOST HIGH we can comprehend nothing)—infraction of whose authority is thereby made, as rather on account of the radically evil SENTIMENT and general turn of the maxims (like UNIVERSAL PRINCIPLES when contrasted with singular transgressions), it would seem to follow, that all mankind could only look forward to an illimitable punishment, and everlasting extrusion from the kingdom of God.

The solution of this difficulty depends upon these following remarks. The final sentence of a Searcher of the Heart must be regarded as bottomed on the general sentiment of the accused, not on its phenomenal appearances—acts at variance or in harmony with the law. In the case considered, however, we assume a dominant good sentiment, which has gained and retains the mastery over the once mighty principle of evil; and thus the question arises, "CAN THE ETHICAL SEQUENTS OF HIS FORMER ESTATE (viz. punishment *qua* effect of the divine displeasure) BE DRAWN OVER AND MADE TO TELL UPON THE BETTERED CONDITION OF HIS PRESENT MAN" where he must be regarded as henceforward an object of the divine complacency. As we do not here inquire, "whether, BEFORE *his change of sentiment, the execution of impending punishment would consist with God's rectitude?*"—(a point about which no man can doubt), we shall take it for granted, in the present investigation, that the punishment due to his misdeeds has not been inflicted prior to repentance. The pains of law cannot, however, be regarded as inflicted AFTER repentance, when the person leads, agreeably to the supposition, a new life, and has become *morally* another man; nevertheless, satisfaction must be given to Supreme Justice, in whose sight no blame-worthy is ever guiltless. Again, since the execution of punishment is, consistently with the Divine Wisdom, to take place neither BEFORE nor yet AFTER a change of heart, and is notwithstanding necessary, it results that we must regard it as suited to Supreme Wisdom to inflict it in the very act of redintegrating one's character. Let us then see if, in such ethic transformation, there are not already, even by the very notion of it, involved those evils which mankind may regard, as due to his previous misdeeds, and as penalties[27] satisfying Divine Justice. A change of heart is an exit out of evil, and entrance into good; a stripping off the old and putting on the new man, so far forth as the individual dies unto sin (and to all appetites misleading into it), and becomes alive unto righteousness. But in this cogitable transit there are not two moral events separated by any distance of time. The whole is but one single act, the departure from evil being effected singly by that good sentiment which wafts us into good, and *vice versa*. The good ideal is consequently included in the abandonment of evil, just as much as in the outset of our pursuit of virtue; and the pain justly annexed to the mortifying of sin, arises exclusively from the clarifying impulses of the latter. Betaking ourselves to the upward road of duty, and dereliction of the ancient haunts of vice, is consequently (*as a death of the old man, and crucifying of the flesh*) in itself a sacrifice, and entrance on a long train of sufferings in life, which the new man, *now like-minded with the Son of God*, undertakes merely for the sake of the ethic good; which suffering and sorrow, however, belonged as PUNISHMENT properly to the old man (now become *morally* another). Although, then, the reformed is *physically* the self-same guilty person as before, and must as such, be equally condemned as obnoxious to punishment, whether before an ethical tribunal, or his own conscience, still his cogitable inward man is, when regard is had to its transformed character, in the eye of a divine judge, with whom the formal of the sentiment comes in room of a defective deed, to be looked upon as MORALLY another; and does in its purity, as a transcript of the examplar of the Son of God, adopted by him into his sentiments, bear,—or by personifying the

---

[27] The hypothesis, that all evils in the world are to be looked upon as punishments for past sins, does not seem to have been invented for the behoof of a Theodicy, neither does it seem a sprig of priestcraft; for the belief is too universally spread to be derived from any artificial origin. Probably it lies just at the door of our understanding, which is apt to connect the course of nature with the Laws of Morality; and thence derives the cogitation, that we must first become better men before we can expect to get rid of the ills of life, or have them counterbalanced by greater goods. Hence the first man is represented (in the Bible) as condemned, upon account of his transgression, to work for his bread, and the first woman to bring forth children with pain, while both are yet farther sentenced ultimately to death; although it is perfectly inconceivable that any other destiny should have awaited animal creatures, constituted with such limbs and organs as we have. The HINDUS suppose that mankind are spirits (called *Dewas*), incarcerated in an animal framework in consequence of some anterior crime; and even MALLEBRANCHE was driven to deny that the irrational part of the creation had souls or feelings, rather than admit that horses should smart under such complicated cruelty, "*without having ever tasted of forbidden hay.*"

idea,—THIS SON OF GOD, does himself, as VICARIOUS SUBSTITUTE, bear for the guilty, and, in like manner, for all who practically believe in him, the penalty of sin;—does, moreover, as REDEEMER, satisfy, by his sufferings and death, Supreme Justice; and does, lastly, as ADVOCATE for the blameworthy, lead them to hope that they may be ultimately absolved and acquitted by their Judge. With this only difference, that in this figurative representation, the suffering continually undergone[28] by the new man while dying to the old, is stated as a death once for all endured by the representative of mankind. Here is something superadded to the desert of good works, not to be met with while considering the two former difficulties, and which is reckoned to us OUT OF GRACE. For, that we should be already held to be what, while on earth (and perhaps in any future world), we are no more than about to *become*, is an adjudication to which we can show no TITLE,[29] and the accuser within would rather move for a condemnatory sentence. Such ABSOLVING SENTENCE must therefore always remain A DECREE OF GRACE, although, as based on satisfaction (extant only in the ideal of an amended sentiment, and known to God alone), it is quite in harmony with everlasting justice when we, for the sake of our faith in that moral good, are acquitted from all farther responsibility.

But here a question may be raised, Does this deduction of the idea of a JUSTIFICATION of the once guilty, but now transmuted to sentiments acceptable in the sight of God, lead to any practical result? and, if so, What may its practical bearing be? It would rather seem, that no POSITIVE use of any sort, can accrue from such an investigation,

---

[28] Even the purest moral sentiment can beget only such actions as consist in a continual transit, on our part, from bad to better. Nevertheless, when regard is had to their supersensible original, this sentiment may and ought to be holy and conformable to the archetypal pattern, and may, as one whole intellectual unit containing the ground of an endless progression, compensate the defects extant at any point of the series, and come in the room of a completed deed. The question, however, here occurs, can he "*to whom there is* (or should be) *now no condemnation*," deem himself justified, and yet regard the *ills* of life that meet him on his course toward good as PUNITIVE? *i. e.* is he to acknowledge a blameworthiness of sentiment, and consequently a state of mind displeasing to God? Yes, but only in his capacity of the man whom he is unremittingly stripping off. What was due to his old man as punishment he joyously stands out and goes through for the sake of that good wherewith his new man is invested; consequently, looking at them under this light, he reckons them not as penal; *i. e.* all those evils and calamities which, befalling the old man, would have been punishments, and still are, so far forth as the old man is not yet altogether put off, his new man willingly accepts, as so many opportunities of testing, exalting, and carrying farther and higher, his moral weal. Whereas the self-same evils would, in his old condition, not merely have been *recompensed* to him as penalties, but would also have been *felt* as such, seeing that as physical evils they are diametrically opposed to that greatest-happiness-amount, which, of the *immorally-minded*, is the exclusive end and aim.

[29] Only SUSCEPTIBILITY; for this is all that we, on our side, can bring towards such *acquittal*. Farther, the Decree of a Superior adjudging to us a good for which, as inferiors, we have nothing more than moral *receptivity*, is called GRACE.

either to religion or to morality, since, by hypothesis, the party interested has already passed into that desiderated moral state, to develope, advance, and bring which about, is already the last end and scope of all analysis and elaboration of ethical ideas; for as to any consolation to be thence drawn, amended moral sentiments do of themselves straightway beget and bring this moral welfare forth (as comfort and hope, though not as certainty). The previous inquiry is therefore no more than the solution of a speculative problem; not to be *silently* overlooked by reason, because then reason might be upbraided with her inability to reconcile her hopes of final absolution from guilt, with the decrees of Divine Justice;—a reproach most hurtful to our rational faculty in many respects, but especially in what regards morality. But whatever may be thought of the POSITIVE value of the above deduction, its NEGATIVE use is of avail to the religion and morals of every man; for now it is most clearly obvious, that, singly, where a total change of heart has taken place, can the guilty cogitate himself as absolved at the bar of Heaven; wherefore no expiations, be they pompous or mournful, no invocations, nor hosannahs (not even of the vicarious Ideal of the Son of God) can supply its want; neither, if such free and incumbent change of heart be there, can those add to its validity before the celestial tribunal, inasmuch as this Ideal must have been adopted, and have passed into our own sentiments, before we can look upon it as coming in the room of our deficient deed.

Different from those interrogatories is the query, what mankind may, at the end of life, have to hope or fear, as consequences of the actions he may have done. To reply to this question, it is first of all requisite that he know his character, at least so far as to be able to strike some tolerable estimate of its worth. Hence, even should he suppose that a reformation of character has taken place, he must notwithstanding, in his estimate, compute likewise the actions of the old man whom he has stripped off, viz. what and how much of the corrupt man he has laid aside, and what purity and degree of strength his supposed new character has attained, so as effectually to counterbalance the depraved bias, and secure him against a return into evil. The estimate must consequently examine in detail his whole life. Again, since he can arrive at no certain or well-defined notion as to the real state of his inward sentiments, but is left to infer this from his course of life, he must hold that the only means of satisfactorily convincing his future Judge (his own awakened conscience rising to sit in judgment on his then recalled actions), will be to place before his mental vision, some time or other, a panorama of HIS WHOLE TRANSACTED LIFE—not a mere segment of it—perhaps the last and most favourable for the accused; for with this latter part he would naturally connect the hope of a still further progression, had his existence lasted longer. When an entire track of behaviour is thus objected to his view, he cannot propose to place his *intentions* in room of his actions, but must, from the aggregate of his actions, conclude upon his *intentions*. WHAT THINKS MY READER? Does not the bare thought that he may one day stand before such a Judge, calling back to memory many things that had long slumbered neglected in its depositories, suggest to him sundry misgivings as to the destiny he may expect as the sequent of his hitherto led life. When we interrogate the monitor who dwells within, an inexorably rigid sentence is always uttered; for no one can bribe his own reason. But if brought before some other judge, such as some pretend to say they know from other sources will be the case, then has he many excuses, taken from the alleged frailty of his nature, to urge against a rigid and severe administration of the law. Either he thinks, by rueful self-compunction (that never springs from a genuine spirit of amendment), to bias his Judge, so as to mitigate his punishment; or else he hopes, by prayers and supplications, or by formulas and confessions, which he gives out he believes, to soften and melt down his purpose; and if such belief is taught and instilled into mankind betimes (conformably to the adage, "*All's well that ends well*"), then does he from the very beginning so take his measures, as not needlessly to abridge his indulgence in voluptuous excess, but waits till near life's termination, in order then, in all haste, to close his ledger with a clear balance anyhow in his favour.[30]

APOTOME II.

OF THE TITLE OF THE EVIL PRINCIPLE TO RULE OVER MANKIND, AND OF THE BATTLE OF THE GOOD WITH THE EVIL PRINCIPLE FOR THE SOVEREIGN EMPIRE OVER THE HUMAN RACE.

The Sacred Volume exhibits this intelligible moral relationship under the Form of a History. It represents the two Principles in man as Persons without him, opposed to one another, and diverse as is Heaven from Hell, who not only prove their strength against each other, but do,

---

[30] The object of those who on death-bed send for a clergyman usually is, to have a Comforter, not for the physical distress which the last illness or even the natural fear of death produces (for here death who ends them may act as Comforter), but for their moral anguish, viz. the stings of conscience. These, however, ought to be rather stirred up and sharpened, so as to goad the person on to do what good he still may—to repair and counteract as far as in him lies the evil springing from his bad actions. It is thus we are warned, "Agree quickly with thine adversary (*him who has a legal claim against thee*) whilst thou art on the way with him (*i. e. so long as thou art alive*), lest he deliver thee to the judge" (*after death*), and so forth. On the other hand, to administer opiates to conscience is a violation of what is due equally to the moribund and his surviving fellow-men, and quite subversive of the true end why such a *curator of conscience* can at all be looked upon as advantageous in one's last moments.

Immanuel Kant

moreover—the one as accuser, the other as advocate—endeavour to make their claims legally valid, as if before a Supreme Judge.

Mankind was originally (*Genesis*, i. 28) invested with the thanage and dominion of all the goods of the earth. Of these, however, he only possessed the fee, and was bound to do homage to his liege Lord and Creator, who retained the overlordship and *dominium directum* of the property. Straightway there appears an evil being (how he became so evil, and broke faith with his Lord, is unknown), who by a lapse forfeited all his estates in heaven, and is now on earth in quest of others in their room. But because this evil person is a spirit of the very highest order, corporeal and terrestrial objects can afford him no delight. He seeks a dominion over the minds and wills, by making the progenitors of our race swerve from their Lord and become subservient to him; by all which he succeeds in being acknowledged as the Superior of the goods of the earth, *i. e.* as the *Prince of this World*. Here a doubt might easily suggest itself, why the Omnipotent should not instantly have crushed this traitor by his might, and overthrown in the beginning the first rudiments of that kingdom[31] he intended to found. But Supreme Wisdom deals with Intelligents agreeably to a Principle of Free Will, and does, in the administration of his empire, allow their good or evil to emanate from and be imputable to themselves. Thus, however, in contempt of the Good Principle, a kingdom of evil was erected, to which all mankind naturally descending from Adam have enthralled themselves, and that, too, with their own consent, the glittering baubles of this world's goods sealing their eyes, lest they should see into the abyss of ruin for which they are reserved. This Good Principle did meanwhile defend itself against the alleged title of the Evil Principle to rule over mankind, by establishing a particular form of government, THE JEWISH THEOCRACY, which was set apart for the public and sole veneration of his name. But since the minds of the subjects in this government were mainly swayed by temporal rewards and punishments; and since the ceremonial law, though containing some few ethical precepts, was essentially civil and forensic; it is plain that such an economy as was the Judaical church and state could not encroach much on the realms of darkness, but served only to prevent the IMPRESCRIPTIBLE RIGHTS of the FIRST OWNER from falling into abeyance.

In course of time the Jews began to feel all the miseries of their Hierarchical Polity, partly perhaps from a sense of the native evils

---

[31] Father Charlevoix relates that, when teaching a wild Iroquese his catechism, and explaining to his pupil all the ruin and evil entailed by the wicked spirit on this originally good world, and the mischiefs still wrought by him frustrative of the best divine institutions, the indignant savage interrupted his instructor with *Why does not God annihilate the Devil?* A home-thrust, which the missionary candidly admits he was unable at the time to parry.

springing from such a course of things, or perhaps they were taught so to regard them by the Greek philosophical speculations concerning political and mental liberty. The soul-thrilling doctrines taught by those immortal sages had flashed out like thunderbolts into all adjoining countries, disturbing ancient heads of Superstition and Tyranny,— awaking the people to a sense of their rights, and rousing them even to the brink of revolution. At such a time as this it was, when the Jewish people were ripe for a rebellion, that all at once there appeared a Person whose wisdom was so much purer than that of any previous philosopher, that it seemed as if it had come down from heaven ! This Person announced himself, both with respect to doctrine and example, as a true man, but yet at the same time as a Divine Ambassador, of such extraction, as, by his originary innocence, not to be included in the covenant which all the rest of mankind had entered into, by their ancestor and representative, with the Evil Principle; and *"in whom, consequently, the Prince of this World had nothing."* The government of the prince was now endangered; for should this man, morally-acceptable to God, withstand all solicitations to join the evil league, and if, in consequence, other men were to adopt a similar cast of thinking, then would he lose all those his subjects, and his kingdom run the risk of being one day utterly subverted. To guard against such an occurrence, the prince offered the ambassador the joint-government with himself, of his whole empire, provided he were by homage acknowledged as the rightful sovereign. But as this experiment did not succeed, he forthwith withdrew from this stranger, while on earth, all that could make life agreeable, plunging him in the deepest poverty, exciting against him the bitterest persecution, calumniating the purity of his intentions and doctrines,—griefs that the moral mind alone can right inly feel,—pursuing him finally even to the most degrading death, without being able, by this violent invasion, to shake him in the least from his constancy and generosity, in advancing the weal of the unworthy by example and precept. And now let us consider the close and issue of this combat. The RESULT may be regarded either under a PHYSICAL or LEGAL aspect. As physical, falling under sense, the Good Principle is worsted. After much endured distress, his life perished[32] in

---

[32] Not, as Dr Bahrdt will have it, that he VOLUNTEERED to die, that he might, by a shining and startling fate, call attention to his good doctrines and designs s such a step would have been self-murder. Mankind may doubtless hazard something, even when the stake perilled is loss of life. We may undergo execution from others, when we cannot escape without betraying a sacred duty; but no one is entitled to dispose of himself or his life as a mere mean toward any end, be that end what it may; for then he would be AUTHOR of his own death. Neither can I coincide with the remark thrown out in the WOLFENBÜTTEL FRAGMENTS, that his life was staked, not on a moral, but on a political and disallowed end, viz. the subverting of the sacerdotal power, and substituting himself as Worldly Head in their room. This latter suspicion is obviated by reflecting that he must already have renounced all hope of life when he exhorted his Disciples at their Last

Immanuel Kant

the conflict, because he sowed sedition in a realm, foreign to his and endowed with force and authority. But since the realm wherein the WILL'S PRINCIPLES,—be they good or evil,—are dominant, is a realm, not of Nature, but of Freedom, *i. e.* a kingdom where *things* can be disposed of, only so far as we are able to maintain sway over the *minds*, and where no one can be enslaved, except him who chooses to be enthralled, and even then only as long as he so wills; it follows that this death,—THE LAST EXTREMITY OF HUMAN SUFFERING,—was an exhibition of mankind's indwelling good principle in its entire moral perfection, as an example displayed for the benefit of every one. It was then, is now, and may be at all times of the greatest possible influence, by setting forth in the most glaring contrast the Freedom of the Children of Heaven, and the Bondage of a mere Son of Earth. But this good principle is not to be regarded as having been manifested at one given particular time only; but must be held, even from the very first origin of our species, to have invisibly come down from heaven, and taken up its abode with man; as any one may immediately convince himself who attends to the final destination of his being—HOLINESS,—and then reflects on the incomprehensible union betwixt such an ethical predisposition and the sensitive nature of man. Appearing, however, in a true and real given person, it may be said of the ideal, that "*he then came unto his own, and his own received him not, although to as many as received him, to them gave he power to become sons of God, even to them that believe on his name;*" *i. e.* he by his example threw open the portals of freedom to all who, like him, chose to die to whatever kept them fettered to this earthly life disadvantageously to their morality, and gathers from among mankind, under his authority, a *peculiar people, zealous of good works*, leaving, the meanwhile, those who prefer the servitude of immorality, to their moral chains.

Consequently, the final close of this moral combat, up to the period of the death of the hero of this history, does not issue in the CONQUEST of the Evil Principle; for his kingdom still endures, and an ulterior epoch is yet expected when it shall be finally subverted. The result of the combat has only been to abridge his power of detaining those whom he enthrals longer than they chose to be his slaves,—a different moral government (and under one or other mankind must at all times stand)

Supper to repeat that ceremony in remembrance of him. Had this been a MEMENTO of failing and defeated worldly designs, it could only have awakened a mortifying and indignant recollection of their framer, and so the exhortation to remember him would have destroyed itself. Nevertheless, such a MEMENTO of the Great Teacher and Master is not inconsistent with his consciousness of having missed of a good and pure moral end, viz. the intent of bringing about a PUBLIC revolution in religion—by abolishing a ceremonial faith that extruded all morality in sentiment, and by overthrowing the authority of its priests—a design that, I regret to think, has not yet gone into execution. It has not, however, been altogether frustrated, but passed, after his death, though slowly and sorrowfully, into a widely self-extending modification of religion.

now awaiting them as an asylum, where refuge and protection can be found for their morality when they come forth from the ancient haunts of bondage. The Evil Principle bears as yet the name of Prince of this World,—a world where the followers of the Good Principle must always be prepared to undergo physical disasters, sacrifices, and mortifications of self-love,—things that are understood to be persecutions on the part of the Evil Principle, because in his kingdom there are. rewards for those only, who make physical wellbeing the scope and aim of their exertions.

Every body must at once perceive, that when this lively and singularly popular narrative is divested of its mystic veil, its spirit and meaning are practically valid and obligatory, at all times, and for the whole world, in as much as they lay before every man a vivid outline of his duty. The moral suggested by the narrative is, that there is absolutely no salvation for mankind apart from their adopting into their inmost sentiments genuine moral principles; that such adoption is withstood, not by the so often blamed sensory, but by a certain self-demerited perversity (satanic guile, or by whatever other name we may term that vitiosity whereby sin entered into the world), to be met with in every man, and capable of being removed by nothing, save by the idea of the moral good in its entire purity, attended, however, with the inward conviction that this IDEAL really belongs to the originary predispositions of our personality; and that all we need do, after having deeply engraven it on our soul, is to keep it clear from foreign admixture, in order that we may, by the effect it gradually takes upon the mind, become perfectly assured that the dreaded powers of evil never can deface it, and that the gates of hell shall not ultimately prevail against us. Again, lest we beat about for some substitute to supply the want of this assurance,—either, first, SUPERSTITIOUSLY, by expiations, that presuppose no change of heart, or, second, FANATICALLY, by imagined passive inward illuminations, both which withdraw mankind to a distance, from good grounded on his own self-activity—the history reminds us that no criterion of this assurance can be morally allowed, other than the criterion of a well-regulated exemplary life.

Finally, an endeavour, such as the present, to find in the Scripture that sense[33] which best harmonizes with the tenets, taught by Reason, and looked upon as in her eye amongst the Holiest of Holies, is not only allowed, but must be deemed a duty; and mankind may remind themselves of what the WISE TEACHER once said to his disciples, touching some one who struck into a path of his own' but which eventually led to the same goal, *"Forbid him not; for he that is not against us, is for us."*

---

[33] Which sense, it is at once conceded, is not the only one.

GENERAL SCHOLION.

Whenever a moral religion (consisting, as it does, not in rites, observances, or traditions, but in the cordial intent of fulfilling all our duties, as if divinely commanded) is to be established, then must even the miracles that may be historically connected with its introduction become ultimately superfluous. Moral religion tends eventually to displace and dispense with all miraculous beliefs whatever; for mankind betrays a culpable state of moral unbelief, when he refuses to acknowledge the paramount authority of those behests of duty primordially insculpted on his heart, unless he see them accredited and enforced by miracles—"*Except ye see signs and wonders, ye will not believe.*" It is, however, quite consistent with the common opinions of mankind to hold, that when a religion of mere rites and ceremonies is to be abolished, and one in the spirit and truth of a moral sentiment is to be introduced in its stead, the historical introduction of this last may be accompanied and adorned with miracles, in order to proclaim the expiry of the former, which, apart from miracles, never would have had any authority. Again, in order to win over the adherents of the old system to the new order of affairs, it is quite conceivable that the spiritual worship might be represented as the fulfilling antitype, foreordained of old, of those ceremonies, and which was, even under the old economy? the last end and design of Providence. Since these matters can be thus accommodated to the notices of reason, it can serve no purpose whatever now to call in question the accuracy of those narrations, or of such allegorical interpretation, provided only we have fairly attained a true religion, which can subsist henceforward by itself, and on its own evidence in reason, although once upon a time it may have required such adminicles to aid it; and provided always that people will not insist, that the bare believing and rehearsal of matters incomprehensible (which any one may believe and repeat without being or ever becoming thereby a better man) is to be deemed a mode, or perhaps the only mode, of acceptably worshipping God; this being an opinion that is most strenuously to be impugned. It may, therefore, perhaps be all very true that the PERSON of the Teacher of the alone true and universally valid religion is an impenetrable mystery; that his advent and departure from earth were miraculous; that his eventful life and death were likewise miracles; nay, that the very history documentarily attesting the narrative of all those wonders, is again itself a miracle (*i. e.* SUPERNATURAL REVELATION); nay, we may concede to such alleged facts whatever worth they claim, and even venerate the vehicle that has brought into public currency, a doctrine, that needs neither sign nor wonder for its credential, being insculpted indefaceably on every human soul. All this, it is conceded, may be done, so long as those historic documents are not perverted into elements of religion, and mankind taught that the knowing, believing, and professing their contents, is in itself something whereby we can render ourselves acceptable to God.

Concerning miracles generally, I am inclined to think, that although sensible people refuse absolutely to deny them, they do nevertheless object to cultivating any practical belief in the marvellous; that is to say, they willingly admit IN THEORY that miracles are possible, but IN THE BUSINESS OF LIFE they count upon none. Enlightened governments have upon this ground at once *conceded*, or even decided and enacted, when legislating in ecclesiastical matters, that miracles happened *in days of yore;* but that *now-a-days* no NEW miracle can be permitted.[34] Prodigies, indeed, were of old so fixed, and gradually circumscribed, by the magistrate, that no confusion could ever accrue through such anomalous means to the commonwealth; whereas if any one were of new to display signs and wonders, the government would naturally be apprehensive whereunto such things might grow, and anxious as to the effect that such preternatural manifestations might exert on public tranquillity and the existing constitution. Were the question raised, "*What is a miracle?*" then— since all we are concerned about knowing is, what miracles are in reference to us, *i. e.* when regard is had to the practical use of our own understanding—the following answer might be given, viz. they are events brought about by causes, with the laws of whose efficiency we

---

[34] Orthodox religious teachers who attach themselves to the articles of a church-creed established by law and supported by government, observe this maxim in the case of all supposed new miracles. They thus left room for MR. PFENNINGER to defend his friend MR. LAVATER, who had declared his belief that miracles were still possible. Mr. P. reproached the orthodox with their inconsistency, in giving out that some seventeen centuries ago there were actual workers of miracles in the Christian congregations, and yet refusing to admit that miraculous gifts existed in the church now. He remarked to them, that they had succeeded in proving from the Scripture, NEITHER that miracles were totally to cease, NOR *when* their termination was to be expected. This proof still remains a desideratum; for the quibble, that miraculous interposition is now no longer necessary, is an assumption of higher knowledge than befits any man. Their conduct in this particular indicates what the dictate of reason is, namely, not practically to admit that such things happen *now*, although the objective insight that miracles are impossible is unattainable. But if this be the only rational dictate to be followed, lest the commonwealth be thrown into continued perturbation, ought not a similar maxim to obtain for the protection of philosophy, and indeed of every rational and reflecting society. They who deny GRAND miracles, but admit the SMALL, under the name of extraordinary Providences (because, as merely directing or influencing the course of events, little expenditure of supernatural agency is required), talk beside the purpose; the question does not regard the volume or intensity of the effect, but touches the Form of the Flux of Nature in time, *i. e.* depends upon the MODE how the form of the course of events is regulated, viz. whether naturally or supernaturally. As for the MYSTERIOUSNESS of supernatural operations, to fancy any studied concealment (*on the part of the Deity?* Tr.) is quite inconsistent with the importance of a matter of this kind. Farther, in the case of God, no distinction betwixt what is difficult and easy is cogitable.

are and must ever remain totally unacquainted. These miraculous portents may be cogitated as flowing either from GOD or from DEMONS, which latter class again branches out into signs *angelical* and signs *diabolical,* according as the marvels are understood to emanate from a good or an evil spirit (agathodemonian or kakodemonian miracles). The diabolical alone fall under examination; since the good angels (I scarcely know why) are seldom or never heard of acting in this capacity.

THEISTICAL MIRACLES can by all means be figured as cogitable; nay, we can even frame to ourselves a *negative* and merely general notion of the law of the agency of the Divine Causality, as the causal-agency of an Almighty and Moral Being, at once Creator and Governor of the intellectual and material worlds; for of the laws of his ethical administration we are intimately aware, and possess a standing perception, that is quite available to reason. On the hypothesis that, in some particular cases, it should seem fit to the Divine Wisdom to control and modify the course of the physical system in that sensible effect called a miracle, then we have not the smallest notion, neither can we ever hope to attain any, of the law agreeably to which God conducts the operation of such sign; we have no more than a general moral notion, that whatever God does, will be all very good—a representation that defines nothing with respect to any singular event. Here the understanding is brought at once to a stand, and shackled in its ordinary avocation of referring phenomena to their known antecedents, and sees no prospect of ever gaining any insight that might compensate for this disturbance. Among the various kinds of possible miracles, the demonian are the most irreconcileable with the exercise of reason. For, touching the theistical, reason is always in possession of a negative criterion, whereby to test their divine original; inasmuch as, if any thing were held to be commanded by God himself immediately appearing, which commandment were, however, directly subversive of morality, then how imposing and majestic soever might be the miraculous appearance of the divine semblance, it is absolutely certain that this supposed preternatural hut immoral behest, never could have proceeded from the Supreme (*e. g.* if a father were desired to slay his perfectly innocent son). But in the case of any fancied demonian miracle, even this negative criterion is wanting; and were we to attempt to introduce the contrary and positive rule, viz. that when the sign invites to a good action, already incumbent on us, as our duty, it cannot possibly have come from an evil being, then may we just as easily go wrong; for this last, as we are told, does sometimes transform himself into an angel of light.

In the business and practical conduct of life, miracles are not to be counted on; neither can they tell in any way upon the suggestions of our understanding, with whose directions, from day to day, we never can dispense. Judges (although, as members of the church, most orthodox believers in miracles) listen to the excuses of a culprit who urges in alleviation of his crime a temptation from the devil, with ears as deaf as if nothing had been said, although, if they really considered such preternatural seduction possible, it would not be undeserving of attention, that a simple common man had fallen into the snares of a most astute and abandoned villain. But then this outlaw cannot be cited to their bar; the prisoner and his spiritual accomplice cannot be confronted; in a single word, no judge can make any rational application of any such alleged defence. Sensible divines will therefore take good heed how they cram and bewilder the heads of their flock with infernal stories about this occult PROTEUS. Again, as for benignant miracles, when men of business talk of them, that is no more than a mode of speaking. Thus a physician says, without a miracle the patient is gone,—he must certainly die; where by a miracle is merely understood an unusual occurrence. To the real business of life belongs the occupation of the natural philosopher, in endeavouring to detect the causes and laws of cosmical phenomena: such physical laws of those events, I say, as he can authenticate and prove by observation and experience, although he renounces every pretence to know, what that which works agreeably to those laws, may be in itself, or what it might be, were we gifted with an added sense. In exactly the same way, each man's moral amendment, is part of the solemn business of life; and whether celestial influences work along with us, or be even deemed needful, toward an explanation of the possibility of so desirable an event, still mankind cannot comprehend them, neither can he certainly distinguish the extraordinary aid, from his own natural operations, nor yet superinduce them upon himself, and so as it were draw down the heavens and put them within his grasp. In as much, then, as no practical benefit can accrue from such tenets, he sets to work as if there were no moral miracles,[35] and, in obeying the decrees of reason, proceeds exactly as if the whole change and amendment of his inner man depended singly on his own strenuous and diligent exertions. Lastly, the imagination, that any one can by dint of A FIRM THEORETICAL FAITH in miraculous events, himself possess the practical gift of performing them, and take as it were the kingdom of heaven by violence, is so very unexpected an evagation from all bounds of common sense, as to render it needless for us to tarry even for a moment on so preposterous a whimsey.

---

[35] That is to say, mankind refuses to admit a miraculous belief into the maxims either of his speculative or practical understanding, without, however, calling in question either the *possibility* or *actuality* of such marvellous demonstrations.

Jugglers, who pretend to magic gifts, have recourse not unfrequently to a subterfuge, in order to impose upon the credulous, viz. they appeal to the confessed ignorance of natural philosophers. We cannot fathom—they cry—the last ground of the attraction of gravitation, nor yet of magnetism; hence, by parity of reason, &c. &c. But the laws of gravitation and magnetism we know in most extensive detail, and are even perfectly acquainted with the limits and conditions under which alone certain given effects take place; and this is enough both for a sure and rational application of those phenomena, and also for a satisfactory explication of them, *secundum quid, i. e.* DOWNWARDS, when using those laws, so as to subsume and arrange the magnetic or other phenomena under them; although certainly not enough for an explication *simpliciter, i. e.* regressively UPWARDS, when we wish to comprehend the last substratal ground of the forces, that we know operate according to those observed laws. This remark likewise serves to throw light on a remarkable peculiarity in our intellectual economy, viz. why the stupendous wonders of Creation, *i. e.* sufficiently attested, though startling and marvellous phenomena, or even unexpectedly emerging appearances, seemingly at variance with nature's known laws, are eagerly laid hold of, as promising enchanting prospects, whereas the announcement of something really miraculous and preternatural, tends rather to abash and deject the mind. The cause is obvious: Natural Wonders unfold in vision farther and exhaustless fields of intellectual research, and ENCOURAGE reason to entertain the HOPE that, by duly tracing the anomalous phenomena, new and hitherto unknown laws may rise to light. Preternatural wonders, on the other hand, rather OVERWHELM the understanding, and give birth to the APPREHENSION that it is about to be bereft of all trust and confidence even in those it believes already investigated and established. Now, whenever the understanding is wrenched away from those laws of experience and observation, which by its categories it prescribes and imposes on all cosmical events whatsoever, then may it be said to have breathed out its last gasp; for in such fairy world its knowledge is useless, and all human wisdom is at once defeated of its ends, seeing that in an order of affairs so loosened and dissolved, even the moral exercise of practical reason, in discharging duty, is subverted; for, now, who can any longer be certain that certain changes may not, quite unknown to us, be miraculously wrought upon our moral springs, where none can tell, whether to ascribe them to himself, or to some higher impenetrable cause. They who are inclined to judge favourably of miracles, think they remove the stumbling-block thrown by them in the way of reason, when they concede that preternatural events are of *seldom* occurrence. Possibly they even insinuate that this *rarity* is covertly involved in the very notion of a miracle, because, if any such event were ordinarily to happen, it would then cease to be a wonder.

Giving them the full benefit of this most sophistical evasion (the sophism of confounding an objective question, viz. *what a thing is?* with one merely subjective, viz. *what the word whereby we indicate that thing signifies?*), it must still be asked, HOW SELDOM? once in a century, or only, perhaps, in the beginning of the world, but now not at all. Here, nothing can be definitively fixed from what we know of the object (for that, by hypothesis, transcends our comprehension); all we can do is to assign a necessary maxim on which we must regulate the use of our understanding, and either admit that they happen *never*, or *daily*, masked under the garb of natural events. The latter alternative is quite incompatible with reason, and hence our only course is to fall back upon the former. This position, however, it must well be noted, is only a self-appointed maxim, regulating our reflex judgments; it must not be mistaken for a positive theoretical assertion. No man is at liberty to frame so exaggerated an opinion of his depth of insight, as to pretend decisively to say that the admirable conservation of species and genera in the animal and vegetable kingdoms, where each successive generation follows the exemplar of its parent kind,—copying with the greatest exactness all the internal mechanism of its originary framework, and even (in the case of plants) adorning itself, every spring, with the most delicate hues that coloured the complexion of the primeval stock, setting at defiance all the desolating fury wherewith the autumnal or wintry blasts of inorganic nature might attack the seeds:—no person, I say, can pretend to know whether all this is operated by the laws and plastic powers of the physical system, or whether the Creator's immediate agency is not invariably required for the annual re-exhibition of this vernal show. But the phenomena are objected to our observation and experience; consequently, *in our eye*, they are seen as effects wrought by nature, and are *by* us never to be otherwise judged of. The modest voice of reason calls upon us to abide within these limits, and to stray beyond this circumscribed barrier, is the step of an understanding at once rash and indecorous; although I am aware, that people who appeal to preternatural explications, often pretend that they do thereby give proof, of their humble and self-denying spirit.

Book III.

OF THE VICTORY OF THE GOOD OVER THE EVIL PRINCIPLE, AND THE FOUNDING OF A KINGDOM OF GOD ON EARTH.

EXORDIUM.

FROM the enduring combat fought by every morally-minded person, under the banners of the principle of good, against the assaults of the principle of evil, no higher advantage is at any time to be expected, than that mankind succeed in achieving his emancipation from the tyranny of the latter. "*To be made free from sin, and a servant of righteousness,*" is the utmost to be gained from the struggle. We remain, notwithstanding, continually exposed to the hostile aggression of our foe; and to maintain a freedom perpetually threatened and endangered, it is necessary that we continue always armed and ready for a conflict.

Into this state of danger, mankind has fallen by his own fault; consequently, he is bound, as much as in him lies, to strain every nerve to extricate himself from it. But how is this extrication to be accomplished? that is the question. Reflecting on the various occasions and circumstances that entangle and detain him in this danger, the conviction arises naturally in his mind, that this his perilous condition is not owing to his own rude isolated nature, but springs from the connection and relationship into which lie is thrown among his fellow-men: no stimulant or instinct of his physical system docs, so long as he lives apart and by himself, stir those emmoved PASSIONS, that spread such desolations amid his originally good predisposition. His wants arc few, and so easily supplied, as to leave his mind unembarrassed and tranquil, in fearless confidence, that as much as man absolutely needs is to be found everywhere. He is only poor (or fancies himself in penury), when he begins to apprehend that others may think him so, and despise him upon that account. Only when mixing in intercourse with his fellow-men, do envy, ambition, avarice, and their train of uncomfortable perturbations, besiege and take his otherwise frugal and contented mind captive. To superinduce upon any one these dire effects, it is by no means necessary that his associates be sunk in evil, or seduce him by their contagious example into crime. It is enough that mankind come together, in order, by their proximity and intercourse, to corrupt themselves mutually, and plunge one another into evil. Unless, then, some method can be devised for guarding against this danger, it would seem that, how successfully soever each individual man may have for a while emancipated himself from the thraldom of the enemy, he is, notwithstanding, in imminent risk of being constantly thrown back into his adversary's snares. The most obvious plan for counteracting this perverted and re-acting bias to spread abroad the seeds of evil, would be to form a general combination, instituted for the express end of warding off the bad, and cultivating what in mankind is good. To combine in such a union is tantamount to instituting a standing society, admitting of gradual and continual extension, intended for the general support of morality, where all the members work in common toward the suppression and overthrow of the wicked principle. The eventual dominion of the Good Principle is, consequently, as far as we mankind can work along with it, no otherwise to be attained than by setting up and spreading a society, combined under laws of virtue, whereof the end is no other than the advancement of virtue as its own and last end. To project and realize such an ethical institution, capable of comprehending the whole human race within its bosom, is therefore propounded to us by legislative reason, at once as Problem and as Duty; for thus alone can the Good Principle hope to triumph over our indwelling principle of evil. Out of and beyond the laws prescribed by morally-legislative reason to each single individual, she unfurls moreover a banner of virtue as a central-point, around which all lovers of good may rally, where each fights no longer alone, but in the escort of allies, all equally intent on crushing the power of their restless and vigilant invader, and securing victory for the Good Principle.

A conjunct association of this sort, regulated on the pattern of the above idea, and combined under its ideal moral laws, may be called AN ETHICAL SOCIETY; and whenever those laws are PUBLICLY announced, it may, in contradistinction to *the juridico-civil* or *political*, be called an *ethico-civil* society, or, in other words, AN ETHICAL COMMONWEAL. This ethic commonwealth may exist in the midst of a political common wealth; nay, the members of both may be the same (however, unless the civil polity be already in existence and serve as groundwork for the other, no ethical polity can ever be figured as realizable by man). But though the one presuppose the other, the ethico-civil polity has its own peculiar and distinguishing principle (the principle of virtue), and consequently a form and constitution essentially different from those of the former. Nevertheless a certain analogy obtains betwixt them, regarded both as commonwealths, upon account of which analogy the latter may be spoken of as AN ETHICAL STATE, *i. e.* A KINGDOM OF VIRTUE (*or of the Good Principle*),—an idea deeply rooted in the reason of man, and possessing full objective reality (viz. as imposing upon mankind a duty of combining in such a moral *civitas maxima*), although subjectively it never can be hoped from the good wills of mankind that they will resolve cordially to co-operate toward the eduction of that end.

APOTOME I.

PHILOSOPHICAL ACCOUNT OF THE VICTORY OF THE GOOD PRINCIPLE, BY FOUNDING A KINGDOM OF GOD ON EARTH.

SECTION I.

OF THE ETHICAL STATE OF NATURE.

A POLITICAL OR JURIDICO-CIVIL STATE denotes the reciprocal relation of man to man, so far as they stand under laws common, public, and forensic (where the laws carry with them an outward title of co-action). AN ETHICO-CIVIL STATE, on the contrary, is one where mankind are combined under the like laws, only these last have not in and for themselves any coercive power of the civil kind, *i. e.* its inherent jurisdiction exists solely under pure laws of virtue.

Again, as to the first, is opposed the juridical (or legal, though not upon that account legitimate) state of nature; so a distinction is to be taken betwixt the latter and the ethical state of nature. In either state of nature each individual appoints to himself his own law, there being no outward legislation extant, to which he, in conjunction with others, could acknowledge himself subject. In both, is each his own judge and avenger, there being as yet no PUBLIC AUTHORITY empowered to act as common arbiter, judicially to apply the rule of right, determine impartially in any emerging crisis what each man's duty may demand, and then enforce its general observance.

Existing political commonwealths have, it is true, departed from the crude inartificial regimen; hut still every member of this civil community remains in his ETHICAL STATE OF NATURE, and is in truth quite entitled to persist in it; for, that any civil polity should be held bound to compel its subjects to form themselves into an ETHIC COMMONWEAL, is a palpable contradiction—the latter society being, by its very idea, distinguished from the other, just by wanting and disclaiming all co-active force. Doubtless every political society must wish that there may obtain among its members a government according to laws of virtue, in order that where its own co-active mechanism is invalid,—human tribunals not penetrating into the interior of man,— these virtuous sentiments may bring forth the desired effect. But woe worth the day to that statesman who should dream of violently establishing a society intended simply for ethic ends; for such rude attempt would give birth to anything save a moral community, and would render uncertain and unstable the foundations even of his STATE. Members of a civil polity arc, therefore, quite exempt from any legislatorial compulsion, or subjection to the decrees of an ethical society, and retain full and unshackled option, whether they will, with their fellow-citizens, frame, moreover, a moral association, or continue in the first and original ethical state of nature. On the other hand, as soon as an ethical commonwealth, based on PUBLIC laws, has been arranged, and possessed of a corresponding public constitution, those who have freely made themselves its members must not suffer themselves to receive orders from any political authority, how to adjust or construct the details of its internal framework. Although they may, indeed must, allow certain limitations to be prescribed, viz. that none of their institutions obstruct that duty already incumbent on each associate as a citizen of state,—a precaution that, where an ethical society is founded on genuine moral principles, is perhaps little better than unnecessary apprehension.

Again, because the offices of virtue extend to the whole human race, the idea of an ethical commonwealth embraces an ideal aggregate of all mankind, and does, by this peculiarity, distinguish itself from all political societies. Hence any assignable number of men, united for this ultimate end, cannot be regarded as THE ETHICAL STATE ITSELF, but only as a branch of it; each partial and more limited society endeavouring to come to a complete uniformity and concordance with every other, in order to arrive at that absolute ethic whole, whereof each lesser association is no more than a *Scheme* or *Effigiation*, each of them again standing to one another in the relationship of an ethical state of nature, and consequently encumbered with all the inconveniences that attach to this imperfect order of things, just as is found to obtain among states totally unconnected by any common international convention.

SECTION II.

MANKIND OUGHT TO QUIT HIS ETHICAL STATE OF NATURE IN ORDER TO BECOME A MEMBER OF AN ETHIC COMMONWEALTH.

The juridical state of nature being, as we have seen, a state of mutual natural hostility, the same remark holds of the ethical state of nature, where each person lies perpetually exposed to assaults from the principle of evil extant in himself, and in every other of his fellows. Mankind (as we observed above) corrupt one another's morality; and, notwithstanding the good-will of individuals, they do, through want of a common central principle, just as were they instruments of the Evil One, distract one another, by having no joint understanding, from pursuing a common good end, and so expose themselves to the risk of again relapsing under the dominion of the evil they had overcome. Again, as a state of lawless freedom, and independency on any co-active rescripts, is a state of open injustice and war declared against each man by his neighbour, which it behoves every one to quit, in order to combine in society political,[36] in exactly the same way the ethical state of nature is tantamount to an open and perpetual invasion of the principles of virtue, and a state of internal immorality, whence each individual ought, with utmost diligence, to come, as speedily as possible.

Here we impinge upon a duty altogether *sui generis*, viz. a duty obtaining not betwixt man and man, but owed by the whole human race to itself. Every class of Intelligents is, agreeably to objective ideas of pure reason, destined to a common and joint end, viz. the pursuit of the SOVEREIGN, *as their common* GOOD. But, since the highest ethic good is not to be attained by each individual's endeavouring separately to carry forward the work of his own moral perfecting, but does, on the contrary, demand for its realization a general union of hearts and minds, combined INTO ONE WHOLE, and purposing the same end, thereby constituting a system, in which, and by the unity whereof, this highest good can alone be brought about, it is manifest to every one that the idea of such a systematic whole, viz. an universal republic under ethic laws, is an idea totally diverse from that of any other moral precept (for those last concern only duties in our power to perform), and one that ordains us to aim at a grand whole, whereof it is uncertain whether its realization may stand within or beyond our power; and consequently the duty imposed by this idea differs entirely, both in kind and principle, from all other duties whatsoever. The reader will, I doubt not, already be aware that this is a duty which will imperatively demand the pre-supposition of a still further IDEA, viz. that of a Supreme Moral Governor, under whose general superintendence and disposing providence the otherwise inadequate efforts of *Particulars* are concentrated, so as to issue in a joint effect. Let us, however, prosecute the inquiry into the rise and source of this our *moral need*, and see whitherward it may guide us.

---

[36] HOBBES' position, "*status hominum naturalis est bellum omnium inter omnes,*" is quite correct when we read "est status belli," &c. For although, betwixt men uncombined by public statutable enactments, actual war may not arise, still their state (*status juridicus*) is one wherein each, as his own judge, decides upon his own rights and property, and has for these no security, except what results from his own strength; and this state of affairs is in very deed an interbelligerent condition, where every one's hand is ready to be turned against his brother. His next position, "*exeundum esse e statu naturals,*" is a corollary from the former, inasmuch as, by this posture of affairs, a perpetual lesion of one another's rights takes place, every one claiming to be judge in his own behalf, and refusing to offer others any security in points of *meum* and *tuum*, save his own arbitrary will.

SECTION III.

THE IDEA OF AN ETHICAL COMMONWEALTH IS THE IDEA OF A PEOPLE OF GOD COMBINED UNDER MORAL LAWS.

In order to found an ethical commonwealth, its individual members must be represented as subjected to a public legislation, and those laws by which singular members are conjoined into a whole must be regarded as commandments issuing from some common lawgiver. When the state to be erected is political, then is the collective will of that artificial body produced by the association, the legislator (*i. e.* author of the constitution):—juridical legislation resting upon the principle, "THAT EACH PERSON'S FREEDOM IS LIMITED, AGREEABLY TO LAW UNIVERSAL, BY THOSE CONDITIONS ACCORDING TO WHICH ALONE IT CAN HARMONIZE WITH EVERY OTHER PERSON'S FREEDOM;—where, consequently the general will extorts outward obedience by virtue of its title of co-action.[37] But if the common wealth is ethical, the people cannot be regarded as themselves legislating; for in this society all laws tend to promote morality—a thing quite internal, and therefore not falling under any public outward human legislation whatsoever, this last concerning itself only with the legality of actions. There must consequently, some one, other than the people itself, be assigned as the public and yet inward legislator of an ethical state. Again, ethic laws arc never understood to emanate ORIGINALLY from the will of a Superior, *i. e.* are not like statutes, which, until embodied and published in an edict, obtain no obligatory force; for statutable decrees of this kind never can become parts of any moral legislation, and the DUTY of obeying them would, however diligently observed, beget no FREE and independent virtue, but would remain always among the offices of CO-ACTION. The Supreme Lawgiver in an ethical society can therefore be such an one alone, in regard of whom, all real duties,[38] whether

---

[37] The above is the Supreme Principle of Law. (The reader will find this position staled and explained in my translation of Kant's Ethics, p. 192 5, B, C, and D.—Tr.)

[38] Whenever any thing is acknowledged to be duty, although only imposed by the arbitrary will of a human lawgiver, then may we forthwith assert that obedience to it is enjoined by the Divine Will. Municipal Enactments are certainly not Divine Commands; and yet, where lawful, it cannot be doubted that obedience to them is divinely commanded. The saying, "*We must hearken to God rather than to man,*" signifies no more than this, viz. that should any earthly legislation enjoin something immediately contradictory of the moral law, obedience is not to be rendered: where, conversely, I take occasion to remark, that when a municipal unimmoral statute is opposed by an alleged statutable divine behest, then is there good ground of suspicion that the declaration of the will of God is supposititious; for then it collides with a clear plain duty; and that any given document really does contain Divine decrees, never can be so authenticated by any experience or observation, as to warrant mankind in setting aside, for its sake, an otherwise plain and existing duty.

juridical or ethical, may be figured as founded on his commandment; who is farther a searcher of the heart, percipient of the inmost sentiments of all, and adjudging—as must take place in every commonwealth,—to each what his actions may be worth. This, however, is the Idea of God[39] as Moral Governor of the World; wherefore we conclude, our ETHICAL STATE can only be cogitated as a FOLK combined by and under a divine commandment, *i. e.* as a People of God standing under ethic laws.

A people of God may no doubt be imagined, combined under legal statutes, where not the morality, but only the legality, of conduct is inquired into. This would be a juridical commonwealth, whereof the legislator is God, and the constitution of such a state would be theocratical; and, in so far as certain men, in the capacity of PRIESTS, immediately receive and communicate his laws, the administration would be aristocratical. An institution of this sort, however, resting, in form and substance, merely on historical events, is not what we are in search of, and cannot be looked upon as solving the problem projected by pure morally legislative reason. In the next apotome, containing a *historical* account of the advent of a Kingdom of God, we shall consider this theocracy as a society regulated by juridico-civil laws, and where the legislator, although God, acts as an outward lawgiver only; whereas in the present apotome, we investigate such a philosophical economy as may depend on a legislation purely inward, and be a society standing under laws of virtue, *i. e.* constituting "*a People of God zealous of good works.*"

Contradistinguished from the notion of a PEOPLE of God, is that of a RABBLE, or MOB, whose Ringleader is the Evil Principle—a gang intent on propagating mischief, and on hindering the other association from taking place, although the principle threatening the sentiments of virtue is also within, and only by a figure spoken of as an extraneous power.

SECTION IV.

THE IDEA OF A PEOPLE OF GOD IS (BY HUMAN ENDEAVOUR) ONLY TO BE REALIZED BY FORMING A CHURCH.

Sublime as is the idea of an ethical commonwealth, it can never be fully attained or realized by man, but dwindles in his hands down to an institution that docs no more than transcribe the Form of the other; for when we come to the materials requisite for instituting such a whole, we find that our means are very much abridged, being contracted by the

---

[39] Any reader who may think the text obscure, would do well to consult Kant's chapter on Conscience, Ethics, p. 277-81, § 13—Tr.

narrow limits of our moral nature.

Establishing a moral people of God, is therefore a work whereof the execution is to be expected, not from man, but only from God himself. It is not, however, upon that account allowable for mankind to resign himself to sloth, and never to bestir himself so as actively to forward this institution, but to devolve all on Providence, each man attending singly to his own private moral necessities, and leaving the supervisorship and care of the ethical interests of the race to the guardianship of a higher wisdom. So far from that, mankind ought to proceed as if every thing depended on himself; and it is only under this condition, that there is room to hope that a Higher Wisdom may crown with success the efforts of our well-meant schemes.

The wish of every honest-minded man therefore is, that "*the Kingdom of God may come and His Will be done on Earth;*" but then, the question arises, what have mankind to do in order that this may come to pass.

An ethical commonwealth under the divine moral legislation is A CHURCH, and in so far as such ideal state is no object of possible experience, it is called THE INVISIBLE CHURCH (a naked idea of the union of all the virtuous under the immediate divine moral government, which idea is the archetype whereon man has to regulate every ecclesiastical institution framed by him). THE VISIBLE CHURCH is an actual combination of given members, in a society, that endeavours to copy the form and feature of the other; and as every association combined by public laws, exhibits differences in rank—those who only obey the law differing in some degree from those who look after its execution—so the collective mass of the church is called the *flock* or *congregation*, while the superiors arc called guides or shepherds, who administer affairs in room of the Invisible Head, and in this latter capacity are styled *ministers* or *servants* of the church. A similar denomination occurs in the political fabric, where the visible Head of the commonwealth not unfrequently styles himself *the first servant of the state*, though he acknowledges no superior, perhaps not even the collective body of the nation. A true visible church is that which represents the moral kingdom of God on earth. Its conditions and criteria arc as follow:

I. UNIVERSALITY, consequently a numerical ONENESS of the church, the groundwork of which unity must spring from the constitution and genius of the church itself; so that, however torn and split by fortuitous sects and differing opinions, its fundamental principles arc such as must eventually bring about unity of view, and lead to a general amalgamation of all parties in one single ecclesiastical society.

II. QUALITY, which is PURITY; the union being held together by no other than ethic laws:—and equally clarified from the timidity of superstition and the whimsies of fanaticism.

III. The RELATIVITY is a mutual relationship of freedom, where not only is the inward relation of members to one another that of equal freedom; but where also the outward relation of the church to the state is based on a free, independent, and reciprocal alliance. (There can therefore be no room, in a well-regulated church, either for HIERARCHY or ILLUMINATISM, which last is a species of DEMOCRATIC inward light, each member claiming particular inspirations, adapted to his own head, and colliding with those of others.)

IV. MODALITY. The church's constitution must be UNCHANGEABLE, admitting, however, from time to time, modifications, according to place and circumstance; for which casual by-laws the church contains a sure and stable groundwork in the *a priori* idea of its own end. (Its establishment rests therefore on primary laws, published, as it were, once for all, in a fixed code: it cannot consequently be founded on arbitrary formulae, for these, wanting the *a priori* authentication of reason, are fortuitous, changeable, and open to contradiction.)

THE CHURCH, or visible ethical commonwealth, regarded as the representative of A CITY OF GOD, has, by dint of those its peculiar principles, a constitution apart and by itself, and betwixt it and any political constitution there is no comparison or similitude at all to be made. It is not MONARCHICAL, under Pope or Patriarch; nor ARISTOCRATICAL, under Bishops and Prelates; nor yet DEMOCRATICAL, as among independent sectarian Illuminati. Its constitutional framework might best be likened to that of a Family under a common, invisible, and moral Father, whose eldest and most holy Son, who best knows his Father's Will, and is by near ties of consanguinity connected with all its branches, does, by unfolding and explaining to the younger brethren what he has more fully learnt of the parental will, occupy the stead of the paternal head. They, upon this account, revere the Father in him, and thus enter into a general fraternal union and lasting alliance of hearts.

SECTION V.

THE CONSTITUTION OF EVERY CHURCH INVARIABLY RESTS ON A HISTORICAL BELIEF (REVEALED FAITH): THIS MAY BE CALLED CHURCH-FAITH, AND IS BEST FOUNDED ON A HOLY WRIT.

PURE RELIGIOUS FAITH, being a naked belief of reason, and capable of being communicated and imparted to every person, is that alone which can serve as a groundwork for a Church Universal. Whereas mere historical belief, grounded only on facts, can spread its influence no farther than the narrative has been carried; and must even then be multifariously limited and circumscribed, as well as by the varying capacity of its auditors to judge of its credibility. And yet experience teaches a faulty weakness of our nature, that must prevent us from ever counting so much on the strength of that pure faith as it well deserves, and induce us to distrust our hope of erecting a church on it alone.

Mankind's short-sightedness in supersensible matters is so great, that even while they justly value and appreciate this pure moral faith (which, upon the whole, is in their eyes, and must indeed be most self-evidently convincing), they are with difficulty brought to admit, that a steady and diligent prosecution of a moral life is really all that God demands to render them his acceptable subjects. Obligation they cannot well figure to themselves, otherwise than as a WORSHIP to be performed toward God, which worship respects not so much the inward moral worth of actions, as looks rather to this, that they are offered TO God, in order by passive resignation and obedience to please him. They will not suffer themselves to be persuaded, that by the fulfilment of their duties to their fellow-men, they do in very deed truly obey the Divine Commands; and that, consequently, in all their actions,—in every thing they morally compass and avoid, they do unremittingly serve and worship God, seeing that it is absolutely impossible to approach him by any closer or nearer worship; our actions affecting mundane Intelligents only, but never placing us in contact with the Deity. A potentate on earth often wishes to be HONOURED and EXTOLLED by professions of subjection, thinking, that without these, he cannot count upon so much obedience to his edicts as he deems necessary for the maintenance of his sway. Besides, mankind, even when most enlightened, take an immediate complacency in demonstrations of respect; and hence duty, so far forth as it is at the same time based on a Divine Behest, comes to be discharged as if it were a CONCERN rather of the Deity than of Humanity; by all which it happens, that the idea of divine worship is placed in room of the idea of a pure moral religion.

Since all religion consists in our regarding God as that awful lawgiver who enjoins upon us all our duties, the next point for consideration in arranging an institution of life, is, "How God WILLS to be feared and obeyed?" Again, the Divine Will commands either by MERELY STATUTABLE or by PURE MORAL laws. Touching the latter, every one may straightway know, from his own reason, what that will of God is which is the substratum of all religion. Indeed the idea of Godhead takes its rise from our consciousness of the Moral Law, coupled with the need felt by reason of assuming somewhere a higher power, able to procure to that law whatever whole and entire effect a created universe will admit of, and to make that effect conspire and harmonize with the moral scope of all things. And as a notion of the Divine Will, framed purely after the standard of the moral law, allows us to have but ONE God, so by necessary consequence can there be room only for ONE religion, and that, too, purely moral. Were it, however, even conceded that there are divine statutable enactments, and religion made to consist in their observance, still an acquaintance with them is attainable, not by any effort of reason, but singly by revelation; and such revelation, whether imparted to the mass publicly, or privately to single individuals for the purpose of being propagated by writing or tradition, would found a HISTORICAL but never a *pure* RATIONAL belief. And although statutable divine laws be admitted (which can be recognised as obligatory, not of themselves, but only by dint of a revelation of the divine will), still the pure MORAL legislation, whereby God's will is originally engraven on our heart, is not only the indefeasible condition precedent of all genuine religion whatsoever, but is just that wherein this last properly consists, and toward which the statutable can only work, as containing a mean of its propagation and advancement.

When therefore a response, valid for every man, REGARDED SIMPLY AS MAN, is to be given to the interrogatory, 11 How God wills to be obeyed and worshipped?" we cannot hesitate in replying, that the legislator's will must be purely MORAL, for the statutable legislation (rested on revelation) can only be looked upon as contingent, and as something that has not yet, and never can, be addressed to all, consequently, as what is not binding upon all mankind generally. Wherefore not they who cry "*Lord, Lord,*" but they "*who do the Will of God;*" *i. e.* not those who, by setting forth his praise conformably to revealed conceptions, which all mankind cannot have (or by lauding his Ambassador as a being of Divine Original), but those who, by good moral deportment (upon which point the divine will is known to all), seek to please him, are they who give that true worship which he exacts.

But when we regard ourselves bound to behave not only as men simply, but likewise as CITIZENS of a divine state on earth, and deem it our duty to promote the existence and wellbeing of that society which we called a church, then it should seem that naked reason can give no answer to the question, "How God may will to be worshipped IN A CHURCH (as a congregation of God)?" and that a statutable legislation, proclaimed by revelation, were indispensable. This again would lay the foundation of a historical belief in the facts revealed, and may, when contradistinguished from the pure religious or ethical belief, be called CHURCH-FAITH. The former is conversant singly with those individual acts which do in their aggregate make up the *matter* of the worship of God, where all our duties arc discharged by the spirit of a moral sentiment, as if they were divine commandments. A church, on the other hand, as a union of many, in an ethic commonweal, requires a PUBLIC obligement, *i. e.* a certain ecclesiastical *Form*, founded on conditions occurring in experience and observation. This form may be various, and being fortuitous, cannot be acknowledged to be obligatory, apart from some statutable divine behest; and yet the fixing of the Form ought not upon this account to be regarded as exclusively devolving upon our heavenly Lawgiver. On the contrary, grounds are not wanting for the assumption, that God's will rather is that we ourselves should carry out into execution reason's idea of such a commonwealth; and that how many forms soever of church polity may hitherto have been tried in vain, mankind are not to cease from pursuing this design by new attempts, avoiding to the uttermost the faults of their predecessors, the end and aim being imperative, and intrusted to their own endeavour. There is, therefore, no insuperable ground for holding the laws forming and instituting any church to have been enacted by divine authority. There is even presumption in declaring them to be so, to the end that we may supersede the toil of labouring steadily to better and improve its form, or perhaps a usurping of higher authority, in order, under the pretence of a divine commission, to impose on the multitude the yoke of ecclesiastical traditions. Nor would there, on the other hand, be less arrogance in peremptorily denying that the mode in which some given church has been framed, may not perhaps be a special arrangement of the Almighty, more particularly should this church, so far as we can see, completely harmonize with natural religion, and be farther distinguished by the characteristic of having appeared all at once, without any assignable march of intellect on the part of the public in theologic matters, that could have prepared the way, or account for its arrival.

Doubts thus obtaining whether God or mankind themselves should institute a church, the latter have betrayed a bias to fall into that RELIGION which consists mainly of a DIVINE WORSHIP (*cultus*); and as all worships rest on arbitrary rescripts, they are biassed to believe in divinely-enacted statutes, whence springs the supposition, that above and beyond the best course of life that man can follow agreeably to the dictates of pure moral religion, he must obey a divine law inscrutable by reason, and needing a particular revelation, the observance of which commandment is intended to be a service done for the immediate worship of the Deity (quite apart from the observance of those precepts promulgated by reason as his laws). Thus it happens, that men never will consider church-membership—associations for regulating its *Form*—or even PUBLIC institutions, as things in themselves necessary for forwarding the moral part of religion, but only as things required, in order that, by solemnities, confessions of revealed laws, and the observance of the formal ritual of the church (which last is itself only a mean toward a moral end), they may, as they say, serve their God. Although the whole of these observances are morally-indifferent acts, they are, just upon this very account, that they are done singly with a view to his worship, reputed to be the more acceptable in his sight. The endeavours of mankind to institute an ethical commonwealth have, therefore, naturally[40] gone hand in hand with a historic creed of some sort or other. The creed of the church will always be found anterior to the pure ethical belief. TEMPLES (fanes consecrated to the public worship of the Deity) arc earlier than CHURCHES (congregational assemblies for inculcating and enlivening the sentiments of morality); and PRIESTS (anointed administrators of sacred rites) arc prior to the CLERGY (teachers of pure moral religion); indeed to this day they are in many countries deemed their superior in rank, and usually held in greater estimation by the vulgar.

Since, then, it is now once for all the case, that a statutable church-creed is invariably superadded to the pure *a priori* ethical belief as a vehicle for promulgating this last, and a mean tending to combine mankind in a public association for moral ends; it is obvious enough that not TRADITION, but WRITING, must preserve the faith unchanged, and give it a uniform and general spread. A written revelation alone can inspire contemporaries and posterity with equal veneration, and without it mankind would be left in doubt as to the offices of worship owed to God. A sacred volume is regarded with the greatest awe, even by those (and in particular just by those) who never read it, or who, when they do, can extract from it no coherent notion. With them the edge of all argumentation against its religious tenets is at once dulled by the stunning dictatorial reply—THUS IT IS WRITTEN; and hence those passages which are understood to state an article of faith, go by the name of *proofs* or *warrants*. The established interpreters of such a Holy Writ receive from their office a kind of consecration; and history shows that no ecclesiastical faith, bottomed upon a Scripture, has ever perished, but has survived the most disastrous convulsions of the state; whereas church-creeds, only rested on tradition, and supported by ritual observances handed down by antiquity, have not outlived the decline and death of the community. How fortunate[41] that such a book has been thrown into our hands, containing, side by side with its statutes and belief, a most Complete and pure moral theory of religion, wherewith the other (considered as the vehicle of its introduction) can be shown to be in the fullest harmony—a happy conjunction of events, which, working together with the end aimed at by it, and the difficulty of explaining by natural causes, whence its enlightening efficacy to our race, has enabled it to maintain its credit and authority as if it were a revelation.

---

[40] Morally, this process should be reversed.

[41] An expression intended to apply to every thing that can be wished or hoped for, which we scarcely venture to anticipate, and cannot procure for ourselves, even by the most diligent forecasting of the future. When, therefore, we find that such unlooked-for benefits have really fallen to our lot, we can ascribe the gift to no other cause than the benignity of Providence.

* * *
* *

There are still a few things connected with this notion of a belief in revelation.

There is but ONE (true) RELIGION, although there may be various kinds of BELIEF. We may even add, that notwithstanding the multiplicity of ecclesiastical institutions, kept asunder by diversity of creed, one and the same true religion may be found pervading.

It is therefore more convenient to say *"this individual is of this or that* (Jewish, Mahometan, Christian, Catholic, Lutheran) FAITH," than to say, *"he is of this or that religion."* The term *religion* ought never to be employed in catechisms or addresses to the great bulk of the people. It is too learned and unintelligible. Indeed no modern language possesses a corresponding synonym. The boor invariably understands by religion his church-creed, which can be laid before him in a seen and embodied form; whereas religion lies hidden in the man within, based upon his moral sentiments. Most men were honoured too much by ascribing to them any religion. They neither know nor desire any, and the established church-creed is all that this word suggests to them. Religious wars, by which nations have often been distracted and bloodstained, have never been any thing else than brawls about creeds of form and show, and the persecuted ought properly to have complained, not that the oppressor hindered him from worshipping God according to the dictates of his own conscience (for that no outward force can do), but that he was prevented from publicly celebrating the rituals of his church-creed.

Whenever a Church, as is the general use and wont, claims to be the Only Church Universal (although grounded on the tenets of a particular revelation, which, being historical, cannot reasonably be expected from every one), then are they who refuse in any wise to acknowledge her particular form of creed straightway denounced as INFIDELS, and hated with the whole heart. He who partially swerves from it in unessentials, is held tainted with HETERODOXY, and shunned as contagious. Lastly, should any one, though a member of the church, stumble at any of the essentials of its established faith, then lie is called—especially if he labour to spread abroad his error—A HERETIC,[42] and is, like a traitor, considered far more culpable than any foreign foe;

---

[42] Mongols call THIBET (*according to Gregorii, Alphab. Tibet*, pag. 11) TANGUT-CHADZAR, *i. e.* the land of dwelling-houses, thereby distinguishing its inhabitants from themselves, as the tent-inhabiting Nomades of the wilderness. Hence the THIBETESE are called CHADZARS, which was subsequently corrupted, as in German, into KETZER; and because the Mongols were addicted to the Thibetese faith (in the Great Llama), which seems to approach very near to Manichaeism (possibly Manichæism thence took its origin), and brought it with them when they burst into Europe, it came to pass that, during a long period, the terms *Hæretici* and *Manichæi* were exchangeable.

and as the Roman senate interdicted from fire and water those who, without permission, passed the Rubicon, so, by ecclesiastical censures, the Church puts all heretics, as outlaws from its pale, under the bann; and with cursing and excommunication devotes them to the infernal gods. The assumed infallible accuracy of the teachers or heads of the Church in points of faith, is called ORTHODOXY; and this again may be divided into a *despotic* or *brutal* and a *liberal* orthodoxy. Were that church which proclaims its formula of faith as universally binding styled CATHOLIC, and those churches again which oppose themselves to this universal claim—(although they would willingly advance it for themselves if they durst)—styled PROTESTANT, then may a curious observer detect many instances highly laudable of *Protestant Catholics*, and several most offensive of *Arch-Catholic Protestants*. The former are men of an open and enlarged mind (for which no thanks to their church), and make a singular contrast with the narrow and contracted views of the latter, who certainly gain nothing by the comparison.

SECTION VI.

THE PURE ETHICAL BELIEF IS THE SUPREME EXPOUNDER OF ALL ECCLESIASTICAL CREEDS WHATSOEVER.

Our readers are already aware, that although a church wants one most important mark of its being the true Church, viz. a valid claim to universality, when founded on revealed tenets, inasmuch as their historical groundwork—though clothed in writing—spread far and wide —and thus guaranteed to the latest posterity—never can become the object of a joint and universally-exceptionless conviction; still, such is the inbred infirmity of mankind, as always to require for the last abstractions—the grounds and ideas of naked reason—some tangible cover and confirmation from the testimony of observation and experience (a consideration to which, in *introducing* any doctrine, intended to be of catholic reception, an eye is always to be bad); and hence some one ecclesiastico-historical creed, from among those already extant, must be made available for that purpose.

Successfully to combine with this *a posteriori* belief, which, it would seem, chance had thrown into our hands, a stable moral faith, will depend mainly on the exegetical mode in which the revealed text is expounded and unfolded; which must receive a perpetual interpretation parallel to the known practical behests of the religion of pure reason. The theoretical and speculative parts of any church creed are for us devoid of moral interest, unless they assist us, and arc found conducive to the discharge of all our duties *qua* divinely commanded (regard had to the imperatives of morality, *as if they were* divine commandments, being in fact the very essence of all religion). An interpretation of this sort may, no doubt, not only frequently seem, but often really be strained; and yet the text must be thus forced into a moral dress, in preference to the verbal and literal meaning, whenever this last savours nothing of morality, or perhaps tends even to snap our moral springs.[43]

Upon reflection, it will be found that this has been done, both in ancient and modern times, with every variety of Sacred Scriptures; and that prudent, honest-minded teachers had continued so long to gloss and refine upon the text, that they at length brought it very nearly to square with the general precepts of morality. The sages of Greece and Rome acted thus with their fabulous histories of the gods; and the coarsest polytheism was gradually sublimated into a symbolical representation of the One Divine Essence. The vicious pranks of the gods, as well as the wild but beautiful fancies of the poets, were first shrouded, and then presented to view under a mysterious apparel, that made the popular belief approach the semblance of a sensible and edifying morality. Modern JUDAISM, nay, CHRISTIANITY itself, consists in great measure of such strained senses, although in either case, the contortions of the meaning, have unquestionably led to good and needful ends. Mahometanism itself has been thus dealt with; and the paradise of the faithful, described as abounding with all sensual voluptuousness, is spiritualized as skilfully as the Song of Solomon. In India the same maxims are currently applied in interpreting the Veda, at least when read to the better-educated classes. That this expedient is practicable with so many different creeds, without always disturbing the literal terms of the narrative, arises hence: Long prior to any popular myths, there lay extant in the human mind its primeval substratum for religion, the first rough development of which

---

[43] Take as an instance the fifty-ninth Psalm, ver. 11-16, where a prayer for revenge is pushed to a dreadful length. Michaelis (Morals, part ii. p. 202) approves of this prayer, and adds, The Psalms are INSPIRED; and when we find in them petitions for vengeance, it cannot be improper to call down punishment on the guilty, for WE CANNOT HAVE A HOLIER MORAL SYSTEM THAN THAT IN THE BIBLE. Let us confine our attention to those concluding words, and then ask, is morality to be expounded after the Bible? or ought not rather the Bible to be tested by the standard of morality? I will not here pause to inquire how this Psalm, and another passage deemed equally inspired, are to be reconciled,—"*Ye have heard that it hath been said by them of old time,*" &c; "*but I say unto you, love your enemies; bless them that curse you,*" &c.; but will just at once try how the Psalm can be adapted and accommodated to my existing moral principles (*e. g.* thus it may be assumed, that not personal enemies, but that under such a figure our wicked passions, those invisible and far more ruinous enemies, are attacked and held up to execration). Should this prove impracticable, then I will suppose it has only a political, not a moral sense, and refers to that relation in which the Jews believed themselves to stand with God as their temporal regent. The meaning will then be somewhat not unlike the spirit of that other passage, "*Vengeance is mine, I will repay, saith the Lord,*" commonly understood to warn us against revenging ourselves, although most probably it points to the law obtaining in every country, that satisfaction for injuries is to be sought in the Sovereign's Tribunals, where the Courts do not justify the revengeful malice of the prosecutor, but allow him to conclude for whatever damages and penalty he pleases, and can.

uncultivated susceptibility did, during the early twilight of dawning knowledge, tend merely to superstitious or hero-worships, and occasioned for their behoof just those various mythic revelations; and thus to those textures woven by the plastic energies of depictive fancy, there always has adhered some unconscious trait, sufficiently indicative of the character of their supersensible original. Neither can such exposition be charged with insincerity, provided we do not insist that the sense given by us to the national legends, or to the holy books, was that intended by the authors; but, reserving such question for a future inquiry, insist only that it is POSSIBLE so to construe the intendment of the writer. Even the reading of the Scriptures, and investigations into their import, have no other view than that of rendering us better men. Their historical part not having this effect, is sheerly indifferent, and may be dealt with as we list: (the Historical Belief "*is dead, being alone;*" *i. e.* the profession of it by itself contains nothing,—and leads to no results—but those, in which we are morally unconcerned.)

Admitting that a particular document contains a Divine Revelation, the preliminary ground of this credence must be, that the doctrines taught are worthy of God; and thereof the surest test and criterion is, that "*all Scripture given by inspiration of God must be profitable for doctrine, for reproof, for correction, and instruction in righteousness,*" &c. &c.; and since this last—the moral amendment of our species—is the proper aim of the religion of reason, it results that Natural Religion must supply the Supreme Canon of all Scriptural Exegesis. This religion it is that is "*the Spirit of God guiding us into all truth,*" and that does, by instructing and redressing the depravities of ignorance, quicken us with principles of conduct. Moreover, it refers all the historic contents of the Scripture to the standard and springs of the pure Moral Law of Righteousness, this being that alone in any ecclesiastical confession which is the sum and substance of religion proper. No searching or expounding of the Scriptures can at any time proceed on any other principle, "*and we can only find in them eternal life so far forth as they bear witness to this truth.*"

Joint-interpreter of the written rule is added as subordinate adjunct, BIBLICAL LEARNING. THE AUTHORITY OF HOLY WRIT, the worthiest, and, in this enlightened quarter of the globe, the only instrument fitted to conjoin mankind in church communion, constitutes what we have called FAITH ECCLESIASTICAL. This popular belief cannot be neglected, for the populace are rootedly fixed in the opinion that no tenets based alone on reason are suited to supply them with an infallible rule, and hence clamour for a revelation from God, and insist on having the church formulary of faith historically verified by an inquiry into its origin. Again, since man's wisdom and skill cannot waft him into Heaven, in order to bring thence the credentials authenticating the mission of the first Teacher, he must rest contented with those tests,—

apart from the inward evidence of the matter revealed,—derived from the circumstances under which the new faith appeared. Here he must acquiesce in the narrative of contemporaries; the writers of antiquity must be ransacked, and the dead languages diligently searched, before any estimate can be struck of the credibility of those ancient Annalists. Thus LEARNING and BIBLICAL CRITICISM are indispensable to support A CHURCH rising on a Holy Writ, although superfluous toward either establishing or enforcing the principles of common morality and natural religion. They do, however, effectually prop up the fabric of Church Authority, so long as its first advent is not seen to be attended by some palpable absurdities or deformities, that at once discredit its pretence to be an immediate institution from the Deity; and this should be enough to remove all obstacles out of the way of those who think they experience from this idea a positive confirmation of their moral faith, and do upon that account the more readily embrace it. But learning is needed not only for showing the genuineness and authenticity of the Sacred Writings, but also for their interpretation. How can the unlearned, who reads his Bible only in translations, be certified of the accuracy of the version? Even the biblical expositor who is versant in the ancient tongues must provide himself with very extended historical information; and much critical knowledge is required, to enable him to extract from the state, manners, and opinions of the olden world, such a digested view as may open and unfold to his congregation the spirit and genius of the text.

Natural religion and biblical learning are therefore the only authorized interpreters and guardians of a holy record. Evidently the Divine must not be disturbed by the arm of the magistrate from publicly propounding whatever insight or discoveries he may have reaped in this field, neither is he to be tied to the narrow limits of certain articles of belief; for were the state so to usurp, then would the Laic constrain the Church-man to follow in his wake, and to abide singly by those opinions for which, after all, the laity were first indebted to the learning and instruction of the clergy. If the state is cautious to provide men learned in theology, whose fraudulent and corrupt manners will not discountenance all they would recommend, and to whose conscientious labours it can safely intrust the entire administration of the ecclesiastical commonwealth, then has the sovereign done all which the ends and jurisdiction of Civil Society entitle him to do. But to intrude himself into the schools of divinity, and to force to church-conformity, by taking a share in theological polemic, is a usurpation beneath the dignity of the head of the state, which nothing save the indiscreetness of a mob could ever have demanded; for those literary controversies, when not waged from the pulpit, always leave the church-going public in the security of profound repose.

Pretences, however, are sometimes made to the office of interpreter, where both Reason and Learning are dispensed with, and *an internal feeling* is set up as light sufficient whereby at once to discern the true meaning of the Scripture, and also to perceive its divine original. Questionless it must be conceded, that "whoever obeys its precepts, and does what it prescribes, will by all means find that the doctrine is of God." The very incentive to good actions and upright conduct felt from its perusal, must convince him on whom the Scripture takes such an effect, that its contents are indeed divine; for this feeling is nothing else than the effect of the moral law, which, by transfixing the soul with inliest reverence, is on that very account deservedly esteemed a divine behest. But, little as any feeling can serve for a foundation for any law, or serve as a criterion of that law's morality,— still less can any feeling serve for a certain index, enabling us to conclude upon any immediate illapses of divine influence: for to bring about any change felt in the inner man, obviously more than one single cause may possibly conspire; and, in such a case as that now under consideration, the very morality of the doctrine tallying with the Moral Law of Reason is of itself a sufficient ground to account for such effect; nay, what is more, whenever any experienced moral incentive can by possibility be traced to such an original, it is our imperative duty to deduce our moral feelings from that their legitimate source, unless, indeed, it be contended that we should unlock and throw wide the portals of Unreason to every species of fanaticism, and even hazard bereaving the emotion reverence itself of its *a priori* dignity, by bringing it into ambiguous juxtaposition with every phantastic fit or start of the sensory. Feelings belong to each particular individual for himself alone; even when the law BY WHICH, or according to which, they are originated, has been previously investigated and ascertained; and hence no feeling, be it of what sort soever it may, can be recommended or trusted as a touchstone of revealed truth: feelings convey no information of things beyond and without us; they exhibit to us no more than the manner,—whether agreeable or disagreeable,—in which our own passive subject is affected; and upon our mental states of liking or dislike no knowledge of any object can be based.

HOLY WRIT is therefore the only rule of ecclesiastical belief; nor can it have any expounder save the RELIGION of pure REASON working together with SCRIPTURARY LEARNING (which last concerns itself with the faith's historic part). Of those two interpreters, the former is alone AUTHENTIC and valid universally for the whole world, while the latter is DOCTRINAL only, shaping from time to time, and framing, the church-creed of a particular nation into a permanently fixed and self-conserving system. Touching the last, it seems to be inevitable, that, in the long run, the historical faith should not slide into an empty belief that trusts to the better insight of those learned in the Scripture,—a state of things certainly not over-creditable to human nature, but which may be amply counterbalanced and redressed wherever public freedom of thought obtains. In fact, this unshackled intercourse of thought is a just compensation, that the citizen is rightfully entitled to challenge from the state and church; seeing that it is only where the learned submit their speculations to general examination, remaining, however, themselves all the while open and awake to the increasing illumination of farther lights, that they can count upon the continued confidence of their countrymen, or expect that members of the literary republic will give heed to their decisions.

SECTION VII.

THE OBSERVED TRANSIT OF THE CHURCH-CREED, WHEREBY IT IS SEEN GRADUALLY TO MERGE AND TO BECOME EVENTUALLY SUNK AND LOST IN THE SUPREMACY AND SOVEREIGNTY OF THE PURE *A PRIORI* ETHICAL BELIEF, IS A CERTAIN INDEX THAT THE KINGDOM OF GOD IS AT HAND.

The sign of the true church is its UNIVERSALITY; and of this last, again, the criterion is necessity and determinability in one only mode. A historical belief, on the other hand,—being founded on revelation, *i. e.* on observation and experience,—is particularly valid only, viz. for those to whom the history has come. It is, moreover, like every other *a posteriori* knowledge, unaccompanied by the consciousness that the object, be it of knowledge or faith, MUST of necessity be *thus* constituted, and is impossible ever to be figured in any other manner: it tells us no more than that *so* the case stands: the belief, accordingly, is entertained by the mind with the consciousness of its contingency. ANNALS of past events may therefore suffice for supporting an ecclesiastical creed (whereof there may be several); but pure moral religion alone it is that,—being founded throughout on the *a priori* notices of reason,—can be recognised as necessary, and the single and alone belief characterizing the TRUE church. Nevertheless, a church may assume this name, although (owing to the inevitable limits put to human reason) a historical belief may attend religion as its concomitant and introductory vehicle, provided always that this its latter character never be lost sight of, and that the church-creed contain within, the germ of a principle, whereby it is urged to a continual and more close approximation toward pure ethic and religion, until at length these last being attained, the other be superseded and dispensed with. Again, since, touching historical dogmata of faith, disputes never can be avoided, an ecclesiastical establishment, resting on an *a posteriori* creed, may be called the church MILITANT, hoping, however, when one day become immutable and all-embracing, to wear the insignia of the church TRIUMPHANT. That faith which imparts to him who holds it a moral susceptibility for eternal bliss is called SAVING; and this saving faith can be but one and practical. How manifold soever may be the frames and diversities of church-belief, this practical and saving faith must pervade the whole of them, and constitute the kernel of pure religion, gradually forth-forming itself, and bursting from the vehiculary husk. That religious belief which leads to a statutable worship of the Deity, is a MERCENARY and servile FAITH; nor can it at any time be regarded as SAVING, inasmuch as it is not MORAL. This last is free and ingenuous, springing from the clarified sentiments of the heart. The bondsman expects, by mechanical services of worship—which, though irksome, are destitute of moral worth, and, extorted by fear or hope, may be equally rendered by the greatest scoundrel—to make himself acceptable to God: while that faith which is of ingenuous birth, goes hand in hand with morally good sentiments, as indispensably requisite to our becoming acceptable in his sight.

That saving faith which leads to the hope of future bliss consists of two parts:—the one respects that which we cannot do ourselves, viz. the forensical rescinding of past misdeeds before the eye of our Divine Judge,—the other touches what we ought and must do ourselves, viz. a walk and conversation in a new life, conformably to what is duty. The former part of faith is belief in vicarious satisfaction (acquittal of debt,—redemption,—atonement with God); the latter is the belief in the possibility of our rendering ourselves acceptable to God, by henceforward leading an honest and upright life. These two constituent conditions compose no more than one belief, and belong by inseparable necessity to one another. Now a necessary conjunction is in no other way to be comprehended, than by assuming that the one link can be developed from its counterpart: *i. e.* we must assume either that the belief in absolution from the load of self-entailed guilt will beget good moral conduct; or that the genuine and practically moral course of life will, agreeably to some law of morally-efficient causes, beget and ground a belief in plenary absolution.

Here there emerges a very extraordinary antinomy and debate of human reason with itself; and the solution of this antinomy, or, should this last prove impossible, disposal of the contested question, can alone enable us to determine, whether a historical belief (church-creed) must, as an essential part of saving faith, at all times be superadded to the pure religion of reason; or otherwise, whether the ecclesiastical faith is not, as a mere vehicle, destined ultimately to pass—distant, indeed, though the day be— into a pure *a priori* belief in religious matters.

I. On the hypothesis, that satisfaction has been rendered for the sins of mankind, then can there be no difficulty whatever in conceiving that every sinner would gladly have the benefit of the same; and if this is to be had simply BY BELIEVING (which is tantamount to a mental declaration that the sinner is willing that such redemption shall have taken place for him), no one would hesitate a moment about thus appropriating it. But what I cannot comprehend is, how any man of common sense, who is inwardly aware of being obnoxious to punishment, can, in sound and sober earnest, seriously bring himself to believe that he needs only to credit the message that his debt of sins has been discharged for him, and then (as a lawyer would speak) *utiliter* to accept this satisfaction, in order to regard his guilt as taken away; and that, too, so *radicitus* and *funditus*, that the inevitable effect of this persuasion and acceptation of the offered benefit should be a steady course of good works in all time coming, although hitherto—aye! even up to the immediately preceding moment—he had been utterly regardless of morality. No sensible man can bubble himself successfully into this belief, although self-love often transmutes a wish into hope, and deludes us touching those goods toward whose attainment we contribute, and can contribute nothing; just as if the desired object would come of itself by merely yearning after it. Such a persuasion can only be regarded as possible when a man holds that this very belief itself is something instilled into him from above, and consequently as something whereof no further account need be rendered to his reason. Supposing that he find this impracticable, or that he is still too upright to experiment upon himself, so as to bring about an artificial and counterfeit confidence, as a mean of ingratiating himself into some other person's favour, then he must, notwithstanding the highest awe felt for this transcendent satisfaction, and the keenest wish to participate in its benefits, hold that they are *conditioned*, and that his strenuously amended life must antecede, before he dare entertain the smallest hope that any such higher merit may stand him in stead. Wherefore, since the historical knowledge of the atonement is part of faith ecclesiastical, the redintegration of character, on the contrary, is a branch of pure morality, it follows that this last must, as condition, take precedence of the other, and that repentance must go before forgiveness.

II. *E contra*, mankind being by nature corrupt and depraved, how can he fancy that—let him bestir himself ever so much—he can transform himself into a new man, acceptable to God? Aware of his past transgressions; still under the thrall and sway of the evil principle, and devoid of strength to extricate himself from his grasp; must he not first of all regard the Divine Justice, which he has aroused and set against him, as appeased by vicarious satisfaction? and then by means of this faith consider himself as born anew, and ready to start upon an altered and amended course of life? which life would then result from his reconciliation and union with the good principle. Unless this be conceded, there is absolutely nothing whereupon to found his hope of ever becoming acceptable to God. Consequently his belief in a righteousness not his own, whereby he is reconciled with God, must go first, as a condition precedent of all exertion toward good works; and forgiveness it is that must go before, and bring forth repentance—which, however, is diametrically contrary to the former statement.

This contest cannot be adjusted by dint of any insight into the first causal determinations of the Freedom of the Human Will, *i. e.* by any insight into the causes whence it comes to pass that a given individual is either good or evil; for when question is made as to the last grounds of free optional determination, then we transcend the whole speculative extent of reason. But, practically, where we do not investigate the physical constitution of the will's nature, but consider morally what is first to be done in regulating our free use of choice, viz. whether we are to begin with believing what God has done on our behalf, or should set forthwith about doing what we have to do in order to make ourselves worthy of it (whereinsoever this gift of the Divine Benignity may consist), then, questionless, the latter alternative must be adopted.

To assume the first pre-requisite of our salvation, viz. a belief in vicarious satisfaction, is necessary *notionally* only, *i. e.* for a theoretical behoof, we cannot otherwise depicture to ourselves expurgation; the latter element, however, is practically necessary, and purely moral. 'Tis certain we can never hope to become partakers in the benefit of a foreign satisfactory merit, and so of eternal salvation, unless we qualify ourselves for such a blessing by unremittingly endeavouring to discharge all the offices of humanity; the performance of which duties must spring from our own effort, and not from any foreign influence whereby we arc entirely passive. Again, because the ethical behest is unconditional, it follows of necessity that mankind must lay down, as a ground-work from which all faith must rise, this maxim, viz. that reformation of life is the supreme condition, apart from which there can be no room for any saving faith.

Ethic starts with *a principle of acting;* revelation begins with *a principle of believing.* Faith ecclesiastical, considered as historical, rightly begins with the latter principle; but then, since it contains only the vehicle toward a pure moral religion, it results that what in ethic, as a practical system, is a first condition of incipiency, viz. *the principle of acting,* must also constitute the real and true commencement in the actual working of the other; while *the principle of knowing, i. e.* of theoretical belief, can tend only toward the confirmation and consummation of the other.

We add this farther remark, that, agreeably to the one principle, belief in vicarious satisfaction is represented to mankind as HIS DUTY, while the belief in his ability to do good works is because the strength is lent him from above, reckoned to be OF GRACE. The converse holds true of the other principle. Good moral conduct is here A DUTY absolutely imperative, and a condition indispensable for all aspiring after the favour of God; while the celestial atonement is derived purely from the Divine Benignity, or GRACE. The adherents of the former method are not unfrequently upbraided, and rightly too, with giving way to a superstitious worshipping of the Deity, that is occasionally seen to combine together a blame-worthy ami religious life. Those who profess themselves favourable to the other arc reproached with leaning to an infidel naturalism, in as much as, though their life is exemplary and unexceptionable, they set themselves in an attitude of indifference or antagonism to the claims of revelation. These epithets rather practically cut than theoretically untie the Gordian knot,—a step that, in religious questions, is sometimes the only one that can be taken. Nevertheless, the following remarks may serve as some slender contribution toward resolving the difficulty of this antithetic.[44]

A living belief in the Son of God, considered as the prototypon of that in humanity which alone is well-pleasing to God, does in itself refer directly to an ethical idea, which is at once the standard and spring of conduct; consequently it is immaterial, in fact the same, whether I begin with this RATIONAL belief in the Son, or with the behests of moral life; contrariwise, a belief in this self-same archetype in his phenomenon—as God-man—is *a posteriori* and historical, and not by any means identic with the principle of a moral life, which last is purely rational; and it would be quite a different affair to commence with a belief in Such historic advent, and thence deduce an amended course of conduct. Thus far forth, then, would there be a repugnancy betwixt those two doctrines; and yet in the phenomenon of the God-man, not that of him which falls under sense, but that in him which corresponds to the ethical archetype latent in our own reason, is, properly speaking, THE OBJECT of saving and justifying faith; and such a faith is quite identic with reason's principles of a walk and conversation acceptable to God. Here, then, there are not two antagonist principles, nor do we start in contrary directions, by setting out from one or other of them. In either case we deal with but one and the selfsame practical idea, regarding it, however, first as an ideal archetype extant in the bosom of God, and emanating from the essential character of his person; while, in the other case, the ideal dwells with our own reason,—a difference of

---

[44] TRANSLATOR'S NOTE—Kant might have said something more. The reader will find, in my Appendix to the version of the Ethics, an attempted analysis of the particular frame or states of mind which the Christian faith is fitted to awaken. With an addition I now make, viz. that the renunciation of one's own righteousness, and substitution of vicarious righteousness in its stead, will produce the first state of will there mentioned, or at least one very similar, and scarcely to be distinguished from it,—the reader will, I apprehend, find the obscurities of this question vanish. It is almost superfluous to subjoin, that the total abnegation of all claim to any personal moral worth is quite inconsistent with, and indeed subversive of, Kant's Ethical Theory. *Conf. Critik d. Urtheilskraft*, p. 123, with Beck's Commentary thereon, and Morals, § 11. It is remarkable that Kant has omitted to re-assert this in the text above, where it would have been much more in place than in the *C. d. Urtheilskraft*.

aspect that becomes altogether evanescent, so far forth as in both cases the ideal standard is deemed and represented to be our regulating rule of life. The seeming antinomy thus disappears—the very same practical idea, when levelled at under two different lights, having been mistaken for two diverse and conflicting principles. Should it, however, be contended, that historically to believe in the actual advent and appearance of this THEANTHROPIC PERSON, is a condition precedent of and indispensable to that faith which alone can justify and save; then, indeed, most indisputably would there be two quite contrary principles—the one *a posteriori*, the other *a priori*,—and a true conflict of maxims would arise, viz. whether we were to commence with the experimental or the rational; and this would farther be an oppugnancy which no human reason would ever be able to settle or adjust. The position, it is incumbent upon mankind to believe, that once upon a time there was an individual, who, by his holiness and meritorious life, satisfied, not only for himself, but also for all others, how great soever might be the shortcomings and gaps in the morality of their deportment, before we can hope that we can, through a course of dutiful obedience (which last, moreover, can only emanate from that faith as its source), ultimately reach to the attainment of heavenly beatitude—is a position most contrary to this other—mankind must strive, with all the might of a holy sentiment, to lead a life acceptable to God, in order to expect that his benignant eare (to which our own reason bears immediate witness) will consummate somehow or other the imperfections inevitably attaching to the deeds of the otherwise honest-minded. To entertain the first belief is not within every one's power, e. g. the ignorant and unlettered can know nothing of it; for, as to the existence of this person, reason is altogether silent. History likewise shows that all forms of religion have afforded room for this antagonism of a twofold set of principles of faith. They all delivered a doctrine of expiations of some sort or other; while mankind's original substratum for morality failed not ever and anon to make its imprescriptible *a priori* claim heard in the midst. But the vociferations of the priesthood always drowned the plaint of the moralist; the former advanced with loud outcry to the government to prevent the decline and fall of the ceremonial worship, which had been instituted either to conciliate the gods of the populace, or to avert mischances from the state; the latter bemoaned the overthrow of public morals, ascribing their decay to those very means of expurgation whereby the priests enabled any one, with the utmost case, to regard himself as clarified from the greatest vices, and the Deity as atoned. And, forsooth, if an exhaustless fund is provided for discharging all incurred and hitherto to be contracted debts, upon which we need only draw inimitably to regard ourselves as free and fully acquitted, postponing meanwhile all firm resolutions of amendment till we become assured that we are thus cleansed from every stain of guilt; then is it indeed much to be feared that no better results can naturally or morally flow from such a creed. Again, were it held that this belief did in itself contain such an especial efficacy, or mystic or magic force, as, although merely historical so far as we can see, to be able thoroughly to transform the whole inner into a new man, provided only mankind yield himself up to it, and to the feelings it is calculated to produce; then must such renewing faith be looked upon as a gift immediately sent down from heaven, along with and under cover of the historical belief—a supposition according to which the ethic properties and destiny of mankind must be, in their last resort, resolved into an unconditioned decree of the Almighty, *"who hath mercy on whom he will, and whom he will he hardeneth,"*[45]—a statement which, taken to the letter, is the *salto mortale* of all human understanding.

It is, consequently, a necessary result of our physical and moral nature, which last is at once the support and the interpreter of all religion, that religion become eventually defecated from tentative and experimental springs, and gradually disengage itself from all statutes authenticated by history, which served for a while, through the intervention of faith ecclesiastical, *provisionally* to combine mankind in an ethic association, until, the pure religion of reason reigning, *"God may be all in all."* The swaddling bands beneath which the embryo shot up to manhood must be laid aside when the season of maturity is come. The leading-strings of sacred traditions, together with all appendages, the statutes and observances, which in their time may have been of service, grow by degrees superfluous or even encumbrances to vigorous youth. As long *as mankind* (the human race) *was a child, he understood as a child and thought as a child*, and spake the doctrines which traditionary legends had unawares put into his mouth; *but now, when he is become a man, he puts away childish things.* The humiliating distinction betwixt Laic and Clergy comes to an end, and from true freedom, equality without anarchy arises, every one obeying THE LAW now no longer statutable, but prescribed by him to himself, — which, just upon that very account, he regards as the will of the Creator

---

[45] Possibly this might be expounded as follows: None can certainly undertake to say whence it comes about that one is good and another bad (I speak of course comparatively), since a disposition to one or other of those characters can be traced even in new-born infants; sometimes also strange contingencies of life, which nobody can foresee, are cast into one's lot, and kick the wavering beam. Nor can we foretell how any one may turn out: a judgment, therefore, on this dark and impervious matter must be handed over to the Omniscient; and this judgment, considered as passed before any individual's birth, is looked upon as a decree appointing to every one the part his destiny will one day call him to act. The Creator's FORE-KNOWING of the Order of Sensible Phenomena, Is when we figure him to ourselves *anthropopathically*, likewise a FORE-ORDAINING. But in a Supersensible Order of Things, where time is awanting, and Laws of Freedom govern, it is no more than an ALL-SEEING KNOWLEDGE, not serving to explain to us why one man acts thus and his neighbour the reverse; nor how such explanation, if got, could be brought into harmony with the will's freedom.

revealed to him by reason, conjoining all under an invisible and common government in a *Civitas Dei*, scantily represented previously by the church visible. This transition is not to be accomplished by any I outward revolution, that by storm and impetuous violence sweeps its hasty and rash course of innovation, where, after all, flaws in the new constitution must be retained for centuries, inasmuch as they cannot again be altered, at least not without—what is always to be dreaded—a fresh revolutionary convulsion. The ground leading toward such a transition must be found in the principles of the pure religion of reason—a divine revelation, that has at all times been promulgated (though not historically) to our race. An intention to make this transit, once adopted upon mature deliberation, can be carried through the steady progression of gradual reform, into execution, so far forth as the amending of the church is a work of man: revolutions intended to hasten the tardy steps of reform, depend alone on Providence, neither can they be introduced upon any uniform settled plan, nor can the public freedom escape unhurt.

It may, however, be rightly asserted *that the Kingdom of God has come*, whenever the transition-principle above explained has taken PUBLIC root in any country, and an observed approximation can be descried of church-faith to a rational and universal religion, although its actual arrival may be still deemed incomputably distant. The aforesaid principle affords the ground tending to this perfection, and does therefore, like a self-evolving and ever-on ward forth-fecundifying seed, comprehend all that is one day to illuminate and govern the world. The Fair and Good naturally sprouting from the soil of human nature, engage alike the affections and the understanding, and never fail to gain a general spread, when once they have free course publicly to run. Impediments arising from civil and political causes, that seem from time to time to stop and hinder their success, do in truth rather serve to draw more closely—and even lend an added super-exaltation to—the hearts of those united in good: which good, once seen in an intellectual apprehension, can never afterwards fall altogether from the memory.[46]

---

[46] The Church Creed may, without being either renounced or impugned, be still made serviceable as a vehicle, while the imagination of its belief's being a duty required for the due worship of God, is prevented from affecting our conception of the pure and true moral religion proper. Thus a harmony of opinion may be caused to prevail amid the adherents of the most diverse statutable confessions,—a union of view that all teachers and interpreters of ecclesiastic dogmas ought to labour to bring about, until at length, by general consent (a uniformity resulting from our moral freedom, and brought about by the gradual march and enlightenment of the understanding), the forms and restraints of a degrading extorted faith are exchanged for an ecclesiastical polity suited to the dignity of a moral religion. To combine the unity of church-confessions with perfect religious liberty, is a problem, to solve which we are urged alike by an ethical interest, and by the idea objected to the mind by reason of the necessary and exclusive *oneness* of *a priori*

* * *
* *

Such is the imperceptible but continual struggle made by the good principle to erect for itself, among the human race, an empire and dominion according to moral laws, destined to subdue the opposing evil, and under its victorious sway to give to the world perpetual peace.

APOTOME II.

HISTORICAL ACCOUNT OF THE GRADUAL FOUNDING OF A KINGDOM OF THE GOOD PRINCIPLE ON EARTH.

Of religion, no Universal History can be written: for when this word is understood in its strictest sense, and not used to signify the different *religions* that may have been prevalent on our globe, then it is obvious that such religion can have no public outward states; for, being founded on pure ethical science, and the *a priori* faith in religion, wherein ethic issues, each individual can be conscious to himself alone, of the progression he may have made in it. Ecclesiastical faith, therefore, it is only that admits of being historically pourtrayed, when the various mutations of its form are contrasted and compared with the sole, pure, and unchanging, ethical belief. At that point of time, when the former is made dependant on the restrictive conditions of the latter, and the necessity of its consent therewith becomes publicly recognized, then does the CHURCH UNIVERSAL begin to frame itself into an ethical *civitas Dei*, and to advance toward perfection, under the guidance of one sure and universally valid principle. It may be conjectured beforehand, that this History can contain nothing but a narrative of the perpetual conflicts betwixt a god or hero-worshipping faith, and that

---

religion, although that this last should ever obtain in any visible church, seems more than human nature will allow us to hope for. This idea, like all other representations of the absolute and unconditioned, is one to which nothing adequate can be found as a phenomenon, and which yet, as a practically regulatory principle, has all objective reality, and must ever prompt us to aim at this grand end,—concord and uniformity in religious belief. The lawyer stands in a somewhat similar position with his political idea of *Law International*, so far forth as this last ought to be acknowledged, upheld, and enforced as a universally coercive *Law Cosmopolitical*. Of this, experience and observation cut short our hopes. A bias appears entwined about our race (perhaps intentionally) inducing each individual state, where it can, to subjugate all adjoining, and erect a Universal Monarchy on their ruins; but this, after attaining a certain size, splinters itself down into lesser states. In like manner, each church advances a lofty claim to universality, but whenever it acquires a considerably extended sway, principles of internal dissolution are observed to distract it, after which it speedily falls asunder into various sects.

The premature and therefore hurtful blending of different races (morality not having yet prepared the way for profitable intercourse),—if I may be permitted to hazard a conjecture, and assume in this point a design of Providence,—is chiefly prevented by these two mighty agents, oppugnancy of religions, and diversity of tongues.

faith which is morally-religious. To the historical belief mankind is ever prone to give preference unduly, although the other—being alone competent to better our inner man—never has renounced its title to precedence, which also it will certainly one day thoroughly vindicate and establish.

A coherent view of church-history can only be given by limiting its extent to that quarter of the globe where the church universal is about to develope this its latent principle of uniformity, so far forth as the question touching the boundary of rational and ecclesiastical belief has been openly propounded, and its final enodation represented as a matter of the utmost importance. The story of diverse peoples, whose faiths are totally unconnected, can promise nothing for this behoof. Neither can the history of two churches be unitively comprised under one and the same head, merely because among the self-same race a new belief may have arisen, widely differing from the faith' previously dominant, even although this last should have afforded OCCASION and opportunity for the first beginning of the other. For if the sequence of different forms of belief is to be regarded as a modification of one identic church, this decursion must flow from one sole principle: where this is not the case, the changes of church-worship do not fall within the scope of the present research.

Consistently, then, with our declared object, we can treat only of that ecclesiastical polity which did, even from the very first, tend toward that objective unity of true religion universal to which it has ever since been constantly approaching. This being the case, it is abundantly obvious that JUDAISM is quite detached from that faith ecclesiastical, on whose history we are now to enter. There obtains betwixt them no essential or inner principle of connection, *i. e.* no incomplex unity of idea, although the one was immediately antecedent, and supplied a physical groundwork whence the church Christian ultimately rose.

JUDAICAL BELIEF, in its pristine form, is nothing farther than an aggregate of statutable laws, whereon rested the political constitution. Any moral *additamenta* that may either then or subsequently have been interjected, are most absolutely foreign to *Judaism* as such. Judaism strictly is no religion at all; it is only an association of a number of individuals, who, as they happened to belong to a particular family, formed themselves into a commonweal political, consequently not into a church. Far from that, the community was INTENDED to be temporal, insomuch that, whenever torn by adverse circumstances, there still remained the political belief,—which was of the very essence of the constitution,—of one day restoring it by the Messiah. Its being a theocracy (a visible aristocracy of priests or leaders, who boasted of receiving their instructions immediately from God),—where the name of God was revered as secular head, but quite apart from any inward conscientious veneration,—never can convert it into a religious constitution.

This is easily shown.

FIRST.—All the commandments are such as admit of being politically efforced as laws co-active; for they respect outward actions only. And though the Decalogue, —even when we do not abstract from its public outward promulgation,—is valid as a behest ethical in the eye of reason; still this decenary code challenges no deferential obedience from conscience. It insists only on outward conformity, and takes no note whatever of MORAL INFORMEDNESS of intent in observance, in which latter point alone Christianity afterwards placed the very spirit and genius of morality. Whence results,

SECONDLY.—Every sequent arising from fulfilling or transgressing the edicts of the Pentateuch, *i. e.* the whole system of rewards and punishments, is limited *to this life*, and even then inconsistently with ethical ideas; those momentous sanctions descending like an entail to posterity, even to generations who could not actively have participated in the guilt of their forefathers. *Politically*, this, as a prudential mean of extorting sequacity, may be practised; but, *ethically*, that equity and justice, on which every moral community must be founded, and by which it must be sustained, are utterly subverted and exploded. Again, since, without belief in a future state, religion is altogether incogitable, it follows that naked JUDAISM cannot, under any aspect, be A RELIGION,—a conclusion yet farther confirmed by the following remark, *viz.* doubtless the Jews had, like every other nation, however savage, a belief in future retribution, *i. e.* in a heaven and a hell; for this persuasion does, by dint of man's moral nature, obtrude itself, of its own accord, on every one's thoughts, so that we may be certain that the lawgiver of this race PURPOSELY OMITTED all mention of a hereafter; and since, although represented to have been God himself, lie deliberately excludes a future state from his code, that evinces to a sufficiency, that the design was to institute, not an ethical, but only a political commonwealth,[47] where, to talk to the burghers of

---

[47] TRANSLATOR'S NOTE—In the text Kant proceeds to unload the usual commonplaces of free-thinking. It is, however, curious to observe that he agrees with Warburton in holding that the author of the Pentateuch must *of forethought purpose* have excluded the doctrine of a future state from his code; but when he goes on to argue that there can be *no religion* without a state of future retribution, I fear he contradicts not only the bishop, but—what is far worse—himself. Referring to his chapter on conscience, we have a definition of RELIGION IN GENERAL, where no vista into futurity obtains. As this point is of moment, I make no apology for quoting Warburton's reply to Lord Bolingbroke, who had urged *the omission* as a cardinal objection against the Divine Origin of Judaism. The Doctor answers thus, p. 617, vol. vii. quarto ed. 1788. "Till the coming of this FIRST PHILOSOPHY, *Religion* was understood to rise on that wide basis, on which the *fanatical Knave*, PAUL, had the art to place it; that 'He who cometh to God must believe that he is; and that he is a RE WARDER of them who diligently seek him.' For men who supposed the infinite *goodness and justice* of God to be as demonstrable as his infinite *power and*

punishments and rewards not to be administered in this life, would have been a most inconsequential and injudicious proceeding; and although it cannot be questioned that the Jews may subsequently, each one for himself, have framed a religious belief of some kind or other, which he would fasten on and connect with the articles of his statutable faith, still this super-addition can belong in no sense to the original laws of Judaism.

THIRDLY.—So remote was the Judaica] era from being the epoch fitted for the advent of a church universal, that, on the contrary, the Mosaic economy rather excluded the rest of mankind from its communion; while the Jews, as a people specially chosen by Jehovah for himself, entertained a sullen disregard or even hatred of the whole human race generally, and were in turn cordially detested. Here it must be noted, that the circumstance has been greatly over-rated that they represented to themselves as the Governor of the world the only one unseen God, of whom no sensible likeness was to be made. Most other nations held pretty much the same belief, and only by WORSHIPPING sundry inferior mighty under-gods did they render themselves suspected of Polytheism.[48] A God who demands obedience to such laws solely as require no amended moral sentiments, is not that Moral Being needed by reason to support religion. In fact, religion would thrive better, when various invisible subordinate deities are pre-supposed—provided always the people understood, that, however different their respective departments, domains, and jurisdictions, all concurred in favouring with assistance those only who, with the whole heart, followed after virtue,—than when a single being is believed in, who places the head and front of his religion in a mere mechanic worship.

General church history, when treated systematically, must

---

wisdom, could not but conclude from his *moral attributes* that he REWARDED, as well as from his *natural attributes* that he CREATED.

"On the more complex notion, therefore, of a MORAL GOVERNOR, all mankind supposed RELIGION to arise; while NATURALISM, the Ape of Religion, was seen to spring from the simpler notion of a PHYSICAL PRESERVER; which, however, they were ready to distinguish, on the other hand, from the *Unnaturalism* (if one may so call it) of *ranker Atheism*.

"RELIGION, therefore, stands, and must, I think, for ever stand, on those two immoveable Principles of PRESERVER and REWARDER, in conjunction.

"The *length* or *shortness* of human existence was not primarily in the idea of religion, not even in the complete idea of it as delivered in ST PAUL'S general definition. 'The Religionist,' says he, 'must believe that God is, and that he *rewards*.'

"But when it came to be seen that he was not always a *Rewarder* here, men concluded this life not to be the whole of their existence. And thus a FUTURE STATE was brought into religion, and from thenceforth became a necessary part of it."

[48] "A circumstance plainly too frivolous to deserve attention—being indeed nothing more than this: whether mankind fall down before a dog, a cat, or a monkey, or whether lie worship the God of the Universe." Warburton upon Hume, p. 866, vol. vii. quarto cd. 1788. Tr.

consequently commence with the origin of Christianity, which, as an entire abandonment of that Judaism whence it sprang, was grounded on a quite new principle, and effected a thorough revolution in points of faith. The pains taken by the apostles to connect both together, by painting the olden order of affairs as a preparation for the new, prefiguring in types and shadows the events that had just transpired, clearly shows, that in this they studied singly the best means of INTRODUCING the true moral religion proper, in room of the old worship, to which their countrymen were inveterately attached, without shocking over-violently their prejudices. The disuse of the corporal mark whereby the race of Abraham were wont to distinguish themselves, guides to the inference, that the new belief was detached not alone from the ancient, but from all statutes whatsoever, and was intended to ensoul a religion valid for no one secluded race, but for the whole habitable globe.

From Judaism went forth Christianity, but not from the olden unmixed Mosaic constitutions. This polity had long ere then fallen greatly into decay; its precepts of worship had insensibly become tinctured with various tenets of school morality: the otherwise uncultivated nation having from time to time imported much of Greek philosophy. Some such changes as these had doubtless greatly modified their notions of obligation; and, concurring with the diminished power of the priesthood, the populace, then smarting under the yoke of conquerors, who regarded indifferently all foreign creeds, were prepared and ready to revolt against the heavy pressure of rites and ceremonies which neither they nor their forefathers could at any time well bear: from such elements of explosion there suddenly burst forth the new Christian faith. The teacher of the gospel announced himself as an ambassador from heaven, accrediting his mission by the worthy declaration, that the servile mercenary belief in Holidays, Rites, and Confessions, was in itself vain; and that a moral faith alone, which proved its reality by good deportment, could sanctify and save. The narrative farther bears, that after having, by his doctrine and sufferings, even up to the point of an undeserved and meritorious death,[49] fully

---

[49] Wherewith the story of his public life concludes, at least so much of it as can be held up as a fit example for general imitation. The more secret events—the RESURRECTION and ASCENSION—witnessed only by his immediate friends, cannot come within the sphere of a religion WITHIN the bounds of reason, although, regarded as mere ideas—which may be done without impugning their historical reality—they would suggest to the reader the commencement of another life, and entrance into the mansions and society of the blessed. Howbeit, understood literally, just as they are congruous to our sensitive mode of perception, so much the more do they encumber our intellectual belief in futurity, implying, as they do, the *materialism* of all cosmical Intelligents whatsoever, and guiding, *first*, to the *psychological* notion, that the SUBSTRATUM of mankind's PERSONALITY is MATTER which can continue IDENTIC only while the BODY remains unchanged; and, *second*, to the *cosmological* notion of its SPACIAL PRESENCE in

exhibited and delineated in his own person a transcript of that in humanity which alone is well-pleasing to God, he returned to the celestial mansions whence he came. Before withdrawing finally from earth, he left with his friends the declaration of his Last Will (*as it were* IN A NUNCUPATIVE TESTAMENT), and assured them, that by force of the memory of his desert, doctrine, and example, "He (the embodied ideal of a humanity acceptable to God) would, though gone hence, remain ever with his disciples, even to the end of the world." The account of this transaction, if designed to afford a HISTORICAL BELIEF in the extraction and the possibly supra-terrestrial dignity and rank of his person, would no doubt need to be supported on the buttress of miracles; and although his moral, soul-amending tenets can dispense with all such adminicles of their truth, still the Sacred Volume has accompanied and interwoven them with *miracles* and *mysteries*, whose very notification is furthermore itself a miracle; thus founding a church-creed on the historic content, which last again can only be authenticated by learning, as well in respect of import as of interpretation.

Every belief that, as faith historical, is rested upon books, demands A LEARNED PUBLIC for its surety, whose contemporary writers, beyond any suspicion of lending themselves as accessories to the report, or of being in any secret understanding with the first publishers of the narrative, can check and control the rumours spread. The ethical faith of reason needs no such confirmation, but docs, on the contrary, give evidence to itself. Now although, at the epoch of the religious revolution above alluded to, the Roman people who then governed Palestine, and were even scattered throughout Judæa, did really possess a literary republic, who, through an uninterrupted series of writers, have handed down to our own day the political events affecting the policy

---

all worlds, the universe itself being, agreeably to this principle, nothing but an extent of room. The Hypothesis of the SPIRITUALISM of Intelligents is much more consonant to reason. Here the body lies neglected in the dust, while the living person still survives. The soul of the man, stripped of its sensuous appendages, can be wafted to the realms of celestial beatitude, without being present *locally* in any part of space's illimitable expanse. Nor is this the only advantage accruing to the mind from this latter theory. It rids us of the difficulty of trying to figure to ourselves matter in cogitation, and relieves us from any apprehension of casualties that might happen to our existence after death, were the permanency of our Being dependent on the form and cohesion of certain particles of matter—*the perdurability* of a SIMPLE *substance*, arising immediately from the very notion of its nature. Where the Immateriality of our Person is held, reason is devoid of any interest to find itself throughout eternity co-associated with a body, whereof it never even here below was over fond, and which, how transformed and purified soever it may be, must (so long as personality is made to depend on its identity) consist of the same materials which constitute the basis of its organization. Besides, why the dust and clay whereof our body is composed should be carried into heaven—a region of the universe where probably totally diverse materials are required for the existence and preservation of animated beings—is altogether incomprehensible.

and the constitution of the realm; still it is to be noted, that no writer of that day makes mention either of the alleged miracles, nor yet of the public change produced by them in the religious opinions of their eastern neighbours. A generation had already expired before later inquirers proceeded to investigate what their contemporaneous progenitors had omitted to ascertain. Speculation was now set on foot touching the essence and nature of this hitherto unknown faith, which had not spread without considerable public commotion; but it does not appear that any inquiry was instituted into its historical origin, in order, out of the Jewish annals themselves, to detect its falsehood or confirm its truth. Consequently, from the first beginning of Christianity to the period when the church constituted a learned body of its own, the narrative is obscure; and we cannot even tell what effect the doctrines of Christ had on the morality of his followers—nor whether the first converts were really morally superior to their neighbours, or just people of the ordinary run. Howbeit, from the time when the Christian Church first figures in the history of the empire, it is past all doubt that the effects it produced arc by no means of that beneficial character, justly expected from a moral religion:—they are certainly very far from recommending it.

History teaches how mystical fanaticism gave birth to swarms of monks and hermits, who, for the sake of some fancied sanctity in celibacy, rendered themselves useless to their species. Connected with this abuse, were hatched a brood of pretended miracles, that fettered the nations with the shackles of a blind superstition; while at the same time a Tyrannical Hierarchy, uttering the dreadful voice of ORTHODOXY, obtruded itself on the free conscience of mankind, and did, by the mouth of presumptuous chosen interpreters, convert the whole Christian world into the embittered partizans of conflicting articles of faith—where, indeed, unless pure reason sit as umpire, no general concord can ever be attained. In the East we see the state making itself ridiculous by mixing itself controversially up, with the statutes and brawls of faith sacerdotal, instead of rather compelling churchmen to abide within the due limits of their post, and preventing them from doing that to which they always have betrayed a strong bias, viz. exchanging the character of *Præceptor* for that of *Governor*. While thus distracted, we observe the Asiatic division of the empire become the booty of enemies who ultimately abolish the dominant belief and its disputes. In the West, faith erects its own throne. The soi-*disant* VICAR OF GOD shakes himself loose from, and sets himself above, all worldly dominion, and allows civil order, together with the sciences (which last alone can truly watch and preserve a community), to fall in ruins to the ground. Finally, we perceive how both the Oriental and Occidental States of Christendom, now far gone in decay, did,—like those diseased plants and animals that attract loathsome vermin, to hasten and complete their decline,—become over-run with barbarians. The kings of those barbarous savages arc from time to time chastised like children by the spiritual head, and kept in awe by an enchanted wand,—the threat of excommunication. Now crusades lead them forth to distant' wars, that devastate remote regions of the globe, while anon subjects are excited to revolt against their rulers, and taught to hate their fellow Christians of a different denomination. The root of this multiform turmoil flourishes in the soil of despotically-commanding church-faith, and would even now vegetate into the like excesses, did not political interests and force suppress them. Whoever puts these things together, might well be justified in exclaiming,—*Tantum religio potuit suadere malorum;* did not the original intention most transparently shine through the page of the original record, viz. that the design of the Author of Christianity was to introduce a pure religious faith, touching which there can be no contradictory opinions or disputes; whereas that whole hubbub, whereby humanity has been and still is distracted, arose entirely hence, that, owing to some perverse bias of our nature, what was primarily intended as a mere introductory transit from antiquated faith historical, to religious faith proper, became afterwards mistaken for, and incorporated with, the foundation of religion universal.

Were any one now to ask, "*What period during the whole known history of the church is to be esteemed the best?*" the answer may confidently be,—"THE PRESENT:" a principle of true religious faith has now been publicly recognised in Christianity, which, though long dormant, needs now only to be roused and set free, in order to bring about a continued approach to that all-containing church, which is the visible likeness of the invisible kingdom of God on earth. Reason at length,—in all moral and soul-amending matters,—withdrawn from the load of arbitrarily interpretable creeds, has now established these two maxims, which are in this quarter of the globe universally, although not publicly, received by all true reverers of religion. FIRST, the principle of an equitable RESERVE in speaking of all matters that concern revelation. Seeing that no one can successfully impugn the claim of the Scripture to be (even in respect to its historic content) divine revelation, its practical part being in all points most God-worthy; and seeing furthermore that a religious community can hardly be established and rendered permanent without some Holy Book and corresponding church-creed founded thereon; it does seem the most prudent and reasonable course that can be pursued, to continue to use this book, such as it is, as the text-book of ecclesiastic education. Again, since no one will now-a-days expect a new revelation ushered in by miraculous credentials, it is obvious that the authority of the existing volume ought not to be lessened by petulant or fastidious cavils,—while at the same time (*owing to this modest doubt?* Tr.) belief in its contents is never to be represented as a condition precedent of and indispensably requisite for salvation. The SECOND principle is, that since the Sacred Narrative exists merely for the behoof of Faith Ecclesiastical, and never can or ought to have any influence on the moral maxims we adopt—being subjected to the Church-Creed, with the express view of more vividly delineating the true and real object of all ethical associations (viz. a virtue that presses after holiness), it results that every interpretation of the Scripture must be entirely moral, and that it never can be too strenuously inculcated,—the unlettered betraying a constant bias to lapse into a merely PASSIVE faith,[50]—that true religion consists not in knowing and confessing what God does, or may already have done, for our salvation, but in ourselves doing what must be done in order to make ourselves worthy of this benefit. Indispensably incumbent pursuits and avoidances can be those actions only that do in themselves possess an undoubted UNCONDITIONED WORTH, which can consequently *alone*, render us acceptable to God, and whereof the practical necessity is self-evident to every man, and fully certain, quite apart from any Scripturary doctrines. The Government is bound not to oppose these principles, nor to lett nor hinder their striking root among the public. It is, on the contrary, a most perilous, indeed audacious undertaking, and one whereby heavy responsibility is incurred, when the Regent tampers with the course of the Divine Providence, and does by Test or Corporation Acts, passed out of courtesy to the prevalent Church-Creed, tempt,[51] by putting up to open auction, the

---

[50] One of the causes of this bias lies in the following supposed *Principle of Security*, viz. that the faults of a religion in which I was born and brought up, quite independently of my own option, and whereof the doctrinal entierty I neither make nor mar, are faults not chargeable upon me, but upon my teachers and other publicly installed instructors. This is doubtless also the reason why, in general, a conversion from one form of faith to another is not looked upon with much favour; although here another and a deeper ground may be assigned, viz. that, owing to the uncertainty inwardly felt by every man, which of the Historical Beliefs is the really true, whilst the Ethical Belief is always and everywhere the same, people deem it a matter of unconcern what vehicle their neighbours may think fit to prefer.

[51] When governments pretend that conscience is not coerced, inasmuch as they only forbid the subject to STATE publicly his opinions on religion, but allow him privately to THINK what he likes, one is provoked to smile, and to say that no freedom is hereby conceded by the magistrate to the people—to stop the current of their thoughts being beyond his power. And yet this mental co-action, which cannot be wielded by the *temporal* authorities, is actually put upon mankind by the *clerical*, who are at all times ready to put an effective VETO upon independent liberty of cogitation, and oftentimes succeed in imposing even on the legislature the shackles of this subtile yoke, barring them from so much as thinking otherwise than they prescribe. Mankind's propensity to a mercenary and worshipping religion, and bias to prefer it before the ethical worship of the Deity, is so strong, that they are even prone to regard a ritual of form and show as a matter not only of the utmost magnitude, but as alone of sufficient efficacy to compensate for every other shortcoming; and hence render it most easy for those Soul-Preservers—the Guardians of Orthodoxy—to instil into their flock so pious a dread of swerving, even in the least, from the Articles of a Creed supported upon History, that they never venture, *even in thought*, to allow a single doubt as to their accuracy to gain footing in their minds,

conscientiousness of the subject, offering or withholding civil offices and emoluments, the common right of all, according as individuals accept or decline those tests which, at the very utmost, can have no more than a learned probability in their favour. Even when no regard is had to the detriment thence arising to the sacred cause of freedom, it is worse than doubtful how far such a mode of dealing can procure good citizens to any state. Who is he of those, thus impeding the free development of God's originary arrangements for the welfare of our race, that would willingly,—conscience being consulted,—stand surety and guarantee for all the damage that he may, by such violent invasion of free rights, entail upon his country. For although the predestinated growth of good, pre-appointed by our Creator, never can by any human power or stratagem be altogether frustrated, still it may, by thus forestalling mankind of a free market for opinion, be long stunted, or even forced to retrograde.

Touching the superintending guidance of Providence, THE HISTORY goes on to represent THE KINGDOM OF HEAVEN no longer as for a while postponed, or merely approaching, but discloses to us its actual advent and ingress. We may regard it as merely designed to animate the hope and courage of those who strive to enter thereinto, when, toward the close of the volume, we impinge upon A PROPHECY where, dark as in Sybilline books, are foretold the ultimate consummation of this grand cosmical revulsion, and painted as come a visible kingdom of God on earth (under the rule of his Vicar,—once more descended from on high), together with the happiness enjoyed even here under his sway. After the rebels who attempt a fresh revolt are quelled and cast out, THE APOCALYPSE announces their final doom, viz. to be hurled with their leader to destruction; and THE END OF THE WORLD concludes the scene. The Teacher of the Gospel, however, exhibited to his disciples the Kingdom of God on Earth only in its glorious, soul-exalting, moral phase; *i. e.* he showed them wherein that worthiness consisted whereby alone they could become citizens in the divine state, and what they had to do, not only to enter in themselves, but also to work hand in hand with all others similarly minded, and even if possible with the whole

---

for this would be tantamount to lending ear to the Evil One. True; to rid one's self of this oppression, a man has but so to WILL (a statement that cannot be made with regard to the statutably-ordained confession of the country); but unfortunately this volition is precisely what clerical co-action clogs with its drag. Bad as is this forcing of conscience (which tempts to hypocrisy), it is not so bad as suppressing outward liberty of belief. The warped understanding gradually regains its elasticity as the man advances in moral insight, and awakes consciously to freedom, whence alone true reverence for duty can spring. But the other, which passes an interdict on the press in favour of a given creed, puts an end to all voluntary efforts that might willingly be made by the ethical communion of believers (in which last alone consists the essential of a true church), and makes the church *formally* subservient to political *ordonnances*.

human race. As for happiness,—an inevitable object of mankind's wishes,—he told them beforehand not to count upon it during this earthly life, but rather to be prepared to submit to the greatest sacrifices and tribulations. Again, since a total renunciation of physical enjoyment cannot well be expected from any living man, he qualified this prospect by saying, "*Rejoice and be exceeding glad, for great will be your reward in heaven.*" The above-cited Appendix to the History of the Church, containing the account of its future and last destination, unfolds to view the church at last TRIUMPHANT; *i. e.* after having overcome all hinderances, CROWNED even while on earth with HAPPINESS. The separating the good from the wicked (which, while the church was advancing to perfection, would have been inconsistent with the idea of its end,—the very mixture being needed, partly to test and whet the virtue of the one, and partly by that bright example to draw over the others from vice) now takes place, as the next effect of the completed establishment and institution of the Divine State. The last proof of its stability and fixity, viz. its victorious overthrow of all outward foes,—where the *state infernal* is finally dashed by the might of the *state celestial,*—is now added; this terrestrial order of things has drawn to a close, and fled away, while "*death, the last enemy* (of the good), *being destroyed,*" either party enter upon an immortality, of weal to the one—of woe to the other. The very form of a church is now abolished, mankind, as Citizens of Heaven, assuming that equal rank with the stadtholder and vicarious head, to which he himself has raised them, and *God becomes all in all.*[52]

This Sketch of a History of Futurity, which is after all no History, is a beautiful Ideal of a distant epoch, FORESEEN IN FAITH, that must one day take place, owing to the introduction of the true religion universal. The period of its actual arrival we do not yet descry; but only LOOK FORWARD TO the day, when, through a constant progression and approximation, the highest good realizable on earth may be attained; a prospect in which there is nothing visionary or mystical, but where everything proceeds according to the principles and laws of our moral

---

[52] An expression that may be thus understood (when abstraction is made from its mysterious import, which last, transcending the range of all possible experience, belongs only to the sacred HISTORY of Humanity, and is therefore PRACTICALLY devoid of ethical *purchase* on the will), viz. that the historical belief, which, being a church-creed, required a sacred volume for conducting the education of our race (which volume, however, obstructs the unity and universality of the church), will one day become evanescent,* having finally merged in a universally self-evidencing pure religious faith: to bring about which transit we ought most sedulously to labour, by constantly developing a pure moral religion from a concomitant vehicle that cannot as yet be altogether thrown aside.

* [In the second edition Kant has appended the following *addendum* to the above Note—Tr.] Not exactly that it should cease (for, as a vehicle, it may at all times be useful and necessary), but that possibly it may do so; a contemplation that denotes only the internal fixity of one's pure moral faith.

nature. The Appearance of Antichrist—the Milennium—the End of the World—may receive from Reason excellent symbolic interpretations. The coming of the new heavens and new earth may, just like the uncertain distance or nearness of death, be very easily understood to express the necessity of our being ever ready for so momentous a change; and does in reality, when we lend to such symbol its intellectual meaning, invite us to regard ourselves as at all times the called citizens of a divine ethical state. *"When, therefore, cometh the Kingdom of God?"—The Kingdom of God cometh not in visual form;* FOR BEHOLD THE KINGDOM OF GOD IS WITHIN YOU! (*Luke*, xvii. v. 20, 21.)

* * *
* *

Thus have we represented a kingdom of God on earth, not according to a particular covenant—not a MESSIANIC, but a MORAL kingdom, cognizable by pure reason. The former (*Regnum Divinum Pactitium*) must draw its proofs from history, and is subdivided into the MESSIANIC kingdom, according to the OLD and the NEW covenant. Here it is worthy of remark, that the Jews, who lived under the elder dispensation, are still extant, and, though scattered over the whole globe, still preserve their ancient character; while, on the contrary, nations professing other creeds generally lost their primitive belief, and adopted the current persuasion of the country they were in. To many this phenomenon seems so extraordinary, that they deem it impossible to have happened by any usual course of events, and one immediately arranged by the Deity for certain ends aimed at by Supreme Wisdom. But, on more mature consideration, we observe, that no race possessing a Written Religion (*i. e.* Sacred Book) mixes itself with another (*e. g.* the Roman) that has none. In truth, it rather gains proselytes. And this is the reason why the Jews, who, previous to their captivity in Babylon, were prone to idolatry, abstained subsequently from this vice; since after that catastrophe their sacred books became, for the first time, matter of general and public study. In exactly the same way the PARSEES, attached to the religion of ZOROASTER, preserve up to this very hour their written creed, notwithstanding their dispersion, and are thus kept together by the Zendavesta, which remains under the sacerdotal guardianship of the DESTURS. The HINDUS, on the other hand, who, under the name of GYPSIES, are scattered far and wide, have been in great measure swallowed up by their neighbours. Their native creed, at all events, has perished; since, being PARIAS—the very dregs of the people—they were interdicted from reading their Sacred Volumes. Furthermore, what the Jews in themselves might have been unable to accomplish was done to their hand, first by the Christian, and then afterwards by the Mahometan religions, inasmuch as both sprouted from the old stock of Judaical Belief, and presupposed an acquaintance with the Sacred Books in question; the force of which remark is not impaired by the circumstance that Mahometanism declares the Jews to have vitiated their Writings. Should at any time the Jews, in the course of their peregrinations, have lost all taste or skill in deciphering the text of their earlier history, they could always revive these studies, and procure copies of their sacred documents from Christian communities, thpt had originally emanated from themselves. Hence also it happens, that, in regions unknown to Christianity and Mahometanism, no Jewish wanderers are to be met with, except a few on the coast of Malabar, and a single colony or so in China. The former are in constant commercial intercourse with their brethren settled in Arabia; and the very circumstance that colonial vestiges of this race are to be met with among the Chinese, places it past all doubt that they must have dispersed themselves, at some period or other, throughout that wealthy empire; and that the major part of them, finding no points of sympathy or cognationship betwixt their own and the Chinese creed, became ultimately oblivious of their peculiar tenets, and were swallowed up and absorbed into the great indistinguishable mass around them. Edifying remarks upon this national peculiarity of the *Abrahamides*, and the long survival of their religion, while they themselves are destitute of habitation, country, or international connexion, arc but of doubtful use, since cither party draw inferences consolatory to themselves. The genuine descendant of Abraham secs, in this long preservative against extinction, a promise on the part of benignant Providence that his race is yet destined to the splendours of terrestrial rule; Christians, again, behold only the warning ruins of a state desolate, because it endeavoured to oppose itself to the advent and spread of the Heavenly Kingdom, which Providence still upholds in being, partly to keep in memory the olden MESSIAH-PROPHECIES, and partly to gibbet up in terror to the rest of the world the almost lifeless carcass of the nation, as a dreadful instance of avenging justice; the Jews obstinately persisting in framing to themselves a *political* instead of a *moral* notion of their foretold Messiah.

GENERAL SCHOLION.

In all religious forms of faith, we do, when searching narrowly into their interior texture, invariably arrive at somewhat MYSTERIOUS, *i. e.* at something HOLY, which may be indeed KNOWN by each single individual, but cannot BE MADE KNOWN by him to others, *i. e.* which does not admit of being publicly communicated. As something HOLY, the OBJECT must be MORAL. It must consequently fall under Reason, and be sufficiently cognisable for every practical purpose, while, at the same time, as somewhat HIDDEN, it is impervious to any theory of our speculative understanding: for were the case otherwise, then it would be communicable to every one, and admit of being imparted and made known, as well outwardly as publicly.

Belief in what we consider to be A HOLY MYSTERY, may be regarded either as DIVINELY INFUSED, or as A PURELY-RATIONAL BELIEF. Unless constrained by some urgent necessity to assume the former, we shall lay down the maxim of abiding singly by the latter. Feelings are not knowledge. Upon the same account they teach and indicate no mystery: consequently, since this last stands immediately connected with reason, and is moreover incommunicable generally, it results that each person must search for this mystery (if perchance there be at all any such) within the circuit and extent of his own Reason.

It is impossible to tell *a priori*, from an investigation of the object, whether there be sacred mysteries or no. We are thus constrained diligently to ransack our inner man, in order to see whether, *from the Subjective* of our ethical economy, some imperscrutable may not rise. Here we most assuredly will not class the last grounds of morality along with the Holy Mysteries; for the whole theory of ethic is publicly communicable, although the supersensible causality lying at the bottom of moral conduct is neither known nor given. That alone, therefore, which may be an object of possible, but incommunicable knowledge, will we regard as possessing the dread character of the SACRO-SANCT. Upon this account—FREEDOM, a property revealed to mankind from the determinability of his Will by the unconditionally commanding Law, is no mystery whatever, for it admits of being publicly propounded and communicated to every one. But the last unsearchable ground and root of this property is *mysterious*, not being the object of any possible human inquest, and so quite incommunicable. Again, just this very freedom alone it is, that does, when transferred to the last object of practical reason, viz. the realizing the idea of our chief moral end, issue inevitably in those holy mysteries.[53]

---

[53] In like manner, the CAUSE of gravitation is unknown, so much so, that we are even able to perceive, that it never can become an object of our knowledge; its very notion presupposing a first motive force as a property unconditionally belonging to matter. Notwithstanding, there is here no mystery: for attraction can be made patent to every body, its LAW being amply cognizable. When Newton represents the attraction of gravitation as the phenomenon of the Divine Omnipresence, he does not thereby attempt to explain it (the local presence of God in space involving a contradiction): all he suggests to us is a Sublime Analogy, where, by subjecting the physical system to an immaterial cause, all corporeal entities are conjoined into one mundane whole. It is equally difficult to comprehend the last substratal ground combining all finite Intelligents in an ethical state. All that we recognise is our duty to become members of such a society; although the possibility of fully realizing this union, even when we obey the dictate of our reason, lies beyond the limited insight we enjoy. There are in Nature *arcana*—and in politics there are *secrets* which OUGHT—not to be divulged; but both may possibly become known to us by observation and experience. Touching that which it is every one's duty to know, no secret or mystery obtains: only touching that which God

Seeing that mankind cannot by himself alone realize that idea of the Sovereign and Supreme Good, which is an inseparable concomitant of a pure and moral sentiment; and since he can neither confer upon himself the requisite share of physical happiness, nor cause to come to pass a general union of mankind, aiming at this moral end, and does nevertheless deem himself bound to endeavour after its accomplishment; the consequence is, that he finds himself impelled to believe in the co-operation or disposing guidance of a Moral Governor of the World, by whose superintending aid this last end may be put within his reach. Here there opens to his mental gaze the unveiled abysses of a mystery, viz. *what—how much*, or if indeed *anything* at all, is to be ascribed to God, as done by him for this behoof: for, in all the offices of humanity, we know only what we ourselves have to do, in order that we make ourselves worthy of this unknown—at least incomprehensible—supply.

To fix and define this Idea of a Moral Governor of the World, is a problem proposed to us by practical reason. What we are concerned about knowing is not what the Nature of God may be in itself; but what he is in reference to us as Moral Agents. For this latter behoof, we must so cogitate and represent to ourselves the Divine Nature, as to exhaust all those relations obtaining betwixt our Idea of Him (as Unchangeable, Omniscient, Almighty, &c.), and that entire perfection requisite on our part for thoroughly executing his Will—and, without regarding him under this relative aspect, no fixt or precise moral notion of the Godhead can be framed.

Cogitated conformably to this practical necessity of our reason, the True Catholic Religious Belief must be explained to be THE BELIEF IN GOD, FIRST, as the Omnipotent Creator of Heaven and Earth, *i. e.* morally as a HOLY Lawgiver; SECONDLY, as the Preserver of the Human race, *i. e.* their BENIGNANT Governor and Moral Guardian; THIRDLY, as the administrator of his own Holy Laws, *i. e.* as a RIGHTEOUS Judge.

MYSTERY here there is none, for this threefold belief expresses merely the moral relations understood to obtain betwixt God and the human race. Furthermore it objects itself to every one's thoughts, and hence comes to be met with in the religion of almost every nation above barbarism.[54] The same notion occurs in Constitutional Law,

---

alone can do, and to co-operate wherewith, transcends our power and therefore also our duty, can there be a mystery properly so called, viz. a Holy Mystery in Religion, concerning which it seems enough for us to be aware that there is such a thing—to comprehend it, might perhaps benefit us nothing.

[54] In the narrative, conveyed to us by the history, of what takes place after death, the Judge of the World (strictly he who separates for himself, and takes under his own dominion, those who belong to the kingdom of the Good Principle) is said to be not God, but the Son of Man. This seems to intimate, that human nature, inwardly conscious of its own infirmity, would choose such a judge to pass sentence—a favour which, though granted, would not offend against justice.—The Divine Judge of his intelligent creation

where every COMMONWEALTH must be figured as swayed by such a threefold order of *Authorities*. Only, in the ethic government contemplated, THE SOVEREIGNTY is purely MORAL; whence the re-union of all three functions may take place in the undivided person of the one ethical legislator of our race; whereas, in every *civil polity*, the legislative, executive, and judicial functions, must be figured as wielded by three several juridical personages.[55]

Again, since this belief, which adapts the moral relations obtaining betwixt the Supreme and his Subjects to the uses of religion generally, purging our conceptions of a hurtful anthropomorphism, and shaping them to a meetness for the true morality of *a People of God*, was first embodied in the Christian Creed, and was thus singly by it publicly propounded to the world; it results that such promulgation may not unaptly be styled the revelation of that which, through mankind's own fault, had hitherto lain hidden from him as a mystery.

The Christian Faith teaches, *FIRST*, the Supreme lawgiver is, *as such*, not to be regarded by us as CLEMENT, and consequently INDULGENT, to the frailty of our race,—nor yet as DESPOTIC, imperiously commanding by dint of his absolute and unconditioned right: neither are we to esteem his behest arbitrary, and unrelated to our notions of morality, but as bearing directly upon the HALLOWING of our nature: *SECONDLY*, His Benignity is not to be placed in an unqualified GOOD-WILL toward his creatures; as if he did not first test the morality of their sentiments, and only then—in proportion to his WELL-

---

(*the Holy Ghost*) can only be cogitated as pronouncing doom according to the utmost rigour of law, and giving force to the sentence already passed upon us by conscience, when reckoning up the account of our misdeeds. The reason is, that since we do not know what deductions may equitably be allowed us on the score of human frailty, and are acquainted only with the amount of our deliberate transgressions, we have no data whence to claim any mitigation of the severity otherwise to be dealt out to us as our future lot.

[55] It is hardly possible to assign any cause why so many nations of antiquity have concurred in holding this opinion, unless it spring from some common principle in reason, namely, the idea of a government, whether obtaining in a single country, or throughout the universe. ZOROASTER'S creed has these three divine persons, *Ormuzd, Mithra*, and *Ahriman*. The HINDUS have *Brahma, Vishnu*, and *Siva* (with this difference, however, that the Persians figure to themselves the third Person, not merely as causing those evils which are punishments, but as causing those very moral ills for which mankind are to suffer, whereas in Hindustan he merely judges and hands over to vengeance). The EGYPTIANS had *Phta, Kneph*, and *Neith*, where, so far as we can collect their meaning through the obscure glimmering of ancient history, the first person was an incorporeal spirit, CREATOR OF THE WORLD; the second was a principle of sustaining and GOVERNING benignity; the third a principle of wisdom limitary of the second, who therefore was conceived to administer a JUDICIARY function. The Goths revered *Odin* (*Allfather*), *Freya* (or *Freyer*, kindness), and Thor (the punisher). Even the JEWS seem, toward the close of their polity, to have imbibed these notions; for, when the Pharisees accused Jesus of terming himself the Son of God, the weight of the accusation seems not to be, that God was said to have a Son, but that Christ individually laid claim to be this Son.

PLEASEDNESS with their conduct—supply their inability to become fully commensurate to His Holiness: THIRDLY, in the Administration of His Justice, as he cannot, *on the one hand*, be figured to be deprecatory by ENTREATY (for this were to hold a contradiction); so neither can he, *on the other*, come to judgment clothed with nothing but the HOLINESS of the Lawgiver (for then no man ever could be justified). His Righteousness must rather be regarded as a principle limiting and restraining the exercise of His Benignity to the prior condition of our conformity with his Holy Law,—so far forth as we Sons of Men are capable of harmonizing with its demands. In a single word, we have to serve God under a *Triad* of specifically-different moral aspects, to indicate which, the term of a threefold (*not physical, but moral*) personality of the same one Being is no improper phrase. This symbol may fitly suggest to us the whole of pure moral religion, which, apart from this tripartite division, might easily degenerate into a mere servile anthropomorphism,—mankind being extremely prone to cogitate the Deity pretty much as they do a temporal regent, where occasionally these threefold functions are not duly separated, but crudely mixed up and confounded.

Should, however, this belief in a tri-une God be understood, not as a mere delineation of a practical idea, but as setting forth what God in Himself is, then would this be a mystery transcending all grasp of thought, quite unsusceptible of being made level even by revelation to our comprehension; and would therefore be properly represented as a surd and incogitable Mystery. To believe this tenet as one adding to a man's theoretic knowledge of the Divine Nature, can be nothing more than a confession of an utterly unintelligible Church-Creed; or, should any think he understands it, then he professes an anthropomorphous symbol of faith ecclesiastical; neither of which can benefit in the least his moral amendment. That only, admitting of being practically understood and comprehended, while, in a theoretical respect, surpassing all our notions when we attempt to fix its nature as an object,—is, in one sense, a Mystery, that, *in another sense*, can be revealed. Of this latter kind is the first above mentioned tri-form faith, which serves as a groundwork, whence three mysteries, revealed to us by our own reason, take their rise.

I. The mystery of our (*effectual?* TR.) CALLING—to become the citizens of an Ethical State.—We can only depicture to ourselves our UNCONDITIONED subjection to the Divine Law, by regarding ourselves as God's CREATURES; exactly in the same way as God can only be regarded as the author of the laws of the material universe, when he is regarded as having created all physical entities. But reason cannot by any means comprehend how any being should be so created as to be endowed with the free use of its powers, seeing that, according to every Principle of Causation, no substance can have any internal ground of agency other than that implanted by its originating cause; but then its every action would be already fixed by this inward determinating ground, *i. e.* by *its* foreign cause, and so the being itself would not be free. Consequently a Holy Godlike Legislation, addressed to Intelligents endowed with Spontaneity, is irreconcileable, upon any ground of our reason, with the notion of their Creation. We are consequently to be regarded as Free Agents already extant, *called*, not by any natural dependency arising from one creation, but *called*, by a purely moral co-action, agreeably to Laws of Freedom—to a citizenship in the Divine State. Our vocation is consequently, *morally*, quite clear; but, speculatively, the possibility of such a call is an impenetrable mystery.

II. The Mystery of Redemption.—Mankind is corrupt, and far from tallying with God's holy law; nevertheless, if the divine benignity has called him into being, and invited him to become a member of the heavenly kingdom, there must be some mean patent to God's Supreme Wisdom, for supplying, out of the fulness of His own holiness, the want of our requisite qualifications. But then all the moral good or evil that can attach to mankind must necessarily be brought forth by his own spontaneity, and consequently no moral good can flow to him from another, but must, if it is to be imputed, emanate from himself. So far, therefore, as all human insight reaches, no one can, by any surplus of desert, come vicariously in our room—at least, even were we to concede the possibility of such a substitution, still it is only, for a *moral practical behoof*, an indispensable assumption; *theoretically*, it is a mystery quite unfathomable by any stretch of reason.

III. The Mystery of Election.—Even after vicarious satisfaction has been admitted as possible: still a believing acceptance of it is a determination of will toward good, presupposing in the man a cast of thinking well-pleasing to God, which, however, owing to the depraved bias of his heart, he cannot have produced in himself. Now, that celestial GRACE should bring about this effect within, not according to any works of righteousness that the man has done, but according to an unconditioned DECREE, adjudging this mighty aid to one, and withholding it from another,—thus foredooming one portion of our race to bliss, and the remainder to eternal reprobation,—is a hypothetical idea of a government, conveying to us no notion at all of Divine Justice; but one that would require, in the last resort, to be referred to the Standard of a Wisdom, whereof the Rule, is for us a most inexplicable mystery.

Concerning those mysteries which deeply pervade the moral history of each man's life, viz. whence it happens that moral good and moral evil are to be met with in the world,—how the one can be developed from the other,—and how mankind's re-establishment in good can be brought about,—why, while this redintegration of character obtains in some, others remain unchanged;—touching, I say, those various mysteries, God has revealed nothing, and can in fact grant us no such revelation; for we could not UNDERSTAND it.[56] With equal reason might we attempt to EXPLAIN, by help of the idea *Freedom*, the phases of the human conduct. God's will as to this last is, doubtless, amply revealed to us by the moral law; but what those LAST GROUNDS are, by dint whereof a free act is in time performed or avoided, is a point wrapped in uttermost obscurity. Nor can any sifting research, instituted by man, bring light into these tortuous windings of his history, which derives its double source at once from freedom and from the enchainment of causes and effects.[57] The objective rule of behaviour is (*by Reason and in the Scripture*) sufficiently revealed; and this revelation is, moreover, intelligible to the whole world.

That we, mankind, are by the moral law called to a good life; *that*, by the inextinguishable reverence felt toward this behest, and engraven upon our soul, we bear within a promise, leading us to trust this good spirit, and to hope that somehow or other we may satisfy his demand; lastly, *that*, from combining this expectation with the stern edict, we must constantly examine ourselves, as were we legally summoned to account,—these are points alike strenuously inculcated by Reason, Heart, and Conscience. It were intemperate to seek for farther manifestations; and were any farther disclosures to take place, they could not be regarded as addressed to the general needs and wants of human nature.

Although that Grand Cardinal Mystery, comprising all the rest under its general formula, is made by each man's own reason thoroughly comprehensible, as a practically necessary idea of religion, it may, nevertheless, be said that it was then first revealed, as the moral groundwork of religion, when PUBLICLY taught, and made the characteristic of an epoch in religion altogether new. A SOLEMN FORMULARY is usually couched in peculiar, sometimes mystic phraseology, not understood by every one, and interpreted only to

---

[56] People not unfrequently demand that tyros in religion should assent to mysteries, because, being incomprehensible, we are no more entitled to deny them, than to deny the generative power possessed by organized beings—a thing likewise comprehended by none—but which must still be admitted, although an *arcanum* that must ever remain hidden. Howbeit we thoroughly UNDERSTAND what we mean when we talk of the growth and generation of plants and animals; and we possess an *a posteriori* notion of those objects, and are perfectly aware that they involve no contradiction. Of every mystery offered to our belief, we may insist upon understanding what it means: which is not the case, so long as we merely understand each individual word of the formula under which the mystery is couched—That God can convey to us a mysterious knowledge by *inspiration*, is incogitable; for our understanding is by its nature unfitted for such a deposite.

[57] Hence, what freedom is, is in a practical point of view thoroughly understood; but in a theoretical, the physical constitution of such a causality cannot be thought of, without involving ourselves in contradictions.

those, who compose a particular guild or union. Out of deference, it is seldom or never used, save when some public solemnity is transacted, such as the reception of a new member into the select company. The highest grade of the moral perfection of Finite Creatures —at all times unattainable by man—is THE LOVE OF THE LAW—conformably to this idea, this would become a principle of religious faith, "GOD IS LOVE." In him mankind may revere the loving FATHER (his love being that of moral complacency in creatures, so far forth as they conform themselves to his Holy Law); farther, in him they can venerate, in so far as he exhibits himself agreeably to the idea of his all-preserving character—the beloved and self-begotten archetype of humanity—THE SON; and lastly, inasmuch as he tempers his complacency by regard had to mankind's coincidence with the conditions limitary of that complacential love, and does thereby demonstrate that his Benignity is sustained by Wisdom, they may farther revere in him THE HOLY SPIRIT.[58] Thus they may INVOKE him, not in his threefold capacity

---

[58] This spirit, whereby Love toward God as our Benignant Saviour, making us partakers of his eternal bliss, is combined with awe felt toward him as lawgiver, is the true Judge of Mankind before his own conscience. Judgment may be pronounced in a twofold character. Sentence may pass as to the presence or absence of *good-desert*, and it may also decide upon *innocence* or *guilt*. The Godhead, regarded as LOVE (*in the Son*), passes sentence upon mankind so far as to determine whether, beyond what is of mere debt, any ulterior merit can accrue to them. Here the verdict is WORTHY or UNWORTHY. Those he selects as his own, to whom such a supplementary good can be adjudged. The rest are sent empty away. The RIGHTEOUS judgment pronounced according to the utmost rigour of law (by the judge properly so termed—the Holy Ghost), affects those to whom no foreign merit has been imputed. The sentence here is GUILTY or NOT GUILTY, *i. e. condemnation or acquittal*. JUDGING signifies, in the former case, SEPARATING the deserving from the undeserving, who both strive for the prize of eternal bliss. By the term MERIT or DESERT, is not meant a *surplus of morality* supererogatory of what the law commands (for no accumulated discharge of duties can ever pass beyond what is of mere debt); all that is meant is, that when mankind are compared together, some are, by their moral sentiments, more deserving than others. WORTHINESS has, consequently, no more than a negative import, viz. not unworthy to receive a benefit from God's benignity. The Judge in his former capacity acts as Umpire betwixt *two persons or parties* contending for a prize; but in the second capacity, where he really does administer a judiciary function, the sentence is passed upon *one and the same individual*, tried at the bar of heaven and his own conscience, and is final either in favour of the prosecution or defence. Now, on the hypothesis that all mankind are laden with the guilt of sin, and that some of them are notwithstanding susceptible of an imputed desert, then we have a case, admitting a sentence from that Judge who is love; which failing, the suppliant's application is rejected as incompetent before this tribunal. Thus he falls into the .hands of Justice, where sentence of condemnation must inevitably follow. It is thus that, in my opinion, the following seemingly contrary passages may be reconciled: "*The Son will come again to judge the quick and the dead;*" whereas elsewhere we read, John, iii. 17, "*God sent not his Son into the world to condemn the world, but that the world through him might be saved;*" while both are likewise brought into harmony with what immediately follows (verse 18), "*He that believeth not on him is condemned already,*" viz. by that SPIRIT, of whom it is written, that he will reprove the world because of sin and of righteousness. The anxious solicitude with which such distinctions are made in the fields of pure reason, in whose behalf alone they are here instituted, may seem to some

(which would import a difference of entities, whereas the object is but one and single), although they may do so in the name of that *ideal* which is revered and loved by God himself beyond everything; to come into moral union with which ideal is at once our wish and duty. This theorem of a threefold aspect of the divine nature is merely a Classical Formula in Faith Ecclesiastical, serving as a criterion whereby to distinguish one given Church-Creed from other forms of belief derived from different historic sources. Few men are able to frame to themselves a just and definite conception of the meaning and import of this formula (for it lies open to many a misapprehension); and its investigation would seem rather to devolve on those Teachers who, as philosophical or learned expounders of Holy Writ, endeavour to settle the boundary and line of demarcation obtaining betwixt their respective faculties, in order to arrive at a mutual good understanding touching its true import and intendment. In these ancient formulae some things are past the range of ordinary comprehension, and are no longer adapted to the necessities of the present time: while an empty belief in their letter tends rather to corrupt than better a cast of thinking truly religious.

Book IV.

OF RELIGION AND PRIESTDOM.

EXORDIUM.

THE Good Principle's sovereignty has then begun, and the advent of the kingdom of God is at hand, whenever the principles of its constitution have been set *publicly* abroach; for, in the *world intelligential*, that has already come, whereof the efficient causes have generally taken root, although their full development as phenomena in the *world sensible* may yet be infinitely remote. We saw, in the former book, that to become members of an ethical society, was a duty of its own kind (*officium sui generis*). It likewise appeared, that, although when each individual executed his own private duty, and an *accidental association* of some men in good might then arise, without any special ecclesiastic institution; still the universal concurrence of all mankind could not be expected, unless the erection and spreading of AN ETHICAL

---

useless and irksome subtilty; and so indeed would it be, were they intended for any analysis or inquiry into the Divine Nature. But since mankind are always prone, in matters of religion, to appeal, on account of their transgressions, to the divine benignity, and yet perceive that his justice cannot be baffled or circumvented, they frame to themselves the notion of a benignant judge. Again, since this notion of a benignant judge is a contradiction, it is quite obvious that the opinions commonly current respecting this practical concernment of humanity must be extremely fluctuating and incoherent; wherefore, to correct and accurately define them, must be of the last possible moment and practical importance.

COMMONWEAL were systematically gone about as a particular work; where, combined under moral laws, the conjunct force and virtue of our species is brought to bear against the invasions of the evil principle,—apart from which joint collectedness of opposition, mankind even do, by mutually tempting one another, render themselves the ready tools and instruments of their inward enemy. This ethic state, as A KINGDOM OF GOD, could only be founded on RELIGION. Religion, again, could subsist publicly (which publicity is of the very essence of every commonwealth) only when the moral community framed itself into the sensible shape of a CHURCH: to institute which church, was consequently represented as a duty incumbent upon our race, and as one that, although handed over to our own convenience, could most justly be imperatively demanded from us.

But then, to found or set a church agoing, so far forth as it is a commonwealth regulated upon Laws of Religion, is a proposal that would seem to require more wisdom, depth of insight, and morality of intention, than is either to be met with or expected among our race, especially when it is considered, that the very morality aimed at, in such an institution, would seem to be of necessity presupposed as already extant in those who are to become its members. In effect, it is not a little incongruous to say, that MEN ought to FOUND a kingdom of God—(as were they about to found the dynasty of an earthly potentate)—God himself must be the author and founder of his own kingdom. But, since we do not know what is immediately done by the Almighty, in order to exhibit, in the way of real fact and event, the idea of his kingdom, wherein to become subjects and citizens, we find within a moral call and destination, and are fully cognizant and aware of that only which it behoves us to do, in order to render ourselves thereof the fit members, it results that this idea —be it current, whether by Reason or by the Scripture— must serve as the pattern of our combination ecclesiastical: where, no doubt, should the latter alternative be received, God himself is the Founder and Originator of the CONSTITUTION: we, mankind, however, as the free denizens and called representatives of the state, are, under any circumstances, authors of its ORGANIZATION. Those, again, who manage the public interests of the society, conformably to that its organized framework, do, as *ministers* of the church, compose the ADMINISTRATION: the rest of the ethic confederation, who are merely subject to the laws of the federal league, constitute the CONGREGATION.

A public religious belief, consisting singly of the pure religion of reason, admits nothing more than the bare idea of a church (viz. *invisible*): the visible church, founded upon tradition, alone it is, that can require or receive any organization from man. The worship under the dominion of the good principle, in the church invisible, cannot be regarded as a *church-service;* and the pure *a priori* religion has no installed *ministers* as the OFFICIALS of an ethical commonwealth,—each member receiving immediately for himself the behest of the Supreme Lawgiver. Again, since we are at all times in the service of God when we unremittingly discharge all our duties (fitly regarded as imposed upon us by Divine Commandment), it follows that PURE RATIONAL RELIGION has for its MINISTERS every honest-minded person, though not OFFICIALLY; upon which latter account, they cannot be deemed the officiating servants of a church (viz. of one visible, touching which alone question is here made). Furthermore, since any church rising upon statutable laws can only designate itself the true church, so far forth as it contains within, the germ of a principle inducing it perpetually to approach the creed taught by pure reason (this latter belief, being that in any other, alone constituting thereof, the practical religion), and in due course of time finally to depart from faith ecclesiastical; we may hold that the TRUE SERVICE (*cultus*) of the church, upreared upon such laws and officers, will consist herein, that its ministers shall so adjust their doctrines and ritual as to endeavour to bring about that last end, viz. the dispensing with faith historical, as superfluous, and resolving it into the pure faith intelligential, now at length become generally public. Should, on the contrary, the ecclesiastic officers of a church not only entirely overlook this end, but even denounce the principle of aiming and aspiring after it, as damnable, declaring, on the contrary, the historical and statutory part of the church creed to be the alone saving, then would they, with all justice, be accused of supporting A SPURIOUS SERVICE, in the ethical republic, combined under the government of the good principle. By a spurious service (*false worship*), is understood that delusion, whereby such actions are proffered to another, as, instead of forwarding, actually frustrate his views. In a commonwealth, this perversion takes place when what is only a mean toward satisfying the Will of a Superior, displaces, and is thrust into the room of, that which makes us AT ONCE AND DIRECTLY his acceptable servants—a delusion whereby the ends of the government are defeated.

APOTOME I.

OF THE RELIGIOUS WORSHIP OF THE DEITY.

RELIGION, subjectively considered, is the acknowledgment and recognition of all our duties AS IF THEY WERE divine commandments.[59]

---

[59] This definition serves as a guard against erroneous significations, sometimes put upon the word RELIGION: *First*, Touching what we therein theoretically profess to acknowledge, nothing whatever is asserted, not even the existence of God. In fact, our insight into supersensible matters is so scanty, that confidently to assert such a position, might in many cases be little short of hypocrisy. Our definition contains nothing more

When I must first of all be told that any given edict is a divine commandment, before I can recognise and acknowledge it to be my duty; then is such religious behest REVEALED, or, at least, one standing in need of a revelation to authenticate it. On the contrary, that religion where I first know what are the incumbent offices of humanity, and then, upon that account alone, admit them to be divine behests, is the religion of nature. Whoso declares Natural Religion alone to be morally indispensable, *i. e.* duty, is a RATIONALIST (in matters of faith). Does he, moreover, deny the actuality of any preternatural divine revelation, then he is a NATURALIST. Should he, however, admit a revelation as possible, but contend that an acquaintance with, and acceptance of, it as real, are no necessary constituent elements of religion, then might he be appropriately called A PURE RATIONALIST. But were lie to maintain that a belief in such revelation constituted a necessary part of religion universal, then ought he to be styled A PURE SUPERNATURAL IST in affairs of faith.

Rationalists must, by their very assumption of such a name, confine themselves within the bounds of all human insight. Hence they cannot dogmatize as do the naturalists, nor dispute either the internal possibility of a revelation generally, nor yet the necessity of a revelation regarded as a divine mean toward the introduction of true

---

than that plausible hypothesis problematically assumed by our understanding when speculating upon the probable first cause of all things, which hypothesis, however, with respect to that chief end whitherward our legislative reason directs our aim, becomes a free, assertive, practical belief, promising the realization of that ultimate object. This practical faith demands no more than THE IDEA OF A GOD,—a conception upon which every morally serious mind must inevitably impinge; but without pretending that it can, by any theoretic speculation, ascertain that any objective reality corresponds to this idea. For such an end as can be represented as imperative upon all mankind, even the MINIMUM of information ought to be subjectively sufficient, *i. e.* the possibility that there may be a God, is enough. *Second*, By this definition of religion *in genere*, we guard against the equally erroneous conception, that by religion is meant an aggregate of certain fixed duties to be rendered toward God, and thus enter our *caveat* against the imagination that there are offices of divine worship, which last, however, are not unfrequently supposed, and that, too, of such efficiency, as to supply what is wanting in our discharge of the everyday offices of humanity. In the true Catholic religion there are no special duties toward God, for God can receive nothing from us, and we cannot act upon him, nor yet for him. Were the awe owed him to be called such a specially incumbent and indebted feeling, then what is overlooked in this assertion is, that this mood or frame of the sensory is not any particular religious act, but is that religious and reverential cast of mind that ought to pervade the observance of every duty. The saying, "*God ought to be obeyed rather than man,*" merely implies, that when any human law collides with duty, the former must give place to the latter. But were this maxim to be so interpreted as to make points of obedience, where God not man is to be obeyed, those commandments which a church gives out as laws of God, then would such a dictum scarcely differ from the notorious *church-in-danger* outcry, by which hypocritical and despotic churchmen usually excite the subject to seditious outbreaks against his government. Allowed actions, when commanded by the civil magistrate, become by his ordinance UNDOUBTED duties. But that any *licit* action has been enjoined by God in a special revelation, is in the highest degree *uncertain*.

religion. Upon these points, no one can by any ransacking of his understanding expect to expiscate anything. The controversy must therefore turn on the conflicting positions of the pure rationalists and supernaturalists, and will affect those particulars deemed by the one party necessarily pertaining to the true and alone religion, but held by the other accidental concomitants of a doctrine, complete and sufficient to all moral and religious ends without them.

From the first origin and inward ground of the possibility of RELIGION—giving birth to its division into natural and revealed—we may totally abstract; and consider that its property singly, whereby it is fitted for public outward communication. Contemplated under this light, Religion is either NATURAL—whereof, once extant, every one can become convinced by his own reason—or else a LEARNED religion, whereof we can convince others exclusively by learning, in and by which last they must be led. This distinction is of extreme importance; for, from the bare original of a religion, nothing whatever can be inferred as to its fitness or unfitness for being the universal religion of our race; although such, an inference can very easily be drawn from the characteristic of its being communicable only locally and partially, or communicable universally, which latter property is of the very essence of a religion obligatory upon all mankind.

Agreeably to what has just been laid down, although a religion be natural, it may notwithstanding have moreover been revealed, always provided the revelation exhibit nothing that mankind COULD not, and indeed SHOULD not, have arrived at by the natural exercise of his own powers, although very possibly he MIGHT not so soon and in such wide extent have attained this knowledge. To promulgate religion, by a revelation locally and specially given at a certain time, may consequently have been a wise and salutary measure; and yet when the religion thus ushered in has fairly struck root and become publicly known, conviction of its truth is to be drawn from its own self-evidencing certainty in reason. A religion of this kind would OBJECTIVELY be natural, and only SUBJECTIVELY revealed; wherefore its appropriate style and title would be that of Natural Religion; for even if, in the sequel, it were to pass to oblivion that a preternatural promulgation of it had ever taken place, still would it not on that account lose one tittle of its certainty, its facility of comprehension, or motive force upon the mind. The very contrary holds true of that religion whose inner structure is such as to render it essentially revealed: were it not carefully preserved by accurate traditions, or entrusted to that guardian document—a sacred book—it would pass from the world, and must then from time to time be publicly renewed; or else, privately a continuous preternatural revelation must take place in each individual, since otherwise the faith could neither be spread nor kept alive.

Immanuel Kant

To a certain extent, however, every, even a revealed religion, must present the lineaments of a natural religion. It is only by force of reason that the idea *revelation* can be superadded in thought to that of *religion;* which last, being derived from the idea of our subjection to the Will of a MORAL lawgiver, is a pure rational conception. Hence, even revealed religions must be open to examination, first as *natural,* and, second, as *learned;* so as to enable us to test and discover what and how much from either source have concurred to make up their constitution.

Now that we are about to treat of revealed religion— at least of what is generally deemed a revelation—it may be advisable to select an instance proper for this purpose: we shall therefore take for our example a case such as we find it in the history of our globe: otherwise necessary illustrations must be invented; but then the possibility of such supposed occurrences might not be granted. The best course to pursue, will consequently be to take some book or other that has interspersed its story with moral doctrines allied to the notices of reason, and make this volume serve as a handle whereby to make more readily prehensile this our idea of revealed religion. Being one of the many books treating of godliness and virtue that have long obtained currency under the garb of a revelation, its dissection will clearly and lucidly set forth that most useful and needful process of extracting from its multiform details what is therein to be found of pure, and therefore rational religion universal. It must, however, well be noted, that this experiment does not in the least intromit with the occupation of those to whom the interpretation of the book, as a collection of positive revealed institutes, is entrusted; neither does it attack that exposition which by force of erudition they have drawn from the document. In truth, an essay in the following manner is rather advantageous than otherwise to the church; both revelation and philosophy having but one common end, viz. forwarding the culture of the moral good; only the philosopher proposes by the natural operation of each man's own understanding to bring him to that goal, reached ecclesiastically along the diverse, though not contrary, road of revelation. The book in question shall be THE NEW TESTAMENT, the fountain of faith Christian. Consistently with the plan just sketched, let us scrutinize the principles of Christianity, first, as *natural,* and then, second, as a *learned* religion.

SECTION I.

CHRISTIANITY AS NATURAL RELIGION.

Natural religion, consisting as it does of two parts, FIRST, *morals* (based upon the freedom of the human will), taken, however, SECONDLY, in connection with *ideas,* by pre-supposing or assuming the reality whereof alone, can the last end of our ethic being be figured as attainable, viz. the idea of God as the moral author of the world: together with the representation of such a duration of our existence (*immortality*) as is congruous to such destination;—natural religion, thus understood, is, I say, a pure practical, and moreover rational conception, which, notwithstanding its incomputable ethical fertility, demands so scanty a grasp of speculative understanding, that every person may, to all practical intents and purposes, be amply certiorated of its truth; and the effects of this belief may be expected to tell upon the actual performance of our duty. This natural religion possesses undeniably the first requisite of a true church, viz. a qualification fitting it for universality, so far forth as, by this latter term, we understand that validity for every man (*universitas vel omnitudo distributiva*) which brings with it an absolute and exceptionless mutual understanding. To preserve and spread the religion of nature as a general cosmical religion, would, no doubt, require *Servants*, but not *Officers*, of the church invisible, *i. e.* Teachers, but not Dignitaries; seeing that, through the religion intelligential of each singular individual, no Church, *qua* general association (*omnitudo collectiva*), exists, nor is indeed even intended to be brought forth by that pure *a priori* idea. Again, since a common and jointly clear understanding in religious matters cannot maintain itself by its own self-regulating and perpetuating action; and, in fact, since general concord and uniformity in religion cannot be upheld and spread unless the church become visible, *i. e.* can be upheld only then when a collective or corporate body—consolidating the society of believers into a church visible, regulated upon the principles of pure religion intelligential—has been erected; and no such corporation can spontaneously arise from such bare parallelism and consent of views—nay, what says far more, since, even were a corporate society of this sort once set agoing, still (as was seen above) it could not be brought into a condition of permanency as a standing congregation of the faithful. Since, I say, all this is the case, it is perfectly manifest that, unless above and beyond the natural laws cognizable by naked reason, there be superadded sundry statutable authoritative edicts, something will be still awanting requisite to bring about a permanent and abiding union of mankind in a visible church universal; which union we represented in the former book as a peculiar duty, *sui generis*, and a mean toward attaining the highest and last ends of our moral destination. This super added authority can only flow from the Founder of an Ecclesiastical Polity; and here we must needs impinge upon a FACT, over and above the naked idea of pure reason.

Although it were conceded, that once upon a time there had appeared a teacher, of whom history—or at least a current opinion not satisfactorily overthrown—relates that he promulgated a universally comprehensible and penetrating religion; yet, so far as the fragments of his tenets have been handed down to us, we are quite in a condition to judge for ourselves of the spirit of his doctrines, and can hence more readily assent to what is asserted of him—viz. that he first openly insisted on this moral faith, and that, too, in despite of the dominant church-creed, which was irksome, devoid of every moral content, and consisting in a merely mercenary and servile ritual (which, by the way, may serve extremely well as a specimen illustrative of all other, in the main, merely statutable beliefs—different varieties whereof filled up, at that time, the whole known and civilized parts of the earth);—all this, I say, being conceded, then, although to his moral religion universal, which he represented as the necessary groundwork, and insisted on, as the supreme and irregressible condition, of every other form and sort of religious faith whatsoever—he went on to affix one or two injunctions, containing forms and observances; still, because those last were intended merely as rivets, to keep and fasten together the church, grounded on the aforesaid principles, we cannot dispute nor deny the claims of this his institution to be the true catholic church, nor yet his own claim to carry off the high prize of having then first summoned his fellow-men to rally and combine under its standards, notwithstanding the contingency and arbitrariness of those appended ordinances; for it does not appear that he intended *these* to be amalgamated with the faith, nor that the performance of that slender ceremonial was to be mistaken for a holy act, in itself obligatory, and a constituent element of religion.

The description just given can leave no one in doubt as to the person fitly venerated as the FOUNDER, not by any means of that untraditional RELIGION primordially insculpted on the hearts of all, but as the founder of the first true CHURCH based thereon. In attestation of the dignity of his divine mission, we will cite a few of his sayings, containing passages that undoubtedly authenticate themselves as parts of religion *in genere*. Be it then with the narrative as it may, the ideas do, in themselves, afford ground enough to render them worthy of all acceptation, being in truth decrees of pure reason; and these are they alone, that not only prove themselves, but even lend part of their evidence to accredit the foreign doctrines in whose company they appear.

First, he contends that no observance of statutable church-duties, but only a pure, honest, moral mind, can make mankind acceptable to God (*Matth*. v. 20-48); that transgressions by thought are deemed by God equal to those perpetrated in deed (v. 28); *e. g.* that inwardly to hate is tantamount to murder (v. 22); and that generally, upon the whole, holiness is the grand object toward which the end of every action should be directed (v. 48). Injuries inflicted by us on our neighbour can only be redressed by making *him* due reparation, but not by any ceremonial or ritual of temple or divine worship (v. 24). As for veracity, he teaches, that the common forensic instrument for extorting it—THE OATH[60]—derogates from the reverence due to truth itself (v. 34-37). We likewise read, that the naturally perverse bias of the human heart must be entirely retroverted,—the appetite for secret revenge give place to placability (v. 39, 40), and the hatred of our enemies make a transit to beneficence (v. 44). By such deeds as these he declares his intent of coming to fulfil the whole Jewish law (v. 17), where, however, he obviously must mean to make, not book-learning, but pure rational religion, interpreter of the code; since, taken to the letter, the Pentateuch allowed, and even ordained, the very contrary of most of the above.

By the difference obtaining betwixt the *strait gate* and the *broad way*, he next calls attention to that misconstruction of the law whereby the Jews allowed themselves to overlook real moral duties, and to fancy they compensated for such violations of integrity by a diligent observance of church-duty (vii. 13).[61]

The only admissible proof of pure morality within, are those good works which are its fruit (v. 16 and 20). He consequently cuts short the fraudulent hope of those who imagine they can make up for their want of good deeds by invocations and hosannahs of the Heavenly Lawgiver in the person of his Ambassador, and think by thus fawning and crouching to ingratiate themselves into the Sovereign's favour (v. 21). These good works ought farther to be so performed, that the observed motives whence they sprang, may induce others to glorify God in like manner (v. 16); and that too with a cheerful mind, not as actions sadly and servilely extorted (vi. 16). By the communication and interchange of morally re-acting sentiments and deeds, a commencement of religion

---

[60] It is difficult to account for the little attention paid to this plain prohibition directed against the usual forensic mode of extorting truth—a mode based entirely upon superstition, not upon conscientiousness. That superstition is what is here counted on, may be certainly inferred from this circumstance, that although we assume of a witness that he is not to be trusted when be solemnly affirms somewhat touching the rights of his fellow-men (the most sacred object that we mankind can deal with here below), we do nevertheless hold, that by the Formula of an Oath his statement becomes credible, although the oath does not differ in any respect from the solemn asseveration, except that he calls down upon himself the divine judgments (which, in any event, he cannot evade) if he swerve from truth, just as if it depended upon him to undergo or avoid the ethical vengeance impending over those who violate the rights of their neighbour. In the passage of scripture cited in the text, this practice of swearing is represented as an absurdity void of rhyme or reason, as if we attempted by uttering spells to bring to pass what lies beyond our power. But when the wise teacher says that a communication surpassing the simple YEA, YEA—NAY, NAY, cometh of evil, it is obvious that he calls our attention to the bad consequences arising from oaths, viz. that their imagined greater weight and importance almost seems to lend a sanction to common every-day dog-trot lying.

[61] The STRAIT GATE and narrow way leading unto life, is the path of good moral conduct. The WIDE GATE and broad way, trodden by the majority, is the church: not that the church or its traditions are the efficient causes why mankind are lost, but that the GOING IN thereat, together with confessing the articles of the creed, and celebrating its multiform rites, is mistaken for the mode in which God wills to be worshipped.

will be made, which, however small at first, will, like mustard seed scattered through a field, or leaven hid in meal, gradually swell by its own inward and augmenting power, till it attain the full size and growth of a kingdom of God (xiii. 31—33). Finally, he compendiously comprises all the offices of humanity, *first*, under a rule UNIVERSAL (embracing at once the inward and outward moral relationships of humanity), viz. discharge thy duty from no spring other than an immediate estimation of its worth, *i. e.* Love God (the ethical Legislator) above all; and, *secondly*, under a rule PARTICULAR, treating singly of the special outward relation obtaining betwixt man and man, viz. love thy neighbour as thyself, *i. e.* promote his wellbeing out of immediate unselfish benevolence. These two commandments are not merely laws of virtue, but behests of HOLINESS; our unremitted wrestling and struggling after which last, is what is properly called VIRTUE. They who, with shut eyes and folded hands, wait slothfully for the moral good as a gift to be passively received from above, are informed, that their expectation is no better than the dream of a sluggard. In like manner, whoso leaves uncultivated the original susceptibility of his moral nature toward good (*i. e.* suffers, as it were, his confided talent to rust), in the idle confidence that some higher moral power will supply his thereby begotten moral shortcomings and defects: him doth Christ threaten, that even that good which may nevertheless have sprouted from the original stock of his nature, will just, on account of that very neglect, stand him in no stead, but be deducted from his account (xxv. 29).

Touching the expectation naturally entertained by all men, of a happy lot proportioned to the deserts of their moral conduct (especially when worldly comforts have been renounced for the sake of duty), they are met with a promise (v. 11, 12) that a reward awaits them in a future world. This allotment varies according to the difference of motive, whereby each party's conduct has been actuated. Duty discharged for the sake of reward, and with the view of escaping punishment, is not so recompensed, as where the law has been honoured for its own sake. The Utilitarian, whom self-interest, the God of this world, governs; and who, without renouncing his solipsism, merely extends his selfish calculations beyond the circumscribed boundary of present time, is represented as such a steward (*Luke* xvi. 3-9) as makes that his Lord (*self-interest*) cheat and circumvent himself. For, on reflecting that he must speedily quit this world, and that he cannot take hence what he possessed below, he resolves to make a sacrifice of whatever sums he (or his master—utilitarianism) might legally have exacted from the indigent: for what the needy debtor is permitted to subtract from his account, bills, or acknowledgments of this fancied beneficence, payable in another world, are taken in return; a method of procedure rather CUNNING than MORAL, at least when regard is had to the inward spring of such seeming good-will. The beneficent act is, however, outwardly conformable to the law, and so allows him to hope that his refined and self-seeking charity may not go unrewarded.[62] Let this parable be compared with the one (*Matth.* xxv. 35-40) where the Sovereign Judge of the World declares those who help the needy, without so much as ever thinking that their services merit a reward, or bind heaven to recompense, to be the true elect of his kingdom; and, from this connected comparison, it will be amply obvious, that the Teacher of the Gospel, when speaking of rewards in a world to come, did not intend *them* to incline the will to action; but aimed only at making such soul-exalting representations of the consummated completion of the divine benignity and wisdom, an object of high moral and reverential complacency to that understanding which contemplates the last and chief destination of Agent-Intelligents.

Thus have we found in Christ's tenets a finished sketch and outline of a religion that can be brought home to the convictions and conceptions of every one; and that, by force of his own reason, the practicability whereof has been set forth by an example, making intuitive the possibility and necessity of adopting that ideal prototype as the standard of our manners. The truth of those doctrines, and the authority and dignity of their teacher, require no foreign confirmation, such as miracles or biblical lore, which are not within the reach of all. When appeals arc made to the legislation of an earlier age, and a secondary meaning given to the oracles of the Jewish sages, these arc not to be understood as if they were intended to bear witness to the truth of his doctrines. They are designed only for an introduction or vehicle, procuring them an inlet among people blindly attached to whatever was ancient. To convey truth to those whose heads arc besotted with the statute-articles of a creed, and consequently numb to the religion of reason, is always a far more difficult task than to impart instruction to understandings, which, though uninstructed, arc unbiassed and disengaged. Hence we need not be surprised if a mode of exposition, adapted to the prejudices of the day, should now seem enigmatically dark, and stand much in need of a cautious and elaborate exegesis, although a religion everywhere shines through, that demands no effort or learning to become alike intelligible and convincing.

---

[62] Of futurity we know nothing; and ought indeed to expect no farther information than suffices to assist us in the discharge of duty, or to explain to us our last and chief end. To this class belongs the hypothesis, that every good action done in this world will be met retributively with corresponding good results in another. Now, if this be so, then at the close of life, let a man be found ever so reprobate, still his vicious career ought not to deter him from doing at least ONE good action should it be in his power, as he may thereby hope, that in proportion to the honest-mindedness of his intention, this act will be of some more worth than those deedless penances and expiations, which, without deducting from his guilt, are supposed to compensate for the defects of one's morality.

SECTION II.

CHRISTIANITY AS A LEARNED RELIGION.

Religions that propound certain *credenda* as necessary, although these statute-articles of faith can by no means be recognised as such by reason, must be regarded as sacred goods entrusted to the guardianship of THE LEARNED, of the very essence of whose office it is continually to propel the uncorrupted faith through all present and future times; and apart from their unintermitted agency, it would be requisite to assume the standing miracle of a perpetual revelation: for, although the miraculous events by which it was AT FIRST ushered into the world, may have obtained for such a system a general and cordial reception, even in those its more questionable points, touching which reason is altogether silent; yet, IN THE SEQUEL, the very narrative of those events, and still more the peculiar doctrines founded on them, would need to be fortified by some written institute, affording to subsequent ages the guarantee of unchanging and official documents.

Adopting the principles of a religion is called FAITH, χατ' ἐζοχην (*fides sacra*), whence Christian faith will fall under investigation, partly as pure rational faith, and partly as revealed faith (*fides statutaria*). The former will appear, under the light of one freely and universally assented to (*fides elicita*); the latter, as one statutably ordained (*fides imperata*). Thus, that a germ of evil lies deeply rooted in the heart, from which perverse bias no man is free; that it is impossible to regard our actions as justifying us before God, and yet indispensable that we possess a righteousness valid in his sight, which no church rite or ceremonial can impart; likewise that it is an immediate and inexorable obligation to become better men: these I say—all these, are points patent to the scrutiny of each man's own reason, and it is an essential part of natural religion, that each individual satisfy and certiorate himself of their truth.

At that juncture, however, where the Christian doctrines rise not upon ideas of pure reason, but upon historic facts, there Christianity ceases to be called Christian RELIGION, and becomes Christian FAITH, serving for the ground-work of a church. Church-worship, founded upon such a bi-form belief, will of course present a twofold aspect, the one pourtraying the lineaments of the historic narrative, the other exhibiting the phase of the pure *a priori* ethical belief. Both are intimately blended in the Christian church, nor can either be regarded as subsisting apart: the former cannot be severed from the latter, inasmuch as the *Christian* faith is a *religious* faith, neither can the latter be detached from the former, because the *Christian* faith is furthermore a *learned* faith.

Christianity, considered as a LEARNED faith, rests upon history; wherefore, so far forth as erudition constitutes an element of its composition, it is not in itself A FREE BELIEF, spontaneously emerging from a rational and convincing insight, into any sufficiently established theoretic argumentation (*fides elicita*). Were Christianity nothing but a pure rational belief, then would it undoubtedly—although the moral laws whereon it as belief in a divine lawgiver is grounded command unconditionally—be necessarily regarded as a free belief, under which character, indeed, we treated of it in the former section. Nay, we may even go a great deal farther and say, that had not assent to it been enjoined upon mankind by some, as a duty, then would Christianity as a historical belief be furthermore a free theoretical faith—provided every one were learned. But are we to be told that it is imperatively binding upon every one, even the unlettered, then would it be not only a commanded faith, but also a blind and servile faith, obsequiously obedient to a commandment, although no previous investigation have been made as to whether this alleged commandment really contain a divine behest (*fides servilis*).

Christianity, considered as a revelation, cannot possibly commence with an UNCONDITIONED ASSENT to occult doctrines, said to be communications from on high, and then call in the aid of literature and history to ward off enemies who skirmish on the rear of the revealed truths; for in this case, too, would the Christian faith be not merely *fides imperata;* but, moreover, and in very deed, *fides servilis*. Consequently, it must at all times be taught and propounded as *fides historicé elicita; i. e.* erudition and moral science must lead forward the van, not skulk as the rear-guard of the Christian revealed faith. Were this system of ethical tactics inverted, then would the order of the clergy—(*the Biblical Literati*)—albeit they cannot dispense with profane learning, bring after them the long train of unlearned laics, in which illiterate company, even the Head of the State may at times be seen to figure. Are we intent that this shall not take place, then must historical erudition retire to the second place, and reason and natural religion be recognised and honoured as the supreme dominant principle in Christianity; while those revealed tenets upon which the church rises, and that have learning for their interpreter and preserver, may very well be cherished and cultivated as a highly valuable mean: but still no more than a mere mean, for assisting the propulsion and permanency of the former, and at the same time bringing its doctrines to the smoother level of general comprehension.

This is the true church-service under the dominion of the Good Principle; but when the matter is reversed, and revelation placed before religion, then is the church-service a false and spurious worship; that which is merely a mean, being insisted on absolutely, as were IT in itself the end. Belief in tenets, whereof the uninstructed can know nothing either from WRIT or REASON (the writings standing in need of erudite authentication), is now represented as an unconditioned and immediate duty (*fides imperata*); and, together with a suite of concomitant observances, a mercenary upstart worship is elevated, though its services are void of moral springs, to the rank of the alone justifying and saving faith. A church established upon such statute-articles of belief does not contain ministers, for they arc exclusively peculiar to the other, but high ecclesiastic officers. True, they may not, as in some Protestant churches, shine in the splendour of hierarchs, and appear arrayed with the trappings of external power; nay, they may even in words protest loudly against such abuses they arc notwithstanding ECCLESIASTICKS, who wish to beholden the sole fit interpreters of Holy Writ: pure moral religion having previously been stripped of its dignity and robbed of its title to sit in inappellable judgment on the import and intendment of revelation; while Scripture-learning is thrust into its room, and ordained to make all usurpations tell in favour of the Church-Creed. Thus is the service (*ministerium*) of the Church turned into a lording (*imperium*) it over the flock, although, to conceal the usurpation and encroachment, the former style is sedulously retained. But this sway, easy had it been administered by Reason, becomes extremely costly, and lavishes the resources of much book-learning. For, ignorant of human nature and the sciences, divines have pulled antiquity about their ears, and lie now nearly smothered beneath its rubbish. The course of matters once brought to this pass has been, and is, as follows:

The interpretations of the ancient legends, wisely suggested by the first preachers of Christianity as a stratagem for weaning their countrymen from inveterate prejudices, were subsequently declared integrant elements of religion; so much so, that one would almost be led to suppose *each Christian was first of all a Jew whose Messiah had appeared;* a hypothesis, however, standing in open contradiction with the fact, that Christians are expressly absolved from every law of Judaism, although they receive the Sacred Writings of this people as divinely inspired, and as containing the narrative of matters in which the whole world are concerned.[63] And yet the authenticity of the Books

---

[63] Mendelsohn has dexterously availed himself of this weak side of the common view of Christianity, to repel all proposals made to any descend, ant of Israel for abandoning the faith of his forefathers. Why, says he, agreeably to your own showing, Judaism is the ground-floor above which Christianity is erected; wherefore to leave it is pretty much the same as if one were to pull down his sunk stories in order to sit more commodiously in the attic. His real meaning is tolerably transparent. What he suggests is this: "Do ye first purge your religion of its Jewish leaven, and then we will deliberate upon the nature of your proposal." (In truth, were Christianity thus clarified, a pure unmixed moral religion would remain.) "Our yoke is not lightened by exchanging a cumbrous ritual for a professed faith in sacred traditions, which last hamper conscience far more grievously."

is loaded with many difficulties. Previous to the advent of Christianity, the Jewish records were unknown to the literary world. Hence we have no check upon their accuracy, nor corroborative testimony to their historic truth. Again, even were all those doubts waived, still it is not enough to become acquainted with the text in vernacular translations. The Church-Creed founded on such a volume can only be guarded by learned watchmen, thoroughly versant in the Hebrew tongue (if indeed such knowledge be attainable of a language where only one volume remains extant), and this preservation of the text affects to be regarded not merely as an inquiry in the fields of antiquarian research, but as an investigation of such moment as to be inseparably connected with the salvation of our race; wherefore there must, at all times and in all nations, be a body of men sufficiently read in oriental letters to guarantee to the world what is to pass current as the true religion.

Similarly defective are the evidences of the Christian religion; the sacred events are no doubt reported to have occurred before the very eyes of a learned nation, and yet one generation passed away before the alleged facts were put in possession of the literati of the day; the consequence is, that the credit of the narrative is unsupported and unconfirmed by the concurrent evidence of any contemporary witnesses. Christianity, however, possesses one signal advantage over Judaism; it was promulgated from the lips of its great Author, not as a statutable, but as a moral religion. Hence it goes hand in hand with pure Reason, and can be introduced by it, quite apart from any historic learning, and can be presented on the strength of its own self-evidence to every nation, even to the remotest times. Howbeit the founders of the early CONGREGATIONS found it advisable to weld up therewith the Jewish history; and this amalgam, probably prudent, or even necessary in their day, has been handed down to us along with other sacred RELIQUES. Those who subsequently combined the congregations into one catholic CHURCH mistook this introductory and recommendatory vehicle for an essential article of belief. They next connected it with traditions or expositions, to which Councils gave the force of law. Thus was a Church-Creed fabricated; now hermeneutically treated, either by LEARNING, or by this last's antagonist—THE INWARD LIGHT. These put various constructions on the meaning; and as every layman can provide himself with the magic lantern above mentioned, it is impossible to foresee what changes of configuration may still await the forms of faith ecclesiastical, a thing indeed quite inevitable, so long as we seek the well-springs of religion not within but without us.

The sacred books of this race will always be highly prized and studied by the learned, but not for the sake of their religion. No history ascends with even a semblance of credibility to such remote epochs of pristine time as the Jewish, dating, as it does, downwards even from the beginning of the world. The enormous gap left by the profane writers must necessarily be filled up by something.

APOTOME II.

OF THE SUPERSTITIOUS WORSHIP OF GOD IN A STATUTABLE RELIGION.

The true and alone Religion contains nothing but LAWS, *i. e.* practical principles, whose unconditional necessity we are conscious of, and which therefore we recognise by Reason; not *a posteriori* as revealed. Only for the behoof of a church (whereof there may be various *forms*, all alike good) can there be STATUTES, *i. e.* alleged divine commandments, which are in the eye of ethical judgment arbitrary and contingent. This statutable faith (confined to one particular race, and incapable of being represented as the catholic religion of our globe), when deemed essential to the worship of God, and made the supreme condition of the divine complacency, is a main delusion[64] in religion, and the acting upon it a superstitious worship, by which, in fact, the true real service demanded from us by God is counteracted.

SECTION I.

OF THE SUBJECTIVE GROUND OF A DELUSION IN RELIGION.

Anthropomorphism can hardly be avoided by man, and is, so long as it does not influence his ideas of duty, quite harmless, for then it affects only our theoretic mode of figuring to ourselves God and his essence. But when anthropomorphous fancies begin to vitiate our notions of the practical relation obtaining betwixt us and God's holy will, it then threatens to become highly dangerous to our morality, in as much as we frame to ourselves such a God[65] as is most easily won over

---

[64] DELUSION (imagination, whimsey, conceit, or fancy,—*Germanice*, WAHN, TR.) is that deception whereby a man regards the representation of a thing as equivalent to the thing itself. Thus the miser is blinded and befooled by the avaricious imagination, viz. to hold the representation that he can use his treasures when he pleases, as an equivalent and indemnity for his never doing so. Fantastic imaginary honour places in the praises of others, which at bottom are no more than the outward representation of an esteem (perhaps not at all inwardly felt), a worth attaching only to that esteem itself. It is upon this fancy that the thirst for titles, stars, and garters arises, these last being no more than the outward representations of excellence. Even the whimsical are only so called, and held crazed, because they are in the custom of pursuing empty whims, as had they real objects corresponding to them, *i. e.* of so acting as if they mistook representations for realities. Now, the consciousness of possessing means, to an end is prior to actual use of them, the possession of that end only in a representation: consequently, to content one's self with the latter, as if it could stand in room of the former, is a practical delusion or craze (WAHN); which latter sort of whimsey is what we are about to treat of.

[65] Doubtless it sounds odd to say that we frame to ourselves our God: the expression is, notwithstanding, perfectly correct. In truth, every person must, according to his moral

to our advantage, and imagine that we may dispense with the arduous unremitting exertion to advance the inward intensity of our moral sentiments. The position usually laid down by mankind touching this practical relation is (supposing that the assumed position does not militate against morality, but merely tends in nowise toward it), that what we do with a view to please God, exhibits our readiness to serve him, as obedient, and so his acceptable servants,—by all which God is *in potentia* served. It is not always by sacrifice that mankind fancies he can accomplish and discharge this worship: solemnities, games, as at Greece and Rome, were often resorted to for this purpose. They are, indeed, in some places, still resorted to, to propitiate the Godhead. However, the first kind (penances, formal castigations, pilgrimages, &c.) has usually been held the more powerful to gain the favour of Heaven, and to expurge sin, because they shew forth the more unbounded though not ethical subjection to God's will. The more senseless such self-castigations obviously are, and the less they point at the moral amelioration of the man, so much the more sanctity do they seem to have; which they do, upon this reason, that, since they are useless, and cost merely trouble, therefore their whole end can be singly to shew devotedness to God; for, say they, although in all this God is in no wise served, yet he sees a good will, and regards chiefly the heart, which is too weak to keep his commandments; but which docs, by its willingness shewn in this manner, make up for its defects. This discloses a proneness to a procedure which has in itself no moral worth, except as a mean to exalt the sensory, so as to accompany the intellectual idea of the end, or perhaps to depress the sensory should the ideas re-act against it.[66] This artifice of stirring or compelling our

---

notions, such as they are, figure to himself a Supreme Illimitable Moral Agent, able to bend and control the course of the physical system, so as to make it harmonize with moral ends, and whom he then learns to revere as his Creator. No matter how others may have described God, each individual must first compare this description with his own idea, in order to see if the Being represented, be fit to be acknowledged and worshipped as a Deity. Even were God himself to appear (supposing such a manifestation possible), the same test would still require to be applied. Wherefore, bare revelation, when not based upon that idea previously laid down, could not furnish us with a religion, and, whatever worship it might give rise to, could only be IDOLATRY.

[66] For the sake of those who, not being quite at home in the distinctions betwixt the sensible and intelligential, think they constantly impinge upon contradictions in my writings, I here remark, that, when I talk of sensible means forwarding the intellectual growth of good, or of hindrances thrown by sense in the way of our morality, the action of those heterogeneous principles on one another must never be figured to be *direct*. As sentient beings, we so know and judge of the phenomena of reason's supersensible causality, *i. e.* the determinations of our physical powers by free voluntary choice, as if cause and effect were perfectly homogeneous. As intelligents, again, the subjective principle of morality within, must be placed in that unfathomable property of our nature, freedom. Of this last we know only the regulating law; and its connection with visible effects is quite beyond our insight. Consequently we cannot EXPLAIN those physical events which are imputable to us as our deeds from that ethic peculiarity of our nature.

sentient framework, in order toward a certain end, becomes a procedure that is made to stand in room of the end itself; or, which amounts to the same thing, we attach to a frame of mind which has susceptibility for sentiments of godliness (*called Devotion*), the worth of that last itself; all which procedure is just a fancied delusion in religion, that may assume all kinds of forms, in some of which the delusive imagination may have a more ethical aspect than in others, and yet is, throughout the whole of them, not a mere inadvertency, but a fixed maxim, to ascribe to the means the worth of the end,—a perverse imagination equally absurd in all those forms, and objectionable as a latent bias to self-deception.

SECTION II.

OF THE MORAL PRINCIPLE WHICH REASON OPPOSES TO ALL DELUSIONS IN RELIGION.

I lay down the following preliminary position, as one requiring no proof. EVERYTHING MANKIND FANCIES HE CAN DO, OVER AND ABOVE GOOD MORAL CONDUCT, IN ORDER TO MAKE HIMSELF ACCEPTABLE TO GOD, IS MERE FALSE WORSHIP OF THE DEITY. I say, whatever man fancies he can do; for that something, beyond all our exertions, may lie in the mysteries of supreme wisdom, possible to be performed by God alone, and making us acceptable in his sight, is not denied by me. But even if the church were to promulgate, *as revealed*, any such mystery, still the opinion, that to believe in this revelation, as taught in the sacred volume, and to confess, whether inwardly or outwardly, such belief, were in itself anything rendering us acceptable to God, would be a dangerous delusion in religion. For *this belief*, considered as the inward self-confession of one's stedfast conviction, is so certainly AN ACT, extorted by fear, that an honest upright man would rather accept any other condition; because all outward ceremonial worship mankind need only regard as something supererogatory to be gone through; whereas here he violates his conscience, by declaring in its presence what he is not convinced of. The confession, therefore, with regard to which, he persuades himself, that it (*as the acceptance of a proffered boon*) will make him acceptable to God, is something lie imagines he can do, in addition to the moral conduct that the law ordains him to execute in the world, and which is done for the worship of God singly.

FIRST.—Reason does not leave us without consolation with respect to the want of our own righteousness. Reason says, that he who exerts his whole powers in the discharge of duty, so as constantly to

---

The full *rationale* of all occurrences must at all times be sought for in the sensible system.

approximate toward the law, may hope, that what lies beyond his power will be supplied by the Supreme Wisdom in some way, without pretending to investigate what that mode may be; which may be so mysterious that God can perhaps only show it forth in a symbolical representation, the practical part of which may alone be intelligible to us; whilst the theoretic relation subsisting betwixt God and man may be such, that we could connect no notions therewith, even were such a mystery thoroughly divulged. Suppose, now, a particular church were to undertake to say, that it knew the exact mode how God would supply man's moral defectibility, and were to consign all men ignorant of this foreign principle of justification (a principle indiscernible and unconfessed by reason) to eternal reprobation, who, I ask, were, in such event, the unbeliever? He who trusts, without knowing how, that what he hopes for, will be effected; or he who insists upon knowing, wherein lies this redemption from evil, and without this, despairs of it?—Properly speaking, the latter is at bottom not intent on knowing the mystery (for even *his* reason tells him, that it is altogether profitless to be instructed in what lies far beyond his ken, and his practical ability to reach). He insists on an acquaintance with it, mainly that he may make out of its belief a worship, in the acceptance, confession, and lauding, of all this revelation; which worship is to procure him the favour of Heaven, prior to any use of his own exertions toward a moral life. Possibly this worship may even aim at preternaturally producing an amendment of his inner man, or otherwise, when this latter project fails, make up and compensate for all his violations.

SECOND.—If mankind depart in the least from the above preliminary ethic principle, then superstition has NO LIMITS; the ancient boundary and landmarks of pure reason disappear: and everything superadded besides and beyond, is quite optional and arbitrary (always, however, with this single *proviso*, that it contradict not morality). From the sacrifice of a man's lips, which costs him little, up to the sacrifice of his estate, which might be better bestowed to the use of his fellow-men,—nay, even to the offering up of his own person, as in the Hermit, Fakir, or Monk's caste, where the man is lost to the world; everything is presented to the Deity, only not the man's moral sentiments; and when he says he gives God his heart, he does not mean the sentiments of a walk and conversation acceptable to God, but his hearty wish, that these offerings may be accepted in lieu of the alone ethic acceptable service. (*Natio gratis anhelans, multa agendo, nihil agens.*— PHÆDRUS.)

LASTLY.—Whenever mankind has made a transit to the maxim of a supposed worship, which may be in itself acceptable, or, if need be, propitiatory, in the sight of God (the worship supposed not being purely moral), then is there no essential difference in this kind of mechanic service which could give one sort of it a preference over any other; they all are alike worth, or rather worthless. 'Tis but the fantastic manners of the exquisitely fastidious, when the bigot deems himself more select or choice—by virtue of a more refined and studied apostacy from the alone and single intellectual worship of the Deity,—than they who fall into the more coarse and crass apostasy of sense. Whether the devotee take his statutable walk to Church, to Loretto, or to Palestine; whether he pronounce his forms of prayer by the lip,—inscribe them upon flags to be unfurled, and thence wafted by the winds,—fire them from a blunderbuss,—or, like the untutored Thibetese, whirl them heavenwards from a wheel; or, indeed, whatever the surrogatum of the ethic worship of God be, is quite immaterial, and rested on the same groundless flams. Nothing depends upon the difference of the outward ceremonial, but all upon adhering to the only principle of becoming acceptable to God by moral sentiments, so far as these can be made exhibitive in actions, their phenomena, or else abandoning that principle, and then attempting to please him by pious drivelling and doing nothing.[67]—Is there not, then, some one may ask, a giddy virtuous delusion, exaggerating itself beyond all limits of man's power, that ought, together with the delusion in religion, to be ranked among the class of self-deceptions? No! virtue occupies itself with something real, that is in itself acceptable to God, and in harmony with the general welfare of the whole world. True! no doubt a self-conceited fancy may sometimes accompany it, when any one fondly imagines himself adequate to the idea of his holy duty. But this is only an accident. To attach supreme worth to virtue is no delusion: which it is, to church-ceremonials.

Again, it is customary—especially for the church—to call what can be done by one's own virtuous exertions NATURE; that, on the contrary, which supplies the want of our ethic strength, GRACE (a sufficiency which, since we ought to possess it, can only be wished, or hoped for, or supplicated); whilst both together are regarded as the efficient causes, productive of a sentiment that brings forth a course of life acceptable to God: but then these two are not only contradistinguished; they are not unfrequently opposed to one another.

The imagination that a man can distinguish and separate effects of grace from those of nature, or still more, that lie can beget the former within himself, is FANATICISM; for we cannot recognise a supersensible

---

[67] Here we may note a psychological phenomenon: Those who attach themselves to a confession in which there are but few articles to be believed, feel themselves thereby ennobled, when comparing themselves with others whose creed deals more extensively with details. The reason doubtless is, that they perceive themselves somewhat nearer pure moral religion, although they may have been unable to shake themselves entirely free from the imagination that this religion requires to be propped up by pious rites,—a circumstance that, were it a little more pondered, might prevent Protestants from looking down upon their Catholic brethren as they do.

object by any criterion, much less exert any influence upon it, so as to draw it down to us, although unquestionably there are sometimes emotions in the mind tending to morality, which we cannot explain to ourselves nor account for, and with regard to which our ignorance must confess that *"the wind bloweth where it listeth, but that we know not,"* &c. To pretend to detect celestial influences within, is a kind of phrenzy, in which there may be method (because these imagined inward revelations arc attached to ethical ideas, *i. e.* go hand in hand with representations of pure reason), but which must notwithstanding be reprobated as a self-deception hurtful to religion. To believe that there may be effects of grace—nay, that there must perhaps be such, in order to eke out the shortcoming of our imperfect ethical exertions, is all that can be said about the matter. We are, however, utterly unable to ascertain anything whatever touching their criteria, and still less to co-operate toward their production.

The imagination that we can by religious rites accomplish anything touching our forensic justification in the sight of God, constitutes RELIGIOUS SUPERSTITION; while, again, the imagination that this justification can be achieved by establishing a hidden intercourse and communion with God, constitutes RELIGIOUS FANATICISM. It is a superstitious delusion to suppose we can become accepted with the Almighty by performing actions that any one may do, without thereby becoming morally good. And the rehearsal of statutable creeds, the observance of rituals of form and show, &c. &c. are denominated superstitions, because physical not ethical means are adopted to effect what stands (viz. *the moral good*) in no connection with the physical system. Farther, a delusion is fanatical, when the mean had recourse to, is neither physical nor ethical, but supersensible, *i. e.* quite above and beyond the power of man, to say nothing of the unattainableness of an end, extant only in the realms of the supra-sensible; for this sense of an immediate presence of the Deity, and the distinguishing betwixt such sense and every other, even the moral sense, would import a susceptibility for intuitions, man's nature is unfitted for. The superstitious delusion contains *a mean*, fitted in many cases for counteracting the impediments opposed by the sensory to sentiments acceptable to God, and is consequently to that extent, allied and akin to reason, and only objectionable from this accidental circumstance, that what is but a mean, is regarded as the immediate object of God's complacency. Howbeit the fanatical delusion is the death of moral reason, apart from which last, neither religion nor morality, both which rest on principles, can be supported.

The Principle latent in Faith Ecclesiastical, guarding, preventing, and eventually extirpating all delusions in religion, is therefore this, viz. that over and above the statute-articles of creed, which the Church-Faith cannot as yet dispense with, this last must contain an inwrapt germ, whereby it is continually urged to forth-form itself into the pure religion of a moral life, which proper and last end once gained—every other religion may thenceforward be discarded.

SECTION III.

OF PRIESTDOM,[68] *i. e.* SACERDOTAL DESPOTISM: AN ORDER OF THINGS BASED UPON THE FALSE WORSHIP OF THE GOOD PRINCIPLE.

The worship of mighty invisible beings first arose from helpless man's consciousness of his own weakness, and was literally extorted by the fear that naturally springs from acknowledged imbecility. Hence' religion was not first, but rather a dread of demons led the way, until at length this slavish god-, hero-, or spirit-worship, receiving an official and established shape, consolidated itself into a TEMPLAR SERVICE: this last again, concurring with the moral march of the human understanding, did by degrees transform itself into a CHURCH-WORSHIP. Both church and temple rise upon faith historical: until now at length, in these latter days, it has been BEGUN to be perceived that the historical belief was but of provisional use, being in fact only a symbolic exhibition, auxiliary to the spread of a pure morally religious faith.

Betwixt a Tungusine SHAMAN—and a European PRELATE domineering it at once over both State and Church, there is no doubt a most enormous gap; or if, instead of the heads and leaders of the party, an example be preferred from the common herd, then it still holds equally true, that from the rude, rough WOGULITE, who, day by day, as he rises from his couch, places a bear's paw on his pate, and ejaculates, "*from this sudden death, Good Bear! deliver me,*" up to the supra-subtile PURITAN or sublimated INDEPENDENT in Connecticut, there obtains a most portentous distance in the FASHION, but none whatever in the PRINCIPLES, of their belief: as for their principle, both belong to one and the same class, viz. the class of those, who place the worship of the Deity in those outward rites that cannot morally amend our species; such as the belief in sundry statutable dogmas, and the observance of arbitrary ceremonies of form and show. Those only who make their worship of the Supreme Being consist in having and upholding the

---

[68] This term (PFAFFENTHUM, which may also be rendered POPERY or PAPISTRY, Tr.), denoting the authority of a spiritual father ($\pi\alpha\pi\alpha$), suggests the still farther idea of spiritual tyranny, and does consequently carry with it a certain amount of blame. This despotic sway pervades more or less every church, however unassuming and popular its pretensions. Although I use the word, I do not mean, either here or in the text, to throw any despite upon the very various sects whom I contrast. All those various modifications of belief are entitled to equal respect, so far forth as they are attempts of us poor mortals to realize a kingdom of God on earth; but then they are all open to the same objection, viz. that they give out some particular visible transcript of that idea for the thing itself

sentiments of a walk and conversation morally acceptable to God, are thereby widely separated and distinguished from the former class; inasmuch as they have made a transit to a *principle* totally diverse from, and incomputably advanced above, the other, viz. a principle whereby they profess themselves members of the one invisible church, containing within its pale all the honest-minded, and whereof the inward essential property is such, as to render it alone, the True Church Universal.

To bias the unseen power that governs the world to their own private advantage, is a design that all spurious worshippers aim at accomplishing; but then, how this unknown being is to be propitiated, is a point concerning which they differ. When this SUPREME is figured as endowed with will and understanding, then are all the exertions of mankind directed towards propitiating so mighty an agent, on whose will depend their lot and destiny in life; and for this purpose different and contrary modes may appear at different times and in diverse countries the more eligible. Should, however, the governor of the physical system be deemed a moral person, then is it self-evident at once to every human understanding, that the only condition under which we can recommend ourselves to his favour, is the performance of good moral conduct, at least where such correct and irreproachable deportment springs from purity of sentiment, as its subjective principle and wellspring within. Howbeit, fancy can very easily depicture to us, that the Supreme Being may perchance choose to be served and worshipped, in some yet other manner, not patent to or cognizable by reason, namely, by such actions as, though in themselves quite unrelated to morality, are perhaps commanded by him, or otherwise are, it may be, spontaneously undertaken by ourselves, in order more vividly to demonstrate our subjection to his will: in either of which events, those actions—whether optional or imperative—would, when systematically arranged into one entire whole, constitute the materials of a WORSHIP of the Godhead. Again, upon the hypothesis, that the ethic and non-ethical services are to be conjoined, then must EITHER both lines of worship be figured as directly rendering us acceptable to God, OR the one must be deemed a mean or vehicle toward the other, which last alone, will then be the proper acceptable worship. That the ethical worship of the Deity (*officium liberum*) is immediately well-pleasing in his sight, is manifest of itself; but then morality would cease to be the supreme condition of God's complacency in our race (which, however, is of the very essence of our idea of morality), whenever mercenary hireling services come to be regarded as able by themselves alone, to recommend us to the favour of the Almighty. Should a mechanic non-ethical worship be thus exalted, then could no one tell, when positive and moral precepts clash, which were to be preferred before the other; and in any given collision of ethic and alleged divine behests, the judgment of mankind must remain suspended, as to which course of action, duty would demand. Wherefore actions that in themselves are void of moral worth, can only be admitted into religion with this proviso, that they are found means of forwarding that which in other actions is immediately and unconditionally good, *i. e.* we may hold them not displeasing to God, so far forth as they are instrumental in aiding our performance of his moral worship.

Whoever imagines that he can employ actions devoid in themselves of moral worth, as a mean fitted for procuring the Divine favour, and so of attaining the realization of his wishes, besots himself with the belief that he has possessed himself of an art, by means of merely natural causes to bring about preternatural effects: essays in this kind usually go by the name of SORCERY. But as the term *Sorcerer* usually conveys the accessory notion of intercourse with the Evil One, whereas the attempts now under consideration proceed upon a mistaken fancy, and originate from good moral designs; it will be advisable to drop the above expression, and use in its stead the more familiar phrase of *Fetiche-making*, or FETICISM.[69] A preternatural effect wrought by man would be such an event as the *fetiche-maker* fancies he can cause to come to pass by acting upon the Almighty, and using God as a means to realise those ends which lie alike beyond the strength of man's physical economy and the insight of his understanding, a delusion that is in its very conception preposterous and absurd.

If man, over and above the active sentiment of ethic conduct (which can alone make him acceptable to God), does, by the use of certain forms, seek to make himself worthy of having his ethic weakness strengthened and supplied by supernatural power, and does for this end adopt *observances* tending to advance that ethic sentiment, in order thereby to make himself *susceptible* of being helped on toward the attainment of the object of his good hopes; then does he reckon, no doubt, on some preternatural supply, not, however, effectuated by him (by acting upon the Deity), only received—an eking out of his natural inability which he only hopes for, but does not attempt to con jure up. But if he has recourse to actions that do in themselves, so far as we can see, savour nothing of morality, in the imagination that such ceremonials will serve as a mean, or even be the condition of his obtaining from God the immediate accomplishment of his wishes, then does he proceed upon the practical delusion, that although for this preternatural benefit he is qualified neither by any physical faculty, nor yet by any moral susceptibility, he can nevertheless bring about this supernatural aid by a common physical operation, quite unconnected

---

[69] Translator's Note. *Germanice*, FETISCHDIENST, signifying HEATHENISM. The word *Fetisso* is said to be of Portuguese origin, and most frequently applied to the superstitious rites of the African Negroes. The meaning in the text therefore is—as *Sorcery* with respect to the *Devil*, so *Feticism* in regard of the Deity.

with morality, and that may be performed indifferently by the worst or the best of our race; for when any one fancies he can work upon the preternatural by using formulas of invocation, confessions of church-creeds, and observing rites ecclesiastical, then is he scarcely to be distinguished from those who have recourse to sorcerous incantations, when he thus attempts *magically* to possess himself of assistance from above. No human understanding can frame to itself any notion of a connection or law of synthesis obtaining betwixt a mere bodily act and a morally-working cause, according to which causal-nexus the latter can be so regulated and determined as to produce the effects aimed at by the former.

Wherefore, whoever declares the observation of statutory laws, cognisable only by revelation, a necessary element of religion, and, considering them not merely as a mean toward forwarding the growth of moral sentiments, gives them out as the objective condition of our becoming acceptable to God, and postpones to this historical belief our due exertions after an amended life; he it is that converts the worship of God into FETICISM, and deals out a superstition utterly subversive of all true religion. The former, being only hypothetically well-pleasing to the Deity, must at all times be subordinated to that moral righteousness which in every nation makes and has made its worker accepted with God. Of such extreme moment is the order and arrangement in which these two good principles are combined. In duly prizing this weighty distinction consists the true moral march and insight of an ENLIGHTENED understanding; and only by rigidly subordinating the elements revealed, to the *a priori* laws authenticated by reason, does the worship of God begin to wear the aspect of A FREE, and consequently A MORAL SERVICE. Is the above distinction overlooked, then is there substituted in room of the Freedom of the Children of God, the yoke of a statutable law; and this, because it comes hand in hand with an unconditioned necessitation to believe in what can only be historically known, is a far heavier yoke[70] for the conscientious than any load of ordained ceremonials. With respect to these last, it is

---

[70] "*That yoke is gentle and that burden light*" where the duty imposed by it on us arises from our own legislative reason. Such a commandment is willingly executed. Of this kind are only the moral laws, *qua* divine behests; and of these alone could the Founder of the first pure church say, "*His commandments are not grievous.*" he means, "*they are not irksome,*" because every one perceives the necessity of obeying them, and is also fully aware that no authority is thereby usurped. On the other hand, despotical *ordonnances* (not originated by reason), even although intended for our good, whereof the *rationale* and use is unknown, are, so to speak, PESTS that no one can away with; and yet, in another point of view, actions imperatively ordained by the moral law are just those mankind experience the greatest *difficulty* in performing; and in exchange for these, not unfrequently undergo the most tiresome and vexatious rites of superstition, as if it were possible that such supererogatory and worthless castigations could pass current in room of a moral life.

plainly quite enough that they be performed; and no one need profess, either inwardly or outwardly, belief in the rites, as ordinances of divine appointment. Of all the various possible forms of superstition, ecclesiastical extortion of beliefs and confessions, is by far the most vexatious; for by this oppression conscience is singularly violated.

PRIESTDOM (*Papistry*) obtains wherever a mal-conformation of the church polity has introduced FETICISM; which worship of a fetiche-god is always to be met with whenever statute-laws of the church, formulas of faith, and ceremonial observances, not principles of morality, constitute the groundwork and essentials of the worship. Some churches there are where the fetiche belief is so mechanical and abundant as almost to supplant both morality and religion, and which do, therefore, approach very near to unmixed PAGANISM. But be the sacerdotal statutes to which obedience is demanded few or many, still, whenever the free homage due to the moral law is not first and supreme, then a servile worship, based on a fetiche creed, prevails. By this last, the multitude are governed, and, through obedience extorted by the church (not rendered to religion), stand bereft of all mental and moral freedom. The constitution of such a church may be hierarchical or democratical; that is a matter of utter indifference, and concerns only the mode of its organization. The administration is, under every form of fetiche creed, out and out despotic; and wherever statute articles of belief are interwoven with the constitutional charters of the church, there THE CLERGY have usurped the sway, and domineer. They think to trample on the understandings of their fellows, and even by degrees attempt to get rid of biblical learning: for, being the alone patenteed interpreters and expounders of the will of the Unseen Lawgiver, to them belongs exclusively the right of dealing out the rules of the faith; whence, armed with this authority, they fancy they have not TO CONVINCE, but only TO COMMAND. Again, since beyond CHURCHMEN all else are LAICS (the sovereign head of the realm not excepted), it is plain, that in the long run the church lords it over the state, not necessarily by force or violence, but partly by compressing the minds, partly by air-drawn visions of the benefits accruing to the state, from those habits of blind obedience, to which spiritual discipline moulds and biases even the very THOUGHTS of the populace. But here long and inveterate customs of hypocrisy insensibly undermine the honesty and independence of the subject. Even his civil duties are tainted, by being rendered with eye-service, and thus, like all false principles whatsoever, the spurious church-worship ends by bringing forth the very contrary of what it professed to aim at.

* * *
* *

All these evils are the inevitable consequence of inverting and deranging the due order obtaining betwixt the principles of the several religious faiths, viz. whether the principles of pure rational religion or those of revealed religion were, as supreme conditions, to be allowed the sovereign and highest place. It is most equitable to assume, that not merely the wise or the disputer of this world, is called to be illuminated touching the nature of his true bliss: for of this believing insight the whole race of man are destined to be capable, and even the foolish things of this world—the unlettered, the most circumscribed by limited ideas—may advance a claim to be thus taught and inwardly convinced. For the behoof of those last, a popular historic creed seems preeminently adapted, especially when all the notions needed for its comprehension are quite anthropological, and address themselves directly to the sensory. Nothing can be more easily spread than a simple story thus sensuously clothed; it admits of being constantly discoursed of and imparted, together with the verbal formulas of its mysteries, wherewith it is not absolutely necessary that the speaker connect any sense. How repeatedly do we not perceive statements that accompany a great and general interest acquiring a ready and almost universal reception; and then, when the history is supported by an ancient document, long acknowledged to be authentic, what deep roots must not the belief in its truths have struck. These various concurring circumstances render such a faith as is the Christian, peculiarly on a level with the most ordinary and common apprehension. Farther, although neither the annunciation of those events, nor the belief in rules of life thereon based, may have been originally intended for, or addressed to, the learned and noble, still *they* are not upon that account excluded, much less devoid of interest, to look into the transactions recorded. But then so many doubts arise, *now* touching their truth, *anon* touching their meaning, that it plainly is the most absurd course in the world to lay down, as THE SUPREME CONDITION of saving and universal faith, a historic creed, open to so many controversies, and to learned and scientific doubts most honestly urged and as sincerely felt. Moreover, there is a practical knowledge based entirely upon reason, needing no historic authentication, lying so near every one, even the most simple, that it looks as had it been written in detail on the tablets of his heart: a practical knowledge, I say, of a law that cannot be named without commanding universal assent to its authority, and which is ushered into every one's soul with the IMMEDIATE consciousness of its unconditioned obligatory force. This practical knowledge is besides sufficient of itself to guide to a belief in God; or should this belief have been suggested *aliunde*, then it fixes and defines our idea of him as a moral lawgiver; thus furnishing a religion that is at once comprehensible by all, and that puts on all the greatest dignity and honour that can possibly be represented: nay, the above-mentioned practical knowledge issues so naturally in this religion, that it admits of being questioned Socratically out of every person's understanding, although he had never heard of it before. It is consequently not merely expedient to commence with this obvious truth, and to make the historical belief wherewith it is so much in harmony follow only as an accessory; but is even a very duty to regard those notices, the birthright of every human reason, as the principal and supreme index, pointing out the only legitimate and infallible way, through which we can become partakers of whatever bliss, a historical belief may promise: for, in truth, we can allow a narrated creed to pass validly current, to such extent only, as the former warrants; whereas, whenever this search into its inner texture and contents has been warily gone about, then is THE ETHICAL BELIEVER always left fully open to make a transit to so much of THE HISTORICAL BELIEF as lie may find conducive to the quickening and enlivening of his pure moral and religious sentiments, in which event alone can such belief possess any inward moral worth, as it is then free, and unextorted by any threat.

There is yet another question which may be asked, whether the lectures publicly delivered in a church ought mainly to set forth doctrines of GODLINESS, or those of pure VIRTUE? The former term, *godliness*, is, perhaps, the only one still used that can convey, even in part, the meaning of the foreign term *religio*.

GODLINESS may be figured as containing under it two different mental moods in regard of our relation to the Deity. FEAR OF GOD is such a cast of thinking as obtains when we observe God's Laws as SUBJECTS in his realm, *i. e.* from the awe of duty. LOVE OF GOD, on the other hand, obtains then, when we offer him the obedience of dutiful children, *i. e.* from a free and ingenuous approbation taken in his law. Either frame of mind is consequently, above and beyond the bare moral determination, accompanied by the attendant idea of a supersensible Being, invested with such attributes as may be needed for placing within our reach that Sovereign Good aimed at by a moral mind, and eking out our inability to realise and attain it. This Person's NATURE does, whenever attempted to be fixed by any predicate, save those immediately arising out of the moral relation perceived to obtain betwixt our IDEA of Him and our duty, stand always in the greatest hazard of being anthropomorphously distorted, and so consequently of endangering, displacing, and even supplanting to that extent our moral sentiments. Accordingly we saw in the *Critiques* that this idea could not be received, as of objective validity, by pure speculative Reason, and that its origin, and still more its main use, was grounded entirely on the self-begotten and self-upholding law of our ethical economy. This being the state of matters, what, it will naturally be asked, ought to constitute the first rudiments of instruction when addressing the young, or when prelecting from the pulpit? Ought VIRTUE to be explained before GODLINESS? or GODLINESS in preference to, and perhaps without even so much as once mentioning, VIRTUE? Both go of necessity hand-in-hand together; but a necessary conjunction of this sort can only obtain where the one is THE END, the other no more than A MEAN. Again, the whole theory of virtue has its complete and entire subsistence by itself, dispensing even with the Idea God; whereas tenets of godliness deal only with this idea, so far forth as it serves to depicture to us how the grand end of morality, viz. the Sovereign Good, is to he gained. Hence it is manifest that godliness cannot *by itself* be the aim and end of morality, but can only serve as a mean, strengthening mankind's honest-mindedness, by ascertaining and warranting to him every good, even holiness, for which his natural efforts might be insufficient. The Idea virtue, on the contrary, is exsculpted, in most prominent relief, on every human soul. Each man bears it fully about within, however it may for a while be partially submerged; nor does it need, like the religious Idea, to be arrived at through any chain of ratiocination. In the august magnificence of its purity, arousing consciousness forthwith to the discovery of an otherwise quite unsuspected energy, empowering man to smite down and overthrow the greatest possible obstacles within; in the dignity of his nature which mankind has to uphold inviolate, in order to reach that moral destination after which he strives; in this recognition of his excellency and purity, there does, I say, lie something so soul-exalting, yea heavenwards wafting, placing mankind as it were even in the presence of the Deity, who merely by his holiness and legislative guardianship of virtue is an object of adoration, that everyman, even though as yet far removed from giving this idea any motive-purchase on his maxims, gladly entertains it in his thoughts, as it then fully reveals to him, and stamps on him, the feeling of the original nobility and state of his rank. How different are the inward phenomena when this order is inverted. The idea of a supreme governor, imposing upon us duties by his law, lies primordially at an incomputable distance, and is observed, when we set out with it, to damp and dash man's courage—which, however, is of the very essence of all virtue—and the godliness is exposed to the risk of sliding into an abject, servile, and adulatory submission to the will of a despot. The energetic valour aroused, set free, and disengaged by virtue, encouraging and enabling mankind to trust confidently to his own resources, is likewise capable of becoming fortified and made inexpugnably secure when followed up by a doctrine of expurgation, announcing an amnesty for that in past transgressions, beyond man's power to undo or counteract; whereas even here, were this ethical order transposed, then must inevitably, doubt as to appropriation of the grace, unnerve and break the spirits: abortive expiations to make what has been done undone then creep in; doctrines of our utter inability to perform of ourselves, any spontaneous ingenuous good, follow in their train; these, by begetting anxious and uneasy apprehensions touching his possible lapse backwards into evil, transplant the unhappy sufferer into a whining, whimpering, passive moral state, incapable of aiming at anything either great or good—only of sighing after it with prayers or vows. In founding and uprearing a moral character, everything depends on the leading and dominant idea whereunto everything else must be subordinated. When to the worship of God is allotted the foremost place to which virtue is postponed, then is such DEITY an IDOL; for God is then an agent not to be won by good moral deportment executed in the world, but one whose approbation is to be gained by invocations and adulatory addresses: RELIGION is now IDOLATRY. Godliness can, therefore, never be a *surrogatum* of virtue, assisting us to dispense with it. Godliness can only be its plenary consummation, crowning it with the hope of that ultimate success, which will one day put wholly within our grasp, the chief and last end of all our moral labours.

* * *
* *

The various kinds of faith prevalent among diverse nations, impart to them by degrees certain peculiar characteristic features, which come in the sequel to be regarded as derived from the localities of the soil or climate, or from the physical temperament of the race. Thus JUDAISM being designed to keep separate the family of Abraham, isolating them by every species of rite and ceremonial from their neighbours, entailed upon the inhabitants of Palestine the well-known charge of a misanthropic hatred of the whole human race. MAHOMETANISM is characterized by the HAUGHTINESS it instils into the Moslem,—a PRIDE begotten by its looking for its evidences, not to miracles, but by finding the confirmation of its belief in its victorious subjection of many nations; and this highmindedness is sustained by devotional exercises of a warlike and lofty-spirited turn. The HINDU persuasions have impressed upon the East a character of *pusillanimity*, from causes the exact contrary of those just mentioned.—Assuredly THE CHRISTIAN FAITH is not to blame if it sometimes has given birth to characters chargeable with the like fault. These have arisen from the faulty mode in which it has been made to tell upon the mind. The vices of a false and abject humility have been superinduced upon primitive Christianity, through the mistaken views of many of its most zealous well-wishers; who, commencing with the doctrine of mankind's corruption, despair of and cut short the mind's elastic and undecaying energies for virtue: thus placing the whole of religion in a principle of

PIETISM, by which I mean a principle of *passive* resignation, where all moral good is expected from above. By these portentous doctrines, mankind stand bereaved of all self-confidence and independence: fretted with perpetual anxiety, they sigh and whine after preternatural assistance; and do, even in this very self-abnegation (*which is not humility*), think they possess a mean whereby to recommend themselves to the favour of the Deity. The outward expression, however, of PIETISM and BIGOTISM (*i. e. spurious devotion*), does at all times amply betray the ABJECTNESS of the sentiment within.

This singular phenomenon, that the second of those classes (an ignorant, though shrewd race) should PRIDE themselves upon their faith, may possibly be in part deduced from the imagination of its founder, that he was the grand instrument of reviving the belief in the unity of the Godhead, which image-worship had at that time nearly blotted from the earth. If this merit can be duly ascribed to Mohammed, then doubtless may his followers feel themselves entitled to claim the ascendant in civilization, as they first freed the world from the superstition of the day; and became the first truly successful ICONOCLASTS, by emancipating the nations they overran from the shackles of Polytheism. As for that characteristic of the fourth class, which rises upon misunderstood humility, this ought to be observed; the estimation of our moral worth, intended to prune the overgrowths of self-conceit, should not issue in self-abhorrence, but ought rather to inspire a more firm determination to press after the holiness objected to our mental vision by the law, by so cultivating our confided talent, as to bring forth fruits worthy of the exalted dignity and high destination of our being. But then, unfortunately, VIRTUE has been confounded with ARROGANCE, and its very NAME banished as suspicious into the realms of HEATHENISM. VIRTUE, together with its main constituent VALOUR, has thus been forced to yield place to crouching superstition and craven devoteeism. BIGOTRY or false devotion is rested upon the custom of placing the usages of piety, not in those moral actions that make mankind accepted with his Judge, but in exercises of reverential homage, whereby the devotee fancies he is immediately occupied with God himself. Such worship is plainly abortive (*opus operatum*), although it adds to superstition the fanatical dream of alleged supersensible feelings of the celestial.

SECTION IV.

OF THE CLUE WHEREBY CONSCIENCE CAN THREAD EVERY POSSIBLE LABYRINTH OF FAITH ECCLESIASTICAL.

The question here is not, "How CONSCIENCE OUGHT TO BE GUIDED?" for Conscience is its own General and Leader; it is therefore enough that each man have one. What we want to know is, how conscience can be her own *Ariadne*, and disentangle herself from the mazes even of the most ravelled and complicated casuistical theology.

CONSCIENTIOUSNESS is a state of consciousness, which to possess is at all times our incumbent duty. But how is this to be figured as possible? The consciousness of any representation—be it what it may—is needed only for logical purposes; but if consciousness is needed conditionally only for the behoof of making our perceptions clearer or more perspicuous, then would it seem that no state or modification of consciousness can be stated as an unconditioned duty.

Here is an ethical proposition that stands in need of no proof: NO ACTION MAY AT ANY TIME BE HAZARDED ON THE UNCERTAINTY THAT PERCHANCE IT MAY NOT BE WRONG (*Quod dubitas, ne feceris! Plin.*). Hence the CONSCIOUSNESSS, that ANY ACTION I am about to perform is RIGHT, is in itself a most immediate and imperative duty. What actions are right,—what wrong,—is a matter for the understanding, not for conscience. It certainly is not absolutely necessary for any one to know, touching all possible actions, whether they be right or wrong. But with regard to any given action which I am really about to perform, I must not only BE OF OPINION, but must BE absolutely CERTAIN, that it is right; and this is a postulate conscience opposes to *Jesuitical Probabilism*, which has for its foothold this position, that the bare opinion, that an action may possibly not be wrong, furnishes sufficient warrant for performing it. Conscience might be thus otherwise defined,—IT IS OUR SELF-JUDGING MORAL UNDERSTANDING;—only this definition would, I fear, stand greatly in need of a preliminary clearing up of the conceptions it involves. Conscience docs not sit in judgment on actions, so as to decide whether they are CASES falling under the moral law, or beyond it; *that* is determined by reason, so far forth as this last is subjectively-practical (hence the *casus conscientiæ*, and indeed the whole of casuistry constitute, if I may so speak, A DIALECTIC of conscience); whereas, in the former event, reason passes sentence on itself, to know if, with all diligence, it have sifted and tested the moral worth or unworth of certain acts; and cites each individual man as conclusive evidence, *for* or *against* himself, that such approbatory or reprobating decree, has been duly pronounced, or has unduly been omitted.

Let us take as an example an official of the Inquisition, who has imbibed the inveterate opinion that his creed is the alone true, and who would willingly, in consequence of this belief, suffer martyrdom for its sake. Let there be brought before this ecclesiastic judge an unoffending citizen, who has been denounced as a HERETIC, and is now arraigned at his bar of the capital crime of MISBELIEF; then I raise this query, whether or not he who dooms his neighbour to the pains of death, can be said to have acted conformably to conscience (*confessedly erroneous though it be*); or whether he is not to be charged with AN UTTER WANT OF CONSCIENTIOUSNESS, and that, too, whether he have so acted, knowing his sentence to be unjust, or in the mistaken supposition that this judicial step was right. In effect, it should seem that we might confidently toss the defiance in his face; that in such a case as the one now supposed, he could not but know that he acted wrong, in as much as it is impossible for any man altogether to escape some inward misgiving, when pronouncing the portentous warrant for an *auto da fe*, lest peradventure his judgment prove utterly iniquitous. Doubtless the Grand Inquisitor is fully persuaded that a supernatural revelation of the Divine will—*compellite intrare*—permits him, or, it may be, even ordains him, to extirpate, root and branch, the infidelity of the incredulous, and to raze all unbelievers from the face of the earth. But was he then so perfectly assured that the above formula was a revelation, and so convinced of the accuracy of the interpretation as is absolutely indispensable, before we can hold any one justified in passing sentence of capital condemnation on his fellow-men? That to put any one to death on account of his opinions in religion is a point of high injustice, is obvious to every one; unless, indeed—to grant the very uttermost concession—the divine will have in a special extraordinary revelation ordained it otherwise; farther, that God ever did, at any time, communicate this dreadfully appalling declaration of his will, rests merely on historical documents, and is, therefore, never apodictically certain. This alleged revelation has only been received from, and interpreted by, his fellow-men; or did any one even suppose that he got such a communication immediately from God himself, as Abraham did, to lead his son like a sheep to the slaughter, still, the possibility would remain, that in all this some latent error had unawares crept in; and should there be room for any such possible mistake, then would he hazard an act that might be extremely unjust. But thus to act at random, and in the dark, is of the very essence of unconscientiousness. Again, every one thus behaves, who thinks to perform acts, otherwise clearly immoral, upon the fancied ground of some authority contained, it may be, in a history or a vision. These last may POSSIBLY be tainted by mistake;[71] and if this be indeed so, then

---

[71] Beyond which, all science, and therefore ethical science, is exalted. There are

does it bewray the man's inward want of conscientiousness when he obeys a historical belief; for whoso blindly hazards the violation of one of the known offices of humanity, upon the imagined probability that perchance he may not do wrong, becomes thereby—conscience being judge—A WRONG-DOER. Furthermore, upon the hypothesis that an action commanded by such an alleged positive revealed law, is in itself perfectly allowed, then still I desire to know if clerical superiors and teachers can venture to impose upon the people, as articles of belief, their own opinions and convictions; and that, too, upon the pain of certain civil disabilities. The conviction in question can be grounded upon no other than historic foundations; and the populace cannot but perceive, if they give the subject the most slender and cursory examination, what abundant sources there are for error, either in the story or in the classic exposition of the text. The judgment of the unlettered can consequently be no other than problematic; and yet the clergyman would constrain his flock to confess (at least inwardly) as confidently as they believe in God, *i. e.* to profess, as it were, in the presence of the Almighty, what they cannot certainly know. Thus some ecclesiastics compel their half-learned countrymen to believe in the institution of one day in seven as a constituent element of religion and godliness, immediately ordained by God himself, for the public periodic celebration of his worship; or wring from the flock a solemn confession of a mystery which it cannot so much as comprehend. Clerical superiors do, in these instances, themselves violate and bespot the conscience, obtruding upon the unlettered sciolist a belief in matters whereof they themselves never can become fully certain; and here they ought to take good heed what they are about, as they it is, that will have to render an account for all abuses springing from such feigned and fictitious faith. Wherefore, there may be truth in the things believed, and yet there may be insincerity in the belief itself, *i. e.* want of conscientiousness in the confession declared by the man to himself—an inward guile that is in itself damnable.

Although, as it was remarked above, individuals who have begun to awake to freedom[72] of cogitation, after having long unconsciously

---

only four sciences, logic, mathematics, physics, and ethics: before the demonstrated truths of these *a priori* knowledges, every opposing obstacle must of necessity fall. Tr.

[72] The phrase often used by sagacious politicians, "*such a people are not yet ripe for freedom,*" is, I frankly admit, one with which I cannot concur. The *adscripti glebæ* are said to be thus immature; and in the same way we hear it strenuously contended that the great bulk of the people are still unripe for freedom in ecclesiastical belief. Agreeably to this hypothesis, no season of freedom ever can arrive. How can any one become mature in freedom, unless, first of all, so placed that he can ripen freely? (the free use of our connate powers never can be harmoniously and symmetrically developed till all clog and restraint are removed). The first essays at freedom may no doubt be awkward, and a nation may for a while, in consequence, find itself thrown into a more uncouth or even dangerous condition than while it stood under the authority and guardianship of another.

slumbered under the yoke of a belief (*e. g.* Protestants), do straightway deem themselves ennobled, in proportion as their articles of belief are scanty; yet, singularly enough, they whose understandings still lie dormant, cling to a very different principle of safety. "BETTER BELIEVE TOO MUCH THAN BELIEVE TOO LITTLE," is here the adage; for whatever is done beyond and above what is duty, cannot in any event harm, but may perchance do good. Upon this delusive dream, which would make dishonesty the very spirit and soul of religious confessions, is based the well-known *argumentum a tuto*, which obtains the more easy and extended currency, because religion compensates for every fault, and hence also for dishonesty in adopting it. If, says the sciolist, what I profess to believe concerning the Godhead is correct, then have I precisely hit the very truth. Should, on the other hand, the articles contain an error, still, as there is nothing in them morally improper, then have I merely assented to something superfluous and unnecessary, by all which I have no doubt molested, but certainly not incriminated, myself. The peril arising out of the improbity of his profession—THE LESION OF CONSCIENCE— necessarily undergone, when that is declared in the presence of God to be certain, which mankind must nevertheless know not to be so constituted as to admit of being affirmed with unconditioned certainty, are all overlooked by this dishonest maxim, AND INDEED PASS WITH THE HYPOCRITE FOR NOTHING. The genuine safety-principle of true religion is contrariwise as follows. Whatever is a mean or condition of future bliss, unknown to naked reason, and promulgated singly by revelation, can strike root in my conviction, just like any other history; and so far forth as it does not militate against morality, cannot be either pronounced absolutely certain, nor yet rejected as absolutely false. Besides leaving this point totally undecided, I may unquestionably trust, that whatever of salutary there may lie in the document, will stand me in good stead, provided I do not by my moral short-coming make myself unworthy of it. In this maxim, there is real moral safety, viz. that conscience be not violated; and more cannot be demanded from mankind. There is, moreover, the utmost danger and insecurity in that lauded stratagem of expediency, whereby we think astutely to evade any disadvantageous sequents that may spring from unbelieving nonconformity. Thus tampering with either party, we destroy our credit with both.

Howbeit, no man ever can ripen into the full maturity of reason, save by HIS OWN exertions; to make which exertions, he must be handed entirely over to HIS OWN freedom. I do not deny that the exigency of particular circumstances may compel those invested with authority to postpone, for a long season, the removal of domestic, municipal, or ecclesiastic bonds. But to proceed upon the principle that those subjected to their authority are unfit for freedom, is to usurp a prerogative of Deity, who created mankind for and unto freedom. Questionless, it is much more convenient to lord it, both at home and abroad, over house, state, and church, where we can—But then there is another question—as to its JUSTICE.

Were the author of a creed, or a doctor in theology, or, generally, were any one, who professes inwardly to himself his steadfast belief in tenets, as of divine revelation; were, I say, any such individual interrogated, if he could, before the Searcher of his heart, protest that those tenets are certainly true, renouncing his hope of everything dear and holy, should they, in any event, turn out to be false; then must our opinion of human nature be low and grovelling indeed, not to anticipate, that even the boldest preacher of belief must tremble at the contemplation Of so portentous an alternative.[73] But if this be so indeed, how can it consist with general conscientiousness to urge vehemently an unlimited declaration of adherence to those points of faith, and even to give out the reckless temerity, that alone is able to utter such asseverations, as in itself a duty, and, in fact, part of the worship of the Deity. So violent an invasion of conscience bereaves mankind of his freedom, which, however, is indispensably needed for every moral act—(pre-eminently so when religious principles are to be adopted)—and does not even allow room for the good will that would cry, LORD, I BELIEVE; HELP THOU MINE UNBELIEF.[74]

---

[73] Whoever has the temerity to say, that he who refuses assent to a historical statement, as a certain truth, MUST INFALLIBLY BE DAMNED, must be ready to invert the proposition, and to say in turn, I CONVERSELY AM WILLING TO BE DAMNED if what I now tell you is untrue. Should there perchance be found any person, willing to emit this dreadful declaration, then would I recommend the Persian proverb, as suggesting the only fit mode of treating such a zealot. Has any one gone' ONCE to Mecca on a pilgrimage, then (says the eastern adage) is it high time to quit the house in which he dwells. Has he been there TWICE, quit the very street. But has he journeyed thither THRICE, then abandon the city, or even the very province, where he is to be found.

[74] SINCERITY! thou Astræa! who hast fled this earth, and betaken thyself to heaven, by what means draw we thee down again,—thee! the indispensable groundwork of all conscientiousness, and so by necessary consequence of all heart-felt religion. I admit—though I deem it matter of regret—that a frank absence of all reserve, which tells the WHOLE truth it knows, is not to be met with in human nature. Notwithstanding, SINCERITY is what we are entitled to expect and to exact from all (viz. that whatever is said, be honestly declared); and were there no substratum in our inner man tending to this virtue, whereof the culture only lies neglected, then would the human species become in their own eyes an object of the deepest disgust and disdain. But this desiderated and invaluable frame of thinking is exposed to many assaults of temptation, and costs many a sacrifice; whence also it demands ethic strength, *i. e.* virtue for its acquisition. Again, this virtue needs to be planted and watered much earlier and more assiduously than any other; for when once the contrary bias to self-deceit has insinuated itself, and contaminated the character, it is almost impossible afterwards to eradicate it. This being the case, just let us throw back an eye on the education given us in youth, especially in what relates to religion, or rather, to speak more correctly, in what relates to points of faith. Here faithfulness of recollection is what is mostly prized (viz. that memory supply the answers to the questions); but as for the faithfulness of the confessions uttered, touching this last, no question is ever asked—a good memory is equipment enough for a good believer, although he does not so much as understand the creed to which he is solemnly pledged. With such a retrospect, why should we wonder at the inroads of insincerity, which generates nothing but a race of inward HYPOCRITES.

GENERAL SCHOLION.

Whatever good mankind is *of himself* able to perform, agreeably to Laws of Freedom, may be termed NATURE, in contradistinction from that good which, springing from preternatural aid, may be called GRACE. The former epithet does not, however, mean any physical property different from Freedom; it is only employed because we know the laws of this last's causality, whence also it happens that, in the analogy those bear to the uniform legal sequences of the physical system, Reason possesses an easy, conspicuous, and available gnomon as its guide: whereas, touching any effects of Grace, we are left altogether in the dark; Reason being totally ignorant of the laws of those operations. Indeed, everything hyperphysical flees the scrutiny of our ken, among which transcendent points of cogitation must ever be ranked Morality, qua absolute Sanctity or HOLINESS.

The conception of the supra-accession of preternatural increments to our moral but defective exertions is transcendent, and a bare idea whose reality no experience can confirm. And yet to admit this idea, even in a mere practical point of view, is exceedingly perilous, and almost inconjungible with our own exertions, upon any grounds of our Reason; seeing that whatever good moral conduct is to be imputable to our account, cannot be originated by any foreign sources, but singly by the strenuous and unfailing use of our own energies. The impossibility, however, of such superadded aid cannot be evinced, nor can it be shown, that both our own and extraneous exertions may not perhaps work harmoniously together. Although Freedom does, in its conception, contain nothing supernatural: nevertheless the possibility even of this our very freedom is incomprehensible; in truth, just as incomprehensible as the preternatural supply alleged to concur therewith; helping and eking out our own self-active but defective voluntary determinations.

There is, however, this very marked difference betwixt the two cases. We are perfectly acquainted with Freedom's LAW (viz. the Moral), according to which its causality is determinable: whereas touching the Laws of any preternatural assistance we are left altogether in the dark; whether any perceived moral strength within, really arise from a celestial source: in what circumstances and under what conditions this divine grace is to be expected, is unknown and uninvestigable. We can, consequently, make no use whatever of this Idea, farther than this general hypothesis, viz. that what our own natural energies cannot accomplish will be effected by Grace; provided only we ourselves have done our utmost. Wherefore, beyond an earnest striving after a good life, nothing can by us be done, so as either to draw down hitherward a supernatural operation, or yet to determine at what time, or in what manner, we may expect it. The idea is quite transcendent; and it is even salutary to regard it as a *sanctum*, not to be incautiously approached, lest, by rashly entering in, we fall into the imagination, either of performing miracles ourselves: or into the no less distressing delusion of perceiving fancied miracles wrought upon our inner man, thereby unfitting ourselves for all rational use of our intellectual faculties, and even encouraging ourselves in sloth, passively waiting from above, for what is certainly to be had by our own diligent and strenuously-sustained labour.

MEANS are those intermediate steps toward an end which we mankind have fully WITHIN OUR OWN CONTROL. Now in order to become worthy of celestial aid, there is no other, and there can be no other MEAN than the solemn and earnest endeavour, whereby we better to the uttermost, our moral properties and state, so as to render ourselves susceptible of receiving that complementary supply not within our reach, but which is nevertheless needed for making us the faultless objects of the Divine complacency; the assistance expected, aiming in fact, at nothing else than the forwarding of our morality. That the depraved and insincere will look for this aid anywhere rather than in industrious moral self-culture, might have been expected beforehand; and this anticipation we find confirmed by fact. The sinner in every age has resorted to sundry sensible observances, that never yet made any one a better man, but which are intended *supernaturally* to effect this desired transformation. Hence arises the notion of MEANS OF GRACE, which, though a self-contradicting representation, serves for a self-delusion alike common, and hurtful to true religion.

The true worship of God rendered by the ethical believer —at once a subject in the Divine realm, and at the same time a free denizen of the moral state—is, like the heavenly kingdom, itself invisible, viz. an inward service of the heart, consisting in the spirit and truth of a real moral sentiment within; and this service can alone consist in that moral-mindedness which discharges all the incumbent offices of humanity as if they were Divine commandments, and does not consist in performing certain stated actions exclusively rendered toward God. But then things invisible, always require some sensible effigiation. This practical vehicle, though perhaps indispensable, is a *mode* of depicturing to us, our duties extremely open to misapprehension, inasmuch as those ceremonials that symbolically suggest to us our offices as servants of the Most High, become confounded with those offices themselves. Whence mankind deem them part of the worship of the Deity; by which very name indeed the institutions of a church, are not unfrequently miscalled.

This alleged worship of God, when reduced to its true spirit and original intendment, will admit of a division into four duties, recognised even by our own reason as duties tending to forward the growth of a cast of thinking hallowed by being dedicated to the advancement of the kingdom of God. To these duties a few corresponding rites will be associated, although standing with them in no necessary connection. The *forms* serve as an *ectyposis*, shadowing forth those duties, and serve to rouse and sustain our attention to what is the true worship of God. From remote antiquity the following sensible rites have been found serviceable, and aim all at one common end, viz. the forwarding morality. 1. With the design of firmly grounding and settling this morality *in ourselves*, PRIVATE PRAYER has been had recourse to, the sentiments of morality being thus intentionally enlivened and revivified. 2. With the view of outwardly spreading and propelling the reign of the good sentiment *among others*, ASSEMBLING TOGETHER IN CHURCH has been instituted. There, on stated periodic times, set specially apart for this very purpose, religious doctrines, wishes, and sentiments, are embodied by words, and mutually interchanged. 3. To propagate morality among posterity, the newly-born members are received into the communion of the faithful, where, by some formulary, seniors are admonished of the duty of educating and instructing their youth in the principles of the faith (BAPTISM among Christians). 4. In order to preserve the society of believers, another public ceremonial—the rite of communion—is celebrated. Individuals are thus represented as members of an ethical body; in this they are permanently combined, agreeably to a principle of equal rights, and joint participation in all the fruits of the moral good.

Every undertaking in points of religion, when not purely moral, and yet intended as a mean that is in itself to make us acceptable to God, and so through HIM to procure the satisfaction of all our wishes, springs from what we have called a fetiche-belief. This heathenish belief consists in the persuasion, that we can accomplish what we wish for by resorting to steps that can neither naturally nor morally tend to such result, provided we steadfastly believe that those means will nevertheless bring about those ends, and then combine with this belief sundry outward ceremonials. Even in minds where the conviction has struck deep root, that everything depends upon the self-originated ethic-good, still the sensuous bias of our nature induces an attempt at a sort of contraband morality, whereby we expect to evade the troublesome conditions of genuine integrity, and fancy that if the ceremonial alone be duly celebrated, God will accept *it* in lieu of the deed. This would indeed be a surpassingly transcendent favour on the part of the Deity; or should we not rather call such an imagination a dream, that in fond and arrogant confidence deals with representations of grace, or perhaps even a mere counterfeit and hypocritically feigned confidence? Owing to the above-mentioned causes, mankind have, in every variety of public faith, excogitated sundry usages as means of grace, although those last are not always (as it has been the case with Christianity) related to the ideas of pure practical reason, and the moral sentiments it demands. Of the five great Mahometan commandments, washing, praying, fasting, alms-giving, and pilgrimage to Mecca, not one has the slightest cognationship to morality, unless the alms-giving be excepted; for when the needy are relieved out of a truly virtuous and therefore religious mindedness, then might such eleemosynary arrangement not unfitly deserve the name of *a mean of grace*. And yet since, consistently with the principles of Mahomet's creed, the dealing out of this gratuitous bounty may very well consist and go hand in hand with an extortion from others of what is thus feigned to be offered to God in the person of the poor, it does not appear worthy of ranking as an exception.

The kinds of elusory belief are threefold, each overstepping the limits and barriers of the human understanding in regard of that preternatural, which, consistently with the known laws of our intellectual economy, is no possible object either of theoretic or practical use. First, there may be an imaginary faith, leading us to suppose we know from observation and experience things whereof it is certain that they cannot possibly take place according to the objective laws of the material universe (the belief in MIRACLES). Second, a delusion that seems to render it necessary for us to adopt, among our ethical notions, an idea of something needed for our moral welfare, although reason is unable to frame to itself any intelligible conception of what this may be (belief in MYSTERIES). Third, the delusion of supposing that by merely natural means we can bring about a mysterious effect within, viz. a divine influence operating upon our morality. Of the two first-mentioned kinds of artificial belief, we have already spoken in the scholia to the second and third books. There remains by consequence to be treated of only THE MEANS OF GRACE. These must be distinguished from THE OPERATIONS OF GRACE;[75] for these last are preternatural moral influences, where we are entirely passive, and the imagined experience of such an inward grace is a fanatical delusion, resting merely on some errant feeling.

I. PRAYER, regarded as an internal formal worship of the Deity, and so as a mean of grace, is a superstitious delusion. It is nothing more than an uttered wish: declared moreover in the presence of a Being who stands in need of no information touching the inward sentiments of the declarant. By prayer there is consequently nothing done; and none of those duties, which, as were they commandments of God, are incumbent upon us, are discharged. Wherefore, in real fact and event, God remains all the while morally unserved and unworshipped. The heartfelt wish, that in everything we compass or avoid, we may be

---

[75] *Conf.* Scholion to Book I.

found well-pleasing in God's sight—*i. e.* in other words, the standing bent and ply of mind pervading all our actions, and inducing us to perform them, *as were they* done for the service of God,—is that spirit of prayer that can and ought *without ceasing* to obtain within. To clothe this wish in words or formularies[76] (even were these last no more than

---

[76] By the former wish, considered as the spirit of prayer, mankind endeavours to operate singly *upon himself*, viz. by enlivening his moral sentiments through means of the idea God. But on the latter wish, verbally uttered, he expects, by an outward operation, to work *upon God*. In the first case, prayer may be offered up with perfect sincerity, although the individual does not so much as presume to affirm that God certainly exists; but in the second form, which is an ADDRESS, the Most High is necessarily figured to be personally present; at least the individual makes an inward feint, as if he were persuaded of the presence of the Supreme,—thinking that this little *make-believe* can do no harm, but may perhaps recommend him to God's favour. From all which it is obvious, that in a verbally pronounced prayer, the sincerity is not so unquestionable as in one which confines itself to prayer's spirit. The accuracy of this remark can easily be confirmed by a hypothetical case. Imagine a pious good-meaning man, one, however, whose religious ideas are exceedingly circumscribed, caught unexpectedly by another in the act, I will not say of praying aloud, but merely in an attitude indicating what he is about; and it is scarcely necessary for me to add, that, in the case put, every one would at once anticipate, that the supplicant would betray some awkwardness or confusion, just as had he been detected in some situation whereof he had reason to be ashamed. "What may be the cause of this mental phenomenon? The reason seems to be, that whenever any one is found talking aloud to himself, we very naturally suspect him to be slightly crazed; and, in the same way, a not unsimilar judgment is passed, when we find some one, though alone, performing gesticulations that have only meaning when some one else stands before him. The Teacher of the Gospel expressed the spirit of prayer most admirably in that formula which enables us to dispense with all special prayers, and so even with the formula itself, as a mere verbal accompaniment. It contains nothing except the forethought resolve of leading a morally good life; which resolve, coupled with the consciousness of our frailty, gives birth to the perpetual and constant wish of becoming a worthy member of the kingdom of God. There is therefore no petition presented for anything that God might in his wisdom see meet to refuse; there is only a wish, which, when earnest and active, will of itself bring forth its own desired object, viz. our harmony with that in humanity which is well-pleasing to God. Even the wish for the means of subsistence, limited to one single day, amounts rather to a confession of what our animal economy WANTS, than to any reflex request expressing what the person himself WILLS. A prayer for to-morrow's bread would convey this last, which, however, is manifestly excluded by the very terms of the petition. This kind of prayer, prompted by a purely moral sentiment (quickened by the idea God), it is alone that can be prayed IN FAITH (*i. e.* in the confidence that it will be heard); for it, as the moral spirit of prayer, is of itself able to render the suppliant acceptable to God. The only prayer that will certainly be heard, is such a prayer for morality, as may, by being uttered and acted on, bring forth its own object. No object, other than morality, stands in this predicament; for suppose a solemn petition were presented for bread for any one given day, then is it impossible for any to foresee whether or not his supplication will be heard, *i. e.* no man can tell whether the object requested stands in such necessary conjunction with God's wisdom, as that it must of necessity be granted; on the contrary, it may perhaps be more congruous to the wisdom of the Almighty to allow the petitioner to die that very day for want of food. Again, the proposal is alike frenzied and presumptuous to attempt, by importunate seeking, to move God from his pre-appointed plans to our advantage; wherefore no prayer, unless when directed toward a moral object, will certainly be heard, *i. e.* no object not moral can be supplicated for IN FAITH. Nay, even were the object one pertaining to morality, but possible to be attained by us only through supernatural influence, then is it so exceedingly doubtful if

internally depictured), can, at the very utmost, possess no other worth save that of a mean, awakening and quickening that our moral-mindedness or intent. Directly it cannot relate to the Divine Approbation; and therefore it cannot be an immediate duty incumbent upon every one, seeing that a mean can only be enjoined upon him who requires it for some particular purpose. All, however, do not feel it necessary to resort to this process (strictly speaking, of conversing in and with themselves, under the pretext of communicating more openly

---

God would find it consistent with his wisdom to eke out and preternaturally fulfil the gaps of character arising from our own self-demerited delinquencies, that all mankind must rather see cause to expect the contrary. No man can therefore pray IN FAITH, even for this ethic benefit, still less can he present a believing prayer for those moral goods which it is still his unremitting and incumbent duty himself to bring about within, e. g. the retroversion of his perverted springs of will, and the putting on of the new man, called regeneration. These remarks will farther enable us to strike a due estimate of that so-called miraculous faith, said to be able to move mountains, which, when exercised, must always be accompanied by inward prayer. That God can bestow upon man a power of working preternatural effects, is impossible, for the very conception involves a contradiction. Again, man on his part can frame to himself no such dear notions of the possible good ends that this sublunary state may admit, as to be able, even had he a supernatural gift, to co-operate with what the decrees of Supreme Wisdom may have already determined on, and therefore could not but misapply this Almighty strength to some improper uses. Understood literally, therefore, a miraculous faith of this sort ("*If ye had faith as a grain of mustard-seed, and should say unto this mountain,*" &c.) is absolutely incogitable, viz. a gift of working miracles, where it should lie within the person's own power, by believing prayer, either to possess or be without it. This miracle-working faith must therefore be understood to point, if indeed it mean anything at all, to an idea of the preponderating weight of the moral destination and properties of our race; so that should we ever attain moral perfection acceptable to God (which we never can thoroughly in this life), an ethic qualification of this sort would entirely outweigh every other motive that could be offered to the Divine Wisdom, and thus become a ground of confidence, that, were we altogether what we ought to be, and may (by a continual approximation) become, then the material universe would be compelled to obey our wishes, which last would, however, in such a case, cease to be unwise.

Touching the edification accruing from church frequenting, it must not be fancied that the public prayers there uttered are a mean of grace. They constitute, however, an ethical solemnity, whether by jointly chanting the hymn of faith, or by the set prayer, directed by the pastor in name of the whole congregation toward God, and embracing all the ethical concerns and interests of the flock. This address represents morality as the joint interest of all, and sets openly forth the wish of each individual present, as united and concurring with the wishes of every other toward one common end, viz. the bringing hitherward a kingdom of God on earth. Thus may the feelings be stretched out to the highest moral enthusiasm,—whereas private prayer rather relaxes them, the above sublime idea being awanting, and the frequent repetition wearing out the effect; upon which account public prayer rests upon a deeper ground of reason than private supplications. Furthermore, it clothes that moral wish which constitutes the spirit of prayer into a framed and set address, without *needing* the presence of the Supreme Being, or attaching to a rhetorical figure the force of a mean of grace. The intention is here quite determinate and given, viz. to stir with most emmotive force the inward springs of each individual, by a solemnity outwardly pourtraying the whole society as unitively conjoined by the mutual wish of helping onward the advent of the moral kingdom of God; and this cannot more aptly be accomplished than by invoking its Sovereign Head, *as if he were* specially present in that place.

and directly with God): on the contrary, every one ought, by unremittingly clarifying and elevating the tone of his moral sentiment, to endeavour to reach such a facility in ethical gymnastic, that this spirit of prayer may be sufficiently animated and perpetuated by itself alone, after which its outward letter may entirely fall away. The verbal vehicle must, like every adminicle which works *indirectly* only toward a given end, rather weaken than strengthen the sensitive effect of the ethical idea,—which effect, subjectively considered, is called DEVOTION. Thus, from the contemplation of the unfathomable wisdom observable everywhere throughout the smallest wonders of creation, as well as of the imposing majesty that invests the highest, there springs a feeling of such complex potency, as at once to transplant our race into that sinking frame of mind, bordering almost upon self-annihilation, called ADORATION, in which, however, there is at the same time, when referred to our moral destination, such a soul-exalting power, that even the words of the Royal Psalmist fall like empty sounds, in as much as the effect arising from so marked and displayed an intuition of the finger of the Almighty, is one that speech cannot express. Again, since mankind readily transmute whatever bears upon their moral amelioration into a religious ceremonial, where the professed humiliations and Hosannahs are usually morally the less felt the more they are wordy and rich in sound, it is extremely necessary diligently to inculcate into children, even with their earliest exercises in piety, where a verbal formulary cannot as yet be dispensed with, that all this discourse has no worth of any sort in itself; but is of value only as it tends to enliven the intent of pursuing a walk and conversation acceptable to God. The form of prayer is no more than a leading-string for the imagination; and a similar remark holds of all efforts that a child may make for apprehending in thought the idea God, which last must be brought as near as possible to an intuition: for where this admonition is overlooked or omitted, devout demonstrations of pious homage are but too apt to slide into a hypocritical worship of the Godhead, thereby frustrating his practical and active service, which never consists in mere abortive feelings and frames of the sensory.

II. ASSEMBLING TOGETHER IN CHURCH, regarded as the solemn outward worship of God in a church generally, exhibits a sensible delineation of the communion of believers, and is therefore not only a MEAN of EDIFICATION[77] that may fitly be recommended to each simple

---

[77] When a fit signification is sought for this term, scarce any other can be assigned than this: EDIFICATION IS THE ETHICAL EFFECT WROUGHT UPON OUR OWN INNER MAN BY DEVOTION. This effect cannot be the mental movement or emotion (for this is already involved in the conception of devotion), although the majority of the *soi-disant* devout (called upon this very account DEVOTEES) place all edification just in this sentimental movement. Edification must therefore be understood to mean THE ETHICAL PURCHASE that devotion takes upon the actual amendment and building up of the moral characters of

PARTICULAR, but is an immediate duty incumbent upon ALL, *qua* citizens of a divine state to be founded and upheld on earth: always, however, provided that the church contain no Formulary, that by issuing in IDOLATRY, may burden conscience, *e. g.* adoratory invocations of God under the name of a man, figured as an impersonation of His Infinite Benignity,—a sensible delineation that would be contrary to that behest of reason,—THOU SHALT NOT MAKE UNTO THEE ANY LIKENESS, &c. But to use church-assemblies as a mean of celestial grace, as if God were thereby immediately served, and to suppose that God has connected sundry benefits and favours with the celebration of this solemnity (a mere sensible effigiation of the all-embracing universality of religion), is a delusion that may no doubt consort with the manners and decorum of a good burgher in the COMMON-WEAL POLITICAL; but that not only adds nothing, but that rather detracts from any one's qualifications as a citizen in the KINGDOM OF GOD ON EARTH. This delusion serves only to hide the sorry content of one's moral maxims from the eyes of others, and even from his own, by daubing them over with some deceptive hues.

III. Solemn initiation into church-membership and the society of the faithful (into the Christian church by baptism) is a highly significant rite; imposing grave obligations upon the novice, should he be old enough to take the vows upon himself, when he makes confession of his faith; or otherwise upon his sponsors, who undertake the responsibility of his education. This ceremony aims directly at something HOLY, viz. the building up of an individual to become a pillar in the Divine state; but it is not in itself a holy act; nor does it possess any hallowing efficacy, as if it could procure for the infant subject holiness of nature and susceptibility for the Divine grace: CONSEQUENTLY BAPTISM IS NO MEAN OF GRACE; although in the early Greek church this rite was held in such extravagant honour, that people supposed it could wash away all sins at once,—a hypothesis whereby this delusion openly betrays its intimate affinity with an almost more than heathenish superstition.

IV. The frequently reiterated solemnity of RENEWING, CONTINUING, and PROPAGATING the ecclesiastical association agreeably

---

mankind. A structure of this sort can only then succeed when systematically gone about; firm principles, fashioned after well-understood conceptions, are, first of all, to be laid deep into the foundations of the heart; from these, sentiments corresponding to the weight and magnitude of our several duties must rise, and be protected and watched against the snares and wiles of appetite and passion, thus uprearing and building up, *as it were*, a new man—A TEMPLE OF GOD. Evidently this edifice can advance but slowly, but still some traces of superstructure ought to be perceptible. Many there are, however, who deem themselves much EDIFIED (by a discourse, psalmody, or book) where absolutely nothing has been BUILDED UP, aye! where not even has a finger been stirred to help on the work: possibly they think that the ethic dome will, like the walls of Thebes, rise to the harmonious concert of sighs and yearning wishes.

to laws of equality—THE COMMUNION—presents unquestionably a grand and august cogitation. The communion may, following the example of the Founder of the Church, and also with a view to keep him in remembrance, be celebrated by joint participation in the same elements at the same table. It thus expands the narrow, selfish, and unsociable temper of mankind, which is nowhere more obvious than in religious matters, to the idea of a cosmopolitical moral community; and is a good mean, well fitted for carrying forward the congregation in the culture of that moral and brotherly love, which is thereby so prominently represented. But to hold that there are special favours connected by the Divine Will with the celebration of this ordinance, and to laud and extol it as such, as also to insert among the articles of creed the tenet that this action, which is a mere church-rite, is beside and beyond, A MEAN OF GRACE, are delusions in religion, that must inevitably counteract its true spirit and genius. PRIESTDOM, *i. e.* sacerdotal despotism under the sway of a CLERIARCHY, may consequently be explained yet farther, as the usurped dominion lorded by churchmen over the minds of the laity; the former having arrogated to themselves exclusive possession of THE MEANS OF GRACE.

* * *
* *

All these various kinds of artificial self-deceptions in religion spring from one common source. Of all the moral attributes of the Deity, viz. his holiness, benignity, and justice, mankind commonly address themselves to the second, in order to evade the deterring condition of becoming conformable to the sacro-sanct requirements of the first. It is irksome to make one's self a good and faithful servant— for then duties must be discharged. It is more agreeable to be a FAVOURITE, for then one's shortcomings will be connived at; or should duty have been far too grossly violated to be thus overlooked, why, then, it may be atoned for and made up through the interceding mediation of some one pre-eminently beloved—the unworthy favourite remaining the same unprofitable servant as before. To succeed in this self-delusion, mankind generally transfer their notions of human nature, together with all its failings, to the Godhead. And since in the case of any earthly Governor, the severity of law, benignant grace, and unbending justice, are not administered apart, each for and by itself, as they ought to be, but are all amalgamated into one, when sentence is passed by an earthly tribunal, the sinner hopes to deal in like manner with the divine righteousness. To bias the administrator of human laws, all that is necessary is to circumvent the failing wisdom of his human will, after which the justice and law needs must yield; an experiment that, by parity of reason, it is presumed will tell with equal readiness upon the Divine grace. To obviate a confusion of this sort demanded that wary and careful separation of the three above-named divine attributes prelected on in the scholion to our Third Book, where the triform relationship obtaining betwixt God and man was brought more conspicuously and prominently forward by the analogical idea of a threefold personality. With some such view as the above, every imaginable sort of ceremonial is industriously celebrated, and, by demonstrating the utmost homage toward the divine commandments, the necessity of obeying them is supposed to be supplanted. Again, to the end that deedless wishes may compensate for deliberate transgressions, the sinner cries Lord! Lord! to escape the necessity of doing the will of his Heavenly Father. Hence solemnities, intended as a mode of enlivening sentiments truly practical, are mistaken for rites that are in themselves means of grace. The belief that they possess this efficacy is next given out and declared to be an essential clement of religion (the common people often deem them religion itself, and the whole duties of it), while the sinner trusts to Providence to make out of him a better man, and instead of *virtue* (*i. e.* the active exercise of his own powers in discharging), presses after *piety* (*i. e.* passive veneration of the Divine law), although properly the combination of both is what alone can be termed *godliness, i. e.* a bent and ply of the mind truly religious. When once the phantasms of this supposed favourite of heaven have reached the fanatical *extravaganza* of feeling special works of grace within, and of attaining and establishing a familiar though hidden intercourse and fellowship with the Deity, then does the very term virtue become abominable in his ears, and itself the object of his most superlative disdain. Need any one, then, wonder at the universal complaint, that religion contributes so little to the moral amendment of our race, and that the inward light of those elect is still under the bushel, and will not outwardly shine forth, radiant with good works. And yet the Teacher of the Gospel declared these outward fruits to be the tests whereby each might try and know himself and others. Judging of the elect by their own professions, we might expect to find them exemplary beyond the rest of mankind, who abide by the behests of natural honour; whose religion, moreover, having been adopted, not with the view of supplanting, but of supporting their morality, makes itself visible by a course of good and active deportment. The day has not yet come when it ever was seen that those who deem themselves thus signally favoured and chosen, excelled in any one point the man of plain natural honesty, upon whom we can count in society, in business, or in distress; on the contrary, taken all in all, they can hardly stand out a comparison with their neighbours,—a sufficient proof that it is not the right course to begin with celestial grace, and thence descend to virtue; but rather commencing with virtue, thence rise to the condonation of divine grace.

www.ingramcontent.com/pod-product-compliance
Lightning Source LLC
LaVergne TN
LVHW041624070426
835507LV00008B/446